Crime Trends
and
Criminal Justice

Crime Trends and Criminal Justice

Dr. R C Mishra IPS

AUTHORSPRESS

First Published 2001
by Authorspress

E-35/103, Jawahar Park (Shree Ganesh Complex),
Laxmi Nagar, Delhi-110 092

e-mail: authorspress@yahoo.com
quantum_soul@mantramail.com

Typeset in NewCenturySchlbk by Chitra Computers

Crime Trends and Criminal Justice
ISBN 81-7273-051-9

Printed in India at Mehra Offset Press, Delhi.

Foreword

Crime and society are intertwined and inseparable since time immemorial. Crime mirrors the community and the pulsating feelings such as cultural conflicts, political legacy, vacillating social malady, diminution of ethical ideals, eroding of moral values, explosive outcry of the oppressed, infliction of mayhem and its abstruse resounding echo which are ventilated as crimes. Potentialities, abilities and talents of the human resources are exploited and liquidated by antisocial elements, bad characters and criminals. Unimaginable number of crimes occur in the society and only countable are being worked out. The rate and scale of crime occurrence is such that it has now become necessary to think about its dynamics and it is at this juncture that we postulate theories, build models and suggest policies to reduce crimes.

In this book Dr. R. C. Mishra has attempted single-handedly to establish a detailed study of current trends in crime and criminal justice. The author has taken great pains to make his study as modern as regards methodology as possible. His intensive experience as an eminent IPS officer has enabled him to present a really useful investigation of current crime trends. With his deep knowledge in the subject, he has presented the root causes of various types of crimes in an authoritative and lucid style. He has also suggested crime prevention policies and strategies which may go a long way in reducing the occurrence of crimes. The treatment is exhaustive rather than selective.

The book will have a wide appeal. The author has done this work partly in order to fill the middle ground between the more applied publications and the more specialist books and articles. The book provides a lucid and cogent picture of the vital aspects of crime trends and criminal justice in a wide-angle perspective. The account on cybercrime and investigation in this book is highly informative. Undoubtedly, this work will prove ideal and dependable reference book for crime investigators, academics, policy planners, social scientists, and researchers alike.

15th May, 2001.

M. S. Malik IPS
Director General of Police,
Haryana.

Preface

Crime is a perennial problem for all societies. It can be defined as any act committed in violation of law forbidding or commanding it, and for which punishment is imposed upon conviction. Both the incidents and the patterns of the crime vary in space and time. Technology has transformed the very nature of crime itself. An important conceptual shift is underway in terms of the costs of criminal behaviour and the forms of criminality which merit-state attention.

Criminologists argue that the decision to commit crime is rational. They have spent countless time and resources attempting to validate social explanation of crime. Many of these theories hover around some compelling arguments that social conditions, such as lack of opportunity, lack of physical comfort, lack of education, lack of resources, improper associations and poor environmental conditions cause people to commit crime. In reality, criminal behaviour occurs in all levels of society, possibly at the same rate. The only differences are the type of offences and the payoff.

Crime prevention is the process of elimination or reducing the opportunity to commit an offence, or denial access to crime target. There has been a proliferation of crime prevention, delinquency control, and community organisation projects and programmes that have been pushed and sold for the past few decades. Many of these programmes were base on a number of compelling social theories that did not pan out in the implementation stage. The local government, criminal justice systems and public housing authorities are worn out with many of the tried and failed programme approaches and philosophies. For fruitful results, the prevention of crime needs to become more visible and assertive and accept its internal role in the functions of prevention, detection, suppression, investigation and prosecution. Any serious study looking into the understanding and control of crime should be insighted from a wide variety of disciplines such as history, criminal justice, political science sociology, psychiatry, biology, etc.

The investigation and prosecution of crimes raise fundamental questions about sovereignty, legal jurisdiction and the obligations of states to protect their citizens. Investigation is expensive, particularly in cases where records are encrypted. However, the costs must be balanced against the benefits of mitigating the high personal and financial toll of the offences.

Upon recognising the occasional state and province variations within some nations, there are considerably more legal systems than countries. The term legal system refers to attitudes, values and norms regarding the nature and role of law, including rules and practices for processing, and functioning. Legal traditions offer guidance in designing and establishing structures, both organisational and personnel, for criminal justice systems.

This book focuses on problem areas that exemplify the changing nature of crime as facilitated by the growth of high-technology and on the developments in criminal justice systems. It is an authentic study about the nature and types of crimes and behaviour of justice systems towards criminals, and will be of immense utility to both the public and officials.

I acknowledge with great sense of gratitude I owe to Mr. M.S. Malik IPS Director General of Police, Haryana for his valuable guidance and foreword to the book. Mr. Malik is a unique person endowed with great qualities of head-and-heart. I am also grateful to Mr. Harish Kumar IPS, Director, NCRB, for providing me crime-related data.

I thank Mr. K'cherry Sudarshan of Authorspress who spared no pain in bringing-out the book in such a short-time. Last but not least, thanks are due to my wife Dr. Archana Mishra, without her constant patience and help this book would not have come-out.

R C Mishra

Contents

1

Crime Analysis

Crime is a committed or omitted act of law which is forbidden or commanded and for which punishment is imposed upon conviction. The present chapter attempts to define major crime heads, its causes and *modus operandi* adopted by the criminals. The ingredients of the definition enable the police to lodge First Information Report (FIR) in proper sections, while causes and working plans help in tracing offenders.

MURDER

According to Section 299 and 300 of Indian Penal Code (IPC) whoever causes death by doing an act with the intention of causing death, or with the intention of causing such bodily injury as is likely to cause death, or with the knowledge that he is likely by such act to cause death, commits the offence of culpable homicide. Except in the cases hereinafter, culpable homicide is murder, if the act by which the death is caused is done with the intention of causing death.

The *modus operandi* of the murder generally depends on the means locally available. Moreover, the killer may use a knife, dagger, firearms, poison, methods of throttling, drowning, suffocating, strangulating, cutting veins, hitting with *lathies* or hockey sticks, using a sword, through accident, throwing acid, explosions, etc. Causes of murder vary from case to case and situation to situation. Moreover, the main causes may be the dispute over wealth, property and women. In some cases sudden provocation becomes the cause of murder. The purpose of murder is basically for the gain of either the property, money, women, or to take revenge.

ATTEMPT TO MURDER

Section 307 of IPC states that whoever does any act with such intention or knowledge, and under such circumstances that, if he by that act caused death but does not die, he would be guilty of attempt to murder. When the attempt to cause death fails, it becomes an attempt to murder or if the aggressor hurts the victim or threatens him or to terrorises him and the hurt occurs on the vital part of the body which becomes the grievous hurt but the victim could not loss the life then it is called attempt to murder. Purpose and modus operandi are the same as adopted in case of murder. Causes of attempt to murder are more or less the same as that of the murder.

HURT

According to Sections 323 to 338 of IPC, whoever voluntarily causes body pain disease or infirmity to any person is said to cause hurt. It may be simple or grievous. If the injury caused to the victim is not so grievous as to the victim have die or if it is not at the vital part or it is not a grievous injury, then it is counted a case of hurt. Causes, purposes and working plans are more or less the same as in the case of murder. But to cause hurt the other local instrument or the tools like lathies, chain, rope, etc., may also be used.

ROBBERY

In order to commit the theft or in committing the theft or in carrying away or attempting to carry away property obtained by theft, the offender for that end, voluntarily causes or attempts to cause to any person death or hurt or wrongful restraint or fear of instance death or of instant hurt, or of instant wrongful restraint, such a theft is called robbery.

If the offender at the time of committing the extortion is in the presence of the person put in fear and commits the extortion by putting that person in fear of instant death, or instant hurt or of instant wrongful restraint to that person or to some other persons and by so putting a fear induces the person so put in fear and then and there forces to deliver up the thing extorted then it is the robbery.

If the offender is said to be present and if he is sufficiently near to put the victim in fear of instant death or instant hurt or of instant wrongful restraint, the theft may be treated as robbery.

The causes and purpose of robbery are to take the moveable or the immovable property but the immediate gains remain from the moveable property. Robbers mainly use firearms, knives, daggers, *bhalas*, hockey sticks, lathies, rods, swords, etc. Thus, the main aspect in the robbery is to put a person under very high fear of death or instant hurt and to dispossess him from the property in such an atmosphere.

SNATCHING

According to Section 356 of IPC, whosoever assaults or uses criminal force on any person in attempting to commit theft on any property which that person is then wearing or carrying, then he commits the offence of snatching. If the culprit assaults or uses criminal force to commit theft of any property which that person is then wearing or carrying, it is treated as snatching. Normally, it is not preplanned but in some cases may be preplanned. The main *modus operandi* is that the offender snatches any ornament from the lady, purse or handbag and runs away.

SERVANT THEFTS

Section 381 of IPC states that whoever intending to take dishonestly any movable property out of the possession of any persons without that person's consent, moves that property in order to such taking, is said to commit a theft. If such an act is committed by a clerk or a servant or an employee during the course of their duty, it will be treated as servant theft.

BURGLARY

Burglary is the theft committed in any building, tent or vessel, which is being used as a human dwelling or for the custody of property. Burglary is generally committed either in an unprotected or an unattended house.

PICKPOCKETING

Sections 378 and 379 of IPC defines pickpocketing as follows:

> Whoever intending to take dishonestly any movable property out the possession of any person without that person's consent, moves that property in order to such taking, is said to commit theft. If such theft is committed from the person's exclusive possession without his consent, then it will be treated as pickpocketing.

DACOITY

According to Section 391 of IPC, when five or more persons conjointly commit or attempt to commit a robbery or where the whole number of persons conjointly committing or attempting to commit a robbery and persons present in aiding, such commission or attempt amount to five or more, every person so committing, attempting or aiding, is said to commit dacoity.

Basically, there is no difference between robbery and dacoity, but when five or more persons conjointly commit or attempt to commit a robbery or where the whole number of persons conjointly committing or attempting to commit a robbery and persons present aiding such attempts amount to five or more, every person so committing, attempting or aiding, is said to commit dacoity.

The *modus operandi* more or less is the same as for robbery and the instruments, arms and ammunition are also the same as used in the case of robbery.

RIOT

Guilty of the offence of rioting occurs whenever force or violence is used by an unlawful assembly or by any member thereof, in prosecution of the common object and every member of such assembly. It is only the use of force that distinguishes rioting from an unlawful assembly. If any person hires or imparts connivance to hire a person to join an unlawful assembly then both types of persons are guilty of rioting. If any person malignantly gives provocation to any person knowing it to cause a riot then he will also be held liable for rioting, committed or not. If any person promotes enmity between different groups on grounds of religion, race, place of birth, residence, language, etc., and doing acts against maintenance or harmony then it commits the offence.

Causes of rioting may be the following:

i) Preplanned or immediate due to provocation,

ii) Political or social reasons,

iii) Communal or racial reasons,

iv) Caste or sects reasons,

v) Religious procession, and

vi) Provocating speeches.

The main cause behind riots are communal or religious provocation, caste or racial provocation, communal dispute, group clashes, property dispute, old enmity, prestige issues or ego problems of the groups, etc. Sometimes the riot occurs even on minor and petty altercation or molestation of a girl by another member of the rival group and sometimes over the issue of pigeons.

The purpose of a riot may be to suppress each other, to hurt the feelings of the group of each other for gains and to satisfy their ego. The *modus operandi* of any riot is to plan, assemble and to increase the altercation with the other group by provocating.

RAPE

Sections 375 and 377 of IPC state that a man is said to commit a rape when he except in the case hereinafter excepted has sexual intercourse with a woman under circumstances falling under any of the six following descriptions:

i) against her will,

ii) without her consent,

iii) with her consent, when her consent has been obtained by putting her or any person in whom she is interested in fear of death or of hurt,

iv) with her consent, when the man knows that he is not her husband, and that her consent is given because she believes that he is another man to whom she is or believes herself to be lawfully married,

v) with her consent, when at the time of giving such consent, by reason of unsoundness of mind or intoxication or the administration by him personally or through another of any stupefying or unwholesome substance, she is unable to understand the nature and consequences of that to which she gives consent,

vi) with or without her consent, when she is under 16 years of age.

Based on the opportunity for the offender, the rape may be preplanned or it may be sudden. It is committed to take revenge and to defame the lady and her parents in society or to fulfil the desire of sexual lust. The opportunity factor plays a vital role in this offence, because as and when the culprit finds the victim alone in the house, field or in the way, the rape is committed.

Most of the rape cases are either committed by the relatives, neighbours or the servants. In many cases the friend of the husband or the friend of her brother gets access to the house of the victim and becomes well known to the family who generally do not doubt but after getting the due opportunity, he commits the crime. In some cases rapes have been committed forcefully at the point of a knife or firearms.

MOLESTATION

According to Section 354 IPC, whoever assaults or uses criminal force on any woman, intending to outrage or knowing it to be likely that he will thereby outrage her modesty is treated as molester. To note down the proper causes and purposes of molestation is difficult because there is no definite reasons behind molestation.

Molestation is generally committed by male with female. It has been observed that molestation is committed by youngsters but middle-aged persons also commit this crime. It is generally committed in the peers group in school and colleges, buses, railway stations, bus-stands and at crowded places.

IMMORAL TRAFFIC

Immoral Traffic Prevention Act (ITP Act) prohibits trafficking in women and girls for purposes of prostitution as an organised means of living. Thus, if any woman or girl produces herself for prostitution in consideration of any type of gains then it will be treated as a crime. The place where such a type of act is committed is called a brothel and the person in whose possession is a such place as also equally an offender under this act. If any other person is living on the commission of the gain in lieu of the prostitution he is also an offender. Prostitution is covered under the ITP Act.

If any person induces or seduces the another person for sexual intercourse in lieu of the gains, or if any person produces another person and takes commission from the gain, or any person uses any premises for such acts he is liable to be punished.

KIDNAPPING AND ABDUCTION

According to Sections 359 to 374 of IPC, kidnapping is of two kinds: kidnapping from India, and kidnapping from lawful guardianship. Whoever carries any person beyond the limits of India without the consent of that person, or of some legally authorised person to consent on behalf of that person, is said to kidnap the person from India. Whoever takes or entices any minor under sixteen years of age, if a male, or under eighteen years of age if a female, or any person of unsound mind, out of the keeping of the lawful guardian of such minor or person of unsound mind, without the consent of such guardian, is said to kidnap such a minor or person from lawful guardianship. On the other hand, whoever by force compels, or by any deceitful means induces, any person to go from any place, is said to abduct that person.

The purposes of kidnapping and abduction are to take ransom or revenge, to murder, terrorise, get release of the persons from the government, for some gain, sexual purposes, marriage, prostitution, sale, begging, etc.

The *modus operandi* of kidnapping and abduction is basically forcefully, false promises, like to give the job, for marriage, or real promise for marriage, stimulating the children, by terrorising the person or the children at the point of a knife or gun, by instincting. If the kidnapping and abduction is made forcefully then the vehicle will certainly be used.

CHEATING

According to Section 415 of IPC, whoever, by deceiving any person fraudulently or dishonestly, induces the person so deceived to deliver any property to any person, or to consent that any person shall retain any property, or intensely induces the person so deceived to do or omit or to do anything which he would not do or omit, if he was not so deceived and which act of omission causes or it likely to cause damage or harm to the person in body, mind, reputation or property is said to cheat. A dishonest concealment of facts is a deception within the meaning of cheating. In the offence of cheating, the delivery of property should be by the person who himself was deceived by the accused.

If the following conditions are fulfilled, then it will be cheating:

i) Deception of any person.

ii) a) Fraudulently or distrust by inducing that person; or to deliver any property to any person or to consent that any person shall retain any property,

b) Intentionally inducing that person to do or omit to do anything which he would not to do or omit if he were not so deceived, and which act or omission causes or is likely to cause damage or harm to that person in body, mind, reputation or property.

The basic purpose of cheating is clear that it is commenced for the gain of property and to harm the person in body, mind or reputation.

The main working plans of cheating may be:

i) Inducing person deceived to deliver property,

ii) Misrepresentation as to the case,

iii) Inducing person deceived to do something,

iv) Delivering of property fraudulently or dishonestly,

v) False entries in the record,

vi) Deceiving railways by the passengers,

vii) Attempt to create false evidence,

viii) False representation and abetment to represent at examination as bachelor, etc., and

ix) Forgery made in passports, false documents, false certificates, copies, etc.

GAMBLING

Playing cards or discs used to be important source of entertainment in olden days. Bets used to be held on cock fighting, lamb fighting, bull fighting and wrestling during the medieval period in India.

Gambling includes wagering or betting except wagering or betting upon a horse race on a prescribed date, and such a race is run in an enclosure and has the sanction of the state government. But this does not include a lottery. This crime may be treated as an organised crime when the organised gangs solicit the people for gambling at their *addas*. The game of chance is gambling according to the statute. Thus, if any act is played as a game of chance it will be treated as gambling.

Gambling and betting have drained out the mental solace and the happiness of the poor homes. People who have fallen prey by the alluring tactics of the fortune making which is very attractive at the first instance have never been able to come out from the inextricable web for the whole of their lives and ruined their families. Such activity may be called the social deviance and may be considered as a marginal crime.

EXCISE-RELATED CRIMES

Whoever imports, exports, transports, manufactures, collects or possesses any intoxicant or constructs or works any distillery or brewery, uses, keeps or possesses any material for manufacturing and still possessing utensils or implements of apparatus without any proper licence, permission or pass granted by the government, commits excise-related crimes.

The cases registered in excises are covered under the Punjab Excise Act, 1914, Act 1 of 1914. An offence under this Act is basically termed as bootlegging. Bootlegging has become a menace which is mostly prevalent in the lower class of society. One of the reasons for bootlegging is the exorbitant cost of the English liquor which the poor and the common people are unable to afford. Another reasons is socioeconomic in nature. The criminal tribes earn their bread by means of this trade. The third reason is the connivance of the law enforcing authority with the illicit liquor offenders who encourage their personal ends. The unemployment problem is also playing a vital role in encouraging such illicit trades in an indirect way.

As per the Punjab Excise Act and latest notifications, any person can have a maximum two litres of any type of liquor or 12 bottles of beer. The possession of more than this is treated illegal and he is liable to be prosecuted in the court. The illegal possession may be for two purposes, i.e., for own consumption, parties or for resale.

POSSESSION OF ILLEGAL ARMS

An offence under the Arms Act is presumed if a person even has any knife, dagger, firearms, etc., in his possession without any proper licence.

Causes and purposes to possess unlicensed arms like knife, dagger, small or big firearms which is illegal is basically for one's personal safety, to threaten others, to commit a crime like murder, attempt to murder, hurt, dacoity, robbery, kidnapping and abduction, theft, burglary, rape, etc.

Arms are not possessed openly and offenders keep the arms either in pockets or socks, etc., and use them when needed. Under the Arms Act, mere possession of an unlicensed arm is covered under the Arms Act and is liable to be punished.

POSSESSION OF NARCOTIC DRUGS AND PSYCHOTROPHIC SUBSTANCES

Whosoever cultivates the cocoa plant, opium, poppy or any cannabis plant or produces, manufactures, possesses, sells, purchases, transports, warehouses, uses, consumes, imports, exports or transships any narcotic drug or psychotropic substance except for medical or scientific purposes, commits the crime under the Drug Act.

Narcotic drug means cocoa leaf, cannabis, opium, poppy straw and it includes all manufactured drugs like heroin, smack, cocaine, etc. Psychotropic substance means any substance, natural or synthetic or any one of the 83 natural material (listed in the Act), or any salt or preparation of such substance or material included in the list of psychotropic substance specified in the Schedule One of this Act.

This Act came into existence on 16 September 1985, which is Act no. 61 of 1985. Prior to this Act the cases used to be registered under Opium Act, Drug Act, Dangerous Drug Act and Excise Act. Therefore, reliable segregated data prior to 1985 on narcotic drug, etc., is not available. After 1985 the cases are registered basically against the persons having possession, selling, trafficking, manufacturing of opium, *charas, ganjha*, cocaine, psychotropic substances, etc.

Drug abuse is spreading fast in the countries of origin as well as in the transit countries. There is a growing nexus between the drug traffickers and the terrorists. Drug and psychotropic substance include opium, morphine, heroin, cocaine, cannabis, synthetic drugs, psychotropic substances, i.e., depressants, stimulants and hallucinogens. It is quite obvious that people indulge themselves in pushing drug trafficking through a carrier ship, selling, etc., for monetary purposes, setting aside the natural as well as social feelings at the international as well national level.

The *modus operandi* of trafficking drugs is mainly through concealing it in camouflaged containers. It has been caught in tins of ghee, the bottom of suitcase, the belt of a person, capsules, tiffin carriers, toys, electronic goods, chestguards hollow pipes, sweet boxes, etc.

SIMPLE AND FATAL ACCIDENTS

According to Sections 279, 337 and 338 of IPC, whoever drives any vehicle or rides on any public way in a manner so rash or negligent as to endanger human life, or to be likely to cause hurt or injury to any other person commits a crime of accident. If the defaulter acts to endanger life or personal safety of others or causes hurt by the act endangering life or personal safety of others or causing grievous hurt by the act endangering life or personal safety of others there are counted as simple accidents.

If the defaulter causes the death of any person by doing any rash or negligent act not amounting to culpable homicide commits a crime and this crime is treated as a fatal accident. Accidents, whether fatal and simple, are basically caused due to rash and negligent driving but sometimes due to the negligence of the victim.

Due to the rapid industrialisation and urbanisation, the economic status of the public increases and they need better facilities, which later on become essential needs. A few decades ago very few motor vehicles used to be seen on the roads when they were clear but nowadays the number of vehicles have multiplied at an unparallel rate. The carrying capacity of the roads has got reduced which diminishes after reaching the optimum point. It seems that in the walled city the saturation point has already been reached and there is hardly any scope to increase the capacity of vehicular traffic in those areas.

CASES UNDER TERRORIST DISRUPTIVE ACTIVITIES ACT (TADA)

The terrorist Disruptive Activities Act (TADA) came into existence in 1985. Unlike all the criminals, the terrorists have a different *modus operandi*. They take shelters in the areas of relative isolation to prepare for the crime and escape after the offence is committed. Causes and purposes behind the TADA cases are to terrorise the public, for monitoring gains, to divide the country, to take revenge from the enemy country by sending their own persons, etc.

The *modus operandi* of the terrorists is that they generally take arms and ammunition, explosives and mines from the country which is basically against that country. The enemy country generally sends its own persons to join the enemy country's terrorists. The terrorists are imparted proper training of weapons, explosive, mines and other know-how by the enemy country. Such terrorists sometimes forcefully make the gangsters follow the path of terrorism.

To terrorise the person, specially the innocent and VVIPs, terrorists generally use modern weapons like rifles, rocket launchers, missiles, explosives and mines. Sometimes, they ambush the police, the paramilitary forces and armed forces. Sometimes, they kidnap VVIPs and conduct negotiations for the release of apprehended persons in lieu of the release of the kidnapped person. Sometimes, they hang the kidnapped person or shoot him, so that the persons from the general public would not be courageous against them.

The incidence and rate of violent crimes occurred in Indian states and union territories, during the year 1999, are given in table 1.1. and table 1.2., respectively.

CRIME PREVENTION

Street and domestic crime create loss, inflict physical and psychological wounds, undermine the safety of communities and take lives. The efforts to stem the tide have been insufficient, costly and sometimes threatening to basic human rights. Crime and insecurity also cost the general public and so endanger sustainable development. The failure to use the best know how to reduce crime slows human and economic development, particularly in the large and fast-growing cities that are the economic motors of most countries.

Crime prevention is anything that reduces delinquency, violent crime and insecurity by successful tackling of the scientifically identified causal factors. Academics divide crime prevention into approaches either focused on victims or offenders. They define these categories with reference to whether the strategy applies to all persons in a community, only those "at-risk" or those who have already been involved in offences. The approaches would be summarised as follows:

— *Social development*: reducing the social factors that predispose young persons to become persistent offenders—often focusing on potential offenders;
— *Opportunity reduction*: making crime more difficult, more risky, or less rewarding to potential offenders.

The public participates in crime prevention in a number of ways. The now almost universally accepted model of successful crime prevention is based on: government accountability; investigation, detection and arrest of criminals; trials and sentencing; imprisonment and rehabilitation; partnership policing; and other partnership arrangements.

Table 1.1.

Incidence and rate of violent crimes in Indian states during 1999.

State	*Murder*	*Attempt to murder*	*C.H. not amounting to murder*	*Rape*	*Kidnapping abduction*	*Dacoity*	*Preparation for dacoity*	*Robbery*	*Riots*	*Arson*	*Dowry death*	*Total crime*	*Crime rate*	*% to total crime under IPC*
Andhra P.	2711	1512	135	895	1169	266	7	726	2853	1057	452	11783	15.7	9.8
Arunachal P.	62	53	6	39	70	60	1	71	60	18	0	440	37.6	19.4
Assam	1517	421	74	703	1440	783	20	907	3663	443	40	10011	38.5	26.8
Bihar	5116	3818	742	1447	2599	2153	200	2691	11106	586	1021	31479	31.9	26.5
Goa	38	34	6	18	11	5	0	49	67	28	2	258	16.5	10.0
Gujarat	1353	695	20	331	1336	340	10	1346	2111	693	94	8329	17.4	6.7
Haryana	839	487	104	372	542	112	98	438	970	219	288	4469	22.8	11.3
H.P.	133	79	7	109	126	4	0	17	589	203	5	1272	19.3	11.5
J&K	765	885	26	170	623	40	0	126	869	425	6	3935	40.2	23.0
Karnataka	1651	1662	51	301	630	284	0	1027	7569	278	217	13670	26.5	12.4
Kerala	484	498	91	423	188	112	5	370	6610	390	31	9202	28.7	9.7
M.P.	3225	3082	189	3561	1203	177	154	1698	3358	1145	584	18376	23.3	8.9
Maharastra	3024	1363	91	423	188	112	5	2554	5246	1234	395	17122	18.9	9.6
Manipur	189	88	7	12	73	9	3	26	68	58	0	533	21.6	21.6

(Table 1.1 contd...)

Meghalaya	134	28	6	27	37	105	2	100	16	31	0	486	20.4	28.3
Mizoram	34	21	3	71	3	6	0	10	5	27	0	180	19.4	8.1
Nagaland	128	32	0	11	48	29	0	125	14	10	0	397	24.1	31.8
Orissa	1019	1299	65	820	482	348	14	1195	1443	377	234	7296	20.5	14.5
Punjab	741	528	108	282	423	18	64	58	3	53	193	2471	10.6	12.2
Rajasthan	1520	2024	51	1198	3157	109	25	1209	16598	1230	443	27564	52.1	16.4
Sikkim	15	4	0	7	12	3	0	10	153	20	0	224	40.7	28.9
Tamil Nadu	1726	1992	25	430	1178	171	38	615	5428	1183	197	12983	21.1	8.9
Tripura	277	32	1	72	219	65	0	102	207	143	17	1135	30.7	36.3
U.P.	7850	7849	1354	1593	4158	927	91	4197	6792	1171	2088	38070	22.7	21.9
West Bengal	1902	516	655	819	945	368	475	913	4601	102	257	11553	14.8	17.4
Total States	**36453**	**29002**	**3817**	**15031**	**21797**	**7007**	**1464**	**20580**	**80399**	**11124**	**6564**	**233238**	**24.0**	**13.7**

Table 1.2.

Incidence and rate of violent crimes in union territoires during 1999.

UT	*Murder*	*Attempt to murder*	*C.H. not amounting to murder*	*Rape*	*Kidnapping abduction*	*Dacoity*	*Preparation for dacoity*	*Robbery*	*Riots*	*Arson*	*Dowry death*	*Total crime*	*Crime rate*	*% to total crime under*
A& N Islands	9	4	0	6	4	2	0	1	32	9	0	67	17.6	11.1
Chandigarh	17	18	9	16	48	1	1	6	73	10	7	206	23.7	7.5
D&N Haveli	16	2	0	3	2	1	0	8	37	1	2	72	37.9	17.4
Daman&Diu	5	5	0	4	3	0	0	2	23	2	0	44	31.4	17.8
Delhi	649	579	81	402	1375	63	36	726	199	57	122	4289	31.5	7.3
Lakshadweep	0	0	0	0	0	0	0	0	3	1	3	4	5.7	12.9
Pondicherry	21	18	5	6	7	5	0	9	72	14	4	161	14.8	4.8
Total (UTs)	717	626	95	437	1439	72	37	752	439	94	135	4843	29.7	7.3
Total	**37170**	**29628**	**3912**	**15468**	**23236**	**7079**	**1501**	**21332**	**80838**	**11218**	**6699**	**238081**	**24.1**	**13.5**

The public largely participates in this model by entering into individual and/or group cooperation with the police service and other elements of the justice system. However, in a democratic state, the accountability for crime prevention is ultimately in the hands of the government as a whole. No other entity in a country can exercise this function—or should try to do so. The most important reason for this is that crime prevention and crime control will at some point involve the use of force and coercion—something which only the government can legitimately exercise in respect of its own citizens. The second reason is that many causes of crime can only be removed through government action.

Public involvement in crime prevention will always take the form of a partnership with the agencies of government. According to this model, public confidence in the process is critical. There are several ways of measuring public confidence in crime prevention measures. The most obvious is to ask the respondents how confident they are that crime prevention agencies are coping with crime. Another way is to ask people what can be done about crime. Yet another way of estimating public confidence is to ask people how safe they feel under the existing crime prevention systems. In terms of business perceptions, another indication of confidence is the decision to invest in the expansion of the businesses. Finally, a key indicator of public confidence in the justice system is the willingness to report crime.

Studies of all these types have been carried out recently in South Africa. In particular, a recent University of South Africa study confirmed results from many other countries that only 58 per cent of victims reported to the police crimes committed against them. This varied from 94 per cent for car theft to three per cent for police corruption.

Media plays a very important role. By focusing on crimes that are committed, rather than on arrests and prosecutions, the public perception is that crime occurs without restraint. Also, this creates confidence in criminals who believe they can get away with murder because there is no evidence to the contrary.

REFERENCES

Alvazzi, del Frate A., *Manual International Crime (Victim) Survey*, Rome: UNICRI, 1996.

Clarke, R.V., (ed.), *Situational Crime Prevention: Successful Case Studies*, Albany, New York: Harrow and Heston, Publishers, 1992.

Crime in India-1999, National Crime Record Bureau, Ministry of Home Affairs, 1999.

Kalish, Carol B., *International Crime Rates*, Washington, DC: Bureau of Justice Statistics, 1990.

Shahi, M. P., *Crime and Corruption in Digital Age*, Authorspress, New Delhi, 2000.

2

Homicide—The Most Vulnerable Crime

Homicide is the killing of one human being by another. All homicides are not criminal: they may also be justifiable or excusable. Criminal homicide is the unlawful taking of a human life. There are two kinds of criminal homicide: murder and manslaughter. Murder is the unlawful killing of another human being with malice or premeditation. Killing a person during the commission of a felony also constitutes murder—even when the killing is unintentional. Most murder convictions are for felony murder rather than for premeditated murder. Manslaughter is the unlawful killing of another without intent—express or implied—to effect death.

Intentional but lawful killing of another is termed justifiable homicide. The state commits justifiable homicide in carrying out a death sentence handed down by a judge after conviction. Justifiable homicide is also committed when a police officer kills a bank robber who shoots at the officer while attempting to escape; or when an individual, believing his or her life is being threatened with a weapon, kills in defence of self or family. Excusable homicide involves one person killing another by accident without gross negligence and without intent to injure; for example, the hunter who honestly mistakes another person for game.

Another type of homicide—suicide—is the taking of one's own life. Although not deemed a crime, suicide is considered a grave public wrong in many jurisdictions throughout the world.

Regardless of the classification of an unlawful homicide, the investigator must marshal evidence for each element of the *corpus delicti* in order for the prosecutor to obtain an indictment or for the judge to hand the case over to a jury.

Elements for unlawful homicide are:

i) Death was not the result of suicide, natural causes, or accident, thus establishing that it was a homicide,

ii) Some person was responsible for the unlawful death, and

iii) Circumstances surrounding the death will determine whether charge will be murder or manslaughter.

INVESTIGATIVE ACTIVITIES

Rather the investigator must be prepared to seize upon any development that seems important and see that it is followed through and fully exploited, while remaining watchful for other developments to emerge. One should record the date and time any tactical manoeuvre is taken in response to new information as preparation for a "when" question from defence counsel during a trial or other hearing. There are risks involved in such jumping around—other aspects of the investigation may be eclipsed, ignored, or overlooked. Hence, a comprehensive checklist will not only preclude this unfortunate result, it will serve as a reminder of the fundamentals that are part and parcel of a thorough investigation.

Investigative activities in a homicide are the following:

i) Record crime scene (photographs, sketches, notes).

ii) Recognise, collect, and preserve all physical evidence.

— To facilitate reconstruction of the crime.

— To link a suspect to the victim, crime scene, or both.

— To identify a substance (poison, narcotic, blood, semen), or an object (bludgeon, gun) in order to locate its source and trace its owner.

iii) Identify the victim.

iv) Establish the cause, manner, and time of death.

v) Ascertain the motive for the crime.

— From the way the crime was committed—using evidence at the scene, and trauma inflicted on the victim for psychological profiling.

— From those who had knowledge of the victim's activities (social, familial, business).

— From documents written by or sent to the victim—diaries, letters, or documents relating to financial or business dealings of the victim.

vi) Seek additional information.

— Interview people to check on the background and activities of the victim; obtain leads from those who knew the deceased; seek a possible informant; consider surveillance in some cases.

— Examine records to ascertain business interests of the victim; trace source of murder weapon through manufacturer's records or firearms registration records.

— Review intra-departmental electronic communications on a daily basis. Scan the police information network for possibly related criminal activity in other jurisdictions.

— Obtain exemplars from any suspect for comparison with similar physical evidence discovered at the crime scene.

vii) Allow suspects to make any statement they wish, including those that are exculpatory. Check any statement in regard to the suspect's knowledge of what happened in order to compare it against facts revealed through reconstructing the event, using available autopsy and physical evidence. The forensic pathologist can be very helpful in reconstructing the event; this should be attempted early in the investigation, preferably within the first 48 hours in a conference involving all investigators and technical personnel. Obtain an admission or a confession. During questioning, make use of forensic laboratory reports and other evidence of guilt that link the suspect to the crime.

Investigation of a homicide involve several persons—a crime scene evidence technician, criminalist, forensic pathologist, and detective or investigator. Responsibility for investigative activities in most cases can be partitioned as follows:

— *Evidence technician*: Recording crime scene, recognising, collecting, and preserving evidence.

— *Criminalist*: Recognising, collecting, and preserving physical evidence; recording crime scene.

— *Forensic pathologist*: Identifying the victim, estimating the time of death; establishing the cause and manner of death; contributing to recognising, collecting, and preserving physical evidence; ascertaining the motive for the crime.

— *Forensic anthropologist*: Recognising, collecting, and preserving physical evidence; identifying the victim.

— *Detective*: Recording crime scene; recognising, collecting, and preserving physical evidence; ascertaining the motive for the crime; seeking additional information; questioning suspects; developing authentic information for identifying the victim.

MOTIVES

Often there is a personal relationship between the victim and the perpetrator that, if subjected to stress, m ay impel one of them to kill the other. If the underlying cause can be found, deductive reasoning may lead the investigator back to the one who logically might have been so motivated. Further investigative efforts are then required either to develop additional evidence of guilt or to eliminate the suspect entirely. Because it will provide some focus to the investigative process, it is useful to understand the most common motives for homicide. One person kills another for several reasons such as financial gain, sexual gratification, emotional factors, self-protection, removal of an inconvenience, and sometimes for combination of motives.

A huge number of homicides occurring today is for financial gain. Criminals prompted by the expectation of financial gain include: the beneficiary of a will or insurance policy of a spouse or relative; the surviving spouse in a community property state; the merchant who stands to profit from the death of a business associate. When financial gain is the precipitating factor, deductive reasoning from motive to possible suspect is often fruitful. In robbery cases when the victim resists and is killed, the motive is seldom particularised; then, the answer is to solve the felony utilising techniques appropriate to that felony. This would pertain to a burglary/homicide. The motive of a "Lonely Hearts" killer or poisoner is also financial gain, but in these cases a paper record of financial transactions connecting the killer and the victim is more likely to remain. Such transactions might include signing the home ownership deed over to the killer, opening a new checking or savings account in the name of the victim and killer, or even using a credit card.

In sex-connected homicides lust is the psychological motive. Wanting a new or younger mate has led to the murder of a spouse, particularly in community property states where husband and wife own equal shares in their accumulated wealth. Sadism generally is not carried out to the point of death, yet there are some who do cross the threshold into homicide when not satiated by cruelty alone. Biting and mutilating may precede or follow the actual killing. There often is no prior connection between the offender and the victim, so the motive is not helpful in leading back to the killer. A psychological profile may be constructed using inductive reasoning. It would begin with the recognition and interpretation of the evidence at the crime scene, including the trauma inflicted on the victim. According to the type of offender described, the profile would suggest the most beneficial interrogative approach. Additional data generated might include: the murderer's sex, race, age bracket, employment history, socioeconomic status, sexual adjustment, past record of offences and in some cases, a prediction as to whether the individual will strike again. Some murders are committed simultaneously with or immediately after the sex act, as a concomitant of sexual gratification. In other cases, gratification is achieved through the act of killing rather than through the act of sex; the assertion of power over the victim is the primary motivation—any sexual gratification is secondary. If these cases are initially perceived as ostensible sex homicides, the result may be a misdirected investigative effort. The inaccurately assessed crime scene can allow serial murders to escape detection for long periods of time.

Emotions factors such as anger, jealousy, revenge, envy, hatred, etc., can provoke a person to commit manslaughter or premeditated murder. If the aggrieved partner plans and carries out the killing, it is premeditated murder. Broken nuptial engagements, domestic quarrels, and altercations in general can escalate and lead to homicide when they exceed the bounds of dispute. As a rule, homicides motivated by strong emotion are readily solved, many being manslaughter cases with witnesses present. But even premeditated murder permits potential suspects to be identified deductively once motive is established. Killings that involve the working out of emotional fantasies are called fantasy murders; they are sex-related as a rule, but not always sex-dominated.

Killing of an eyewitness may immediately follow the primary homicide. When homicide-suicide has been ruled out, the case is viewed as a dual criminal homicide. The chance that one of the victims was an eyewitness to the first homicide should also be considered. Checking on the background of each victim often determines who was most likely the intended victim and who the potential eyewitness. Investigative efforts then can be concentrated on solving the initial homicide. When motive for a secondary homicide is silencing of a potential informant, it will have investigative value only if some connection existed between the killer and the secondary victim that made the victim privy to the activities of the killer. Since the secondary victim could have incriminated only a limited number of individuals, the investigator must discover who they might be, and who among them had the opportunity to commit the secondary homicide.

Homicides are usually taking place to remove an inconvenience like a blackmailer, an unwanted child, a feeble parent blocking the takeover of a family business. Once an investigator perceives that the very existence of the deceased was a major inconvenience or impediment to another person, the prospects of solving the homicide are enhanced. Records and people are important sources of information in such cases; they can support the hypothesis that the removal of an obstacle was the motive.

Self-protection is another reason for homicide which should be recognised as a feasibility in specific situations. One example would be the criminal whose escape is interrupted or hampered by the victim. Another would be a murder committed as a result of the realisation of the eventual danger that would be posed by an eyewitness should the offender become a suspect. Another example, perhaps more frequent in occurrence, is that of an offender known to the victim who kills to silence the victim. In such situations, self-protection is the motive for the removal of the eyewitness as a potential informant. Home burglaries are sometimes interrupted by the unforeseen return of the resident; if the burglar's escape is hampered, a homicide can ensue.

Motiveless Crimes

The two distinct kinds of homicide appear motiveless or senseless are: (i) those of stranger killing stranger; and (ii) those in which a person other than the intended victim is killed.

Cases of a stranger killing a stranger is increasing today. The adolescent male acting on a dare or the gang member asserting manliness shoots to kill the first stranger he encounters. Encountering the stranger isn't always necessary; such shootings come from high-rise buildings as well as from passing cars. Nor is it necessary to be a male; adolescent girl gangs are proliferating. Alcohol and other drugs often play a role in these senseless crimes, the fundamental cause of which is probably low self-esteem. The solution of such crimes is frequently based on information obtained through a neighbourhood canvass, from informants motivated by a substantial community reward, from pawn shop records and from people who saw or heard the discharge of a firearm and reported it.

Motiveless homicides occur due to mistaken identity. A homicide will appear to be without motive, and after a thorough check on the victim's background, though the time or site may suggest the killing was intentional, no reason can be found. For example, a businessman was shot upon emerging from his apartment house at about 6:30 a.m., apparently by two men who just before that were observed loitering outside the building. The deceased's business and social background furnishing no possible motive, the case remained unsolved. Several months later, in the vicinity of the first homicide, another man was shot at the same time of the day as he emerged from a building bearing the same house number but on a different street. When apprehended and questioned, the perpetrators confessed that they were hired killers. The first slaying had been a case of mistaken identity; the second was committed to rectify the mistake: this time they got both house and street number correct.

FOCUS OF INVESTIGATION

The crime scene can be a rich source of physical evidence. To reconstruct how the crime was committed, or determine, what actually happened, physical evidence must be recognised before it can be recorded, collected and preserved. In fact, legal requirements can limit the crime scene search to a single opportunity, should the property owner refuse to allow a second search. Other reasons for a thorough initial search include the possibility that the scene may be damaged by weather conditions, building construction in the premises housing the crime scene, or other factors.

The crime scene is the centre point around which important questions revolve:

i) Is this an unlawful homicide?

ii) Is this a homicide disguised as a suicide?

iii) Who is the deceased?

iv) What was the motive for the killing?

v) Is there physical evidence present that may link the killer to the crime scene or the victim?

vi) What happened and/or how was the crime committed?

An element of murder which must be proved in court is whether the death was a result of an action that is neither excusable nor justifiable. This task being the responsibility of the medical examiner's or coroner's office, the forensic pathologist provides expert testimony on the cause and manner of death. To the investigator coming upon a crime scene it is important to point out that appearances are not always what they seem; the cause of death is not necessarily obvious from viewing the body. In one case, an observant police officer saw a man leave an apartment house with a newspaper-wrapped package under his arm, return to the building, and re-emerge 10 minutes later with another package from which some apparently human toes protruded. On accompanying the man back to his apartment, the officer was confronted with the sight of a dismembered female body, a blood-splattered kitchen and bathroom, and what would appear to be an open-and-shut case of criminal homicide.

To cover up a crime, simulating another crime is fairly rare, but it is not unheard of: to cloak homicide, arson, and automobile accidents are the most common expedients; to conceal larceny, especially when an inventory is imminent, burglary may be used. Such crimes are detected because the simulation is often overstated by an offender who is too anxious that investigators not miss the point.

In homicide cases, victim identification is of singular importance. The experience of numerous investigators bears witness to this assertion, for only after an identification has been made can a motive for the killing be established and then utilised to generate potential suspects. Correctly identifying the victim, therefore, is crucial. In addition to its investigative value, the identification is part of the *corpus delicti;* thus, it has probative value as well. In many cases identification is easy. It is speedily accomplished by relatives, friends, neighbours, and business associates who have known the victim for some time and can be relied upon to perform this function.

Identification by two unrelated persons who knew the victim well or by one person and a document in the victim's possession with matching description or photograph is adequate for a "positive ID". Jewelry, although not in itself sufficient for an identification in a criminal homicide, can make a contribution if it is engraved or of unusual design. Fingerprints, useful perhaps 10 per cent of the time, nevertheless should be checked—especially if the body is not readily identified. Missing persons records should be reviewed. The victim's clothing should be examined; if a laundry dry cleaning mark is found and a laundry file is maintained, it must be checked. A photograph of the victim can be distributed in the community, and a public appeal made through newspapers and television.

Any psychological evidence suggestive of the killer's motive must be recognised at the crime scene and interpreted. An informed effort to estimate what kind of a person could have committed the crime is called psychological profiling. Apt to be useful in homicides involving sex, sadistic torture, disembowelment, or genital mutilation, a psychological profile may enable investigators to choose among those likely suspects whose aberrant behaviour has been noted in the community and who appear capable of committing such a crime. Lack of apparent motive in a homicide raises the possibility of a mistake. A neighbourhood canvass should be undertaken in search of a living individual whose description and behaviour are consistent with those of the deceased; then a background check made on that individual. If a motive is found to explain why his or her sudden demise would be desirable, there is some chance that the motiveless crime was a case of mistaken identity.

Evidence linking the perpetrator to the crime scene or victim is of two kinds:

i) Evidence brought to and left at the scene. Examples are: fingerprints; spent bullets and cartridge cases; and blood, hair, and fibres from the person or clothing of the perpetrator.

ii) Evidence taken deliberately or accidentally from the scene. Examples include: easily carried loot such as small appliances; rug and clothing fibres; broken glass particles imbedded in clothing or in the rubber heel of a shoe; smeared fresh paint or blood spattered on clothing; and so on.

Sources of associative evidence suggest what might be looked for at the crime scene:

i) *Traces of the person*: These include finger and palm prints; blood, semen, saliva, hair; bare footprints; other skin patterns such as car prints and lip impressions; teeth marks, etc.

ii) *Traces of wearing apparel*: These include shoe prints; weave pattern and stitching of clothing and gloves; clothing accessories, etc.

iii) *Impressions left by*: These include weapons; tools; shovels, etc.

To determine how the crime was committed and what happened scientific means are used. The purpose is to allow any account of the event advanced by a suspect or witness to be compared with the reconstructed facts. Therefore, before anything is moved it is vital that the initial appearance of the crime scene be faithfully recorded through notes, sketches and particularly photographs. The kinds of clue materials most frequently involved in the reconstruction of a crime are firearms and blood evidence. Other determinations might include: estimating the time needed to perform an act; pinpointing the exact time of a telephone call; making a theoretical analysis of a certain phenomenon; or conducting experiments.

Significant differences between the facts disclosed through scientific reconstruction of evidence, and facts alleged by a suspect or witness, can be put to good use in subsequent interrogations. Owing to its serendipitous nature, physical evidence may, when least expected, bring to light what actually happened. For example, though human hair seldom serves this purpose, when the need arose to determine which of two inebriated individuals was the driver of a car that killed two people in an unwitnessed accident, examination of the hair imbedded in the damaged windshield on the passenger side provided an indisputable answer. The major contribution of the forensic pathologist to homicide investigation rests on the autopsy.

Body as Focus of Investigation

The victim's body can provide evidence of investigative and probative value. The testimony of the forensic pathologist figures significantly in this endeavour; it is required to prove one of the elements of homicide—that death was the result of a criminal act. In addition to shedding light on the cause and manner of death, he may be able to testify about some of the circumstances surrounding the event, thus permitting a reconstruction of the crime—how and when it was committed. An experienced forensic pathologist can provide facts useful in constructing a profile of the killer, for instance, a description of the blows and the way they were inflicted.

The most common means of identifying the victim are successful in permitting investigators to move on to other pressing matters. But sometimes body and facial features are unrecognisable and clothing or jewellery is not present. In these circumstances, the forensic pathologist and forensic odontologist may be able to identify the body through a comparison of skeletal and dental X-rays, or through unique features such as a surgically repaired organ, spinal cord defect, scar, birthmark, or tattoo.

Autopsy

The forensic pathologist, using medical autopsy, determines the cause and manner of death and also evaluates the circumstances of the death. In gunshot cases for instance, the cause and manner are determined in part by the circumstances surrounding the discovery of the body. In addition to its probative value, in the event that death was the result of a criminal act, the autopsy reveals detailed information. This affords the investigator, assisted by the pathologist, an opportunity to reconstruct the crime. The principal purpose of autopsy is the study of disease, particularly terminal disease. A medicolegal autopsy is a postmortem, scientific and systematic, internal and external examination of a corpse by a physician, the forensic pathologist. Involving as it does the practice of medicine, confidentiality must be maintained.

External examination of the dead body is a significant part of autopsy. The pathologist will also want to see the clothing of the deceased and the weapon. Yielding details that facilitate an identification, the external examination also provides what is necessary to reconstruct inductively the circumstances of the death, what happened, how and when it happened and whether the body was moved after death.

Internal examination of the dead body involves making incision to remove organs, tissues, and fluids. Following a gross visual inspection, samples are taken for further study under the microscope and for chemical analysis by a toxicologist. The test results and the external examination allow for the formation of an expert opinion on the cause and manner of death.

Autopsy evidence and its interpretation will help the investigator to reconstruct a homicide.

After committing a crime, a killer may move the victim's body to create the appearance of accidental death. To accomplish this, other aspects of the crime scene will have to be staged. Another reason for moving a victim's body is to limit the scope of the investigation; a sudden disappearance can look like a missing person case instead of a homicide. Serial killers sometimes bury their victims in remote, unfrequented places to avoid detection. Another compelling reason for moving a body from the site of a homicide is the perpetrator's realisation of the close connection between himself or herself and the crime scene. Investigators have some means for determining whether a body has been moved from the site of the killing. One involves the circumstances surrounding the discovery and the place of the discovery; another, the phenomenon known as postmortem lividity.

Appropriateness of the dead body's clothing, considered in conjunction with the place of discovery of the body, may suggest that the crime was committed elsewhere. For instance, a dead woman found in a garbage dumpster clothed in a nightdress more than likely was killed somewhere else. The chances of solving such cases are improved if the site of the murder can be determined. If the site is under private control or ownership, and there is a known connection between the controller and the victim, questioning that individual is in order. If the site is theoretically open to the public but seldom used, the investigator should determine who knew the victim and who had access to that locale and would feel safe from detection while committing the crime.

Postmortem lividity describes the bluish-purple colour that develops after death in the undermost parts of the body. A living person's blood circulates under pressure from the heart muscle, but a dead person's pressure drops to zero and gravity causes the blood cells to sink to the bottom of the circulatory pipelines. Lividity can be evident within 30 minutes of death and, because of clotting, it will remain where it started, even if the body is subsequently moved. If signs of lividity can be seen on the top and side surfaces of the body, the inference can be drawn that it was moved after death.

Forensic entomology helps to find the kind of insect(s) found on a body which may prove it was moved. The environment influences the kind of insect species to be found on decomposing bodies. When the entomologist fails to find insects on a body, this may indicate that the body was indeed moved, and that the suspect's denial is false. Entomologists study where a body is discovered as an ecological problem, then interpret their findings in terms of locality. If it is not, then one can surmise that the body was moved from somewhere else. When a body has been moved, locating the site of the homicide can be critically important.

The presence of the body may affect the species composition of the soil beneath it, and these changes will remain detectable after the body has been moved. In indoor situations, the presence of certain corpse-associated insects will reveal the fact that a body had been placed there at some earlier time. There are even cases in which it was shown that murder victims were transported from place to place in a particular car. Very small insects and other organisms can be inadvertently collected on the clothes or in cars and other vehicles. The presence of these insects can often show that the person or vehicle frequented a particular locality. This kind of associative evidence has largely been overlooked, in spite of its great potential.

Entomologists may be able to provide information about how the death occurred. Was the body mutilated after death? Was this animal, especially a species protected by law, killed illegally? Entomological information is most effectively utilised in the interrogative stage of an investigation.

In cases of homicide it is important to know the time of death. Some reasons include:

i) To question the individual who appears to be the last one to have seen or talked with the victim.

ii) To look for flaws in a witness's account when it is in conflict with the forensic pathologist's estimated time of death.

iii) To protect the innocent, one person immediately seems the likely suspect and the sequence of events relative to the homicide can have inculpatory or exculpatory consequences.

Besides the killer, the last person who see the victim alive not realising that he possesses information of value, may have useful clues that remain undiscovered unless sought by the investigator. Hence, it is important to allow witnesses to recall the last contact with the victim in their own way.

Time of death

The time of death is accurately determined in manslaughter cases than in murder cases. In the absence of a witness, the forensic pathologist estimates the time of death, basing it on as many factors as possible. Rigor mortis, body temperature, and other factors are used for this purpose.

Rigor mortis is the result of chemical changes within the muscle tissue. Evident at first in the small muscles of the hands and jaws (in two to four hours), it becomes more obvious in the larger muscles (in four to six hours) and is fully developed in 12 hours, where it remains until postmortem decomposition begins. Decomposition is affected by extremes of heat and cold;

it occurs very slowly in cold weather, more rapidly in hot weather.

A live body is able to maintain a constant temperature of about 98 degrees Fahrenheit regardless of weather and type of clothing. After death, its temperature falls to that of the surrounding medium. The rate of fall can be affected by several factors, but for a clothed adult body in a room with normal heat, the formula below allows for an estimate of the interval between time of death and time of recording of rectal temperature. It assumes an average drop in temperature to be 1.5 degrees Fahrenheit per hour, that the ambient temperature was about 70 degrees Fahrenheit, and that the deceased had a normal body temperature of 98.6 degrees Fahrenheit at death.

$$\frac{98.6 - T}{1.5} = N$$

Where:

T = body rectal temperature in degrees Fahrenheit

N = number of hours elapsed since death.

Other factors that can help in estimating time of death include stomach content, insect growth and external factors.

Stomach content: The stomach and small intestines are examined for undigested food; its presence provides two important pieces of information—what the deceased ate for the last meal and how long ago it was eaten. When what is coupled with where—the victim's home or a restaurant he frequented—the information obtained can affect the outcome of the investigation.

Insect growth: The forensic entomologist studies insects from egg laying and larvae growth to fully developed adulthood. Entomologists regard the human cadaver as an ecosystem in which certain insects appear and depart on a predictable schedule; they know, for example, that the eggs of houseflies hatch into maggots in 24 hours. Specific knowledge about the time required for each growth stage permits the specialist to estimate the time of death for a body on which insect specimens were observed, recorded and collected. If practicable, the entomologist should visit the crime scene to collect specimens and do so at the autopsy as well. For such evidence to be reliable, the lifecycles of the specific insects obtained from the cadaver must be replicated.

External factors: Evidences from victim's residence and personal habits can be of assistance in estimating the time of death. Gathering this information is the function of the investigator who then shares it with the pathologist. Neighbours are often able to state when the victim was last seen alive. Additional information can be gleaned from such observations as: any food on the table, dishes in the sink, newspapers or mail not picked up, blinds or shades drawn or open, electric lights on or off, or a watch or clock stopped by its having been damaged. If the deceased habitually performed certain daily tasks, e.g., walking the dog, leaving the house to buy cigarettes, going to work, picking up the mail, telephoning friends and family, or receiving calls from them, failure to do so establishes boundaries for estimating time of death.

In some homicides the time available to the killer to carry out the crime can become an important issue, in others, there may be evidence that the killer delayed in leaving the scene. In either event the investigator should appreciate the implications of the time factor. Forensic pathologists cannot pinpoint the time of death; rather, based on when the victim was last seen alive and when the victim was found dead, they can state the interval of time during which death could have occurred. When the timespan is great, the forensic pathologist may be able to narrow these limits.

Events surrounding a homicide can be of great importance in fulfilling the obligation to protect the innocent. The investigator should ascertain whether the interval of time was sufficient for the suspect to inflict the injuries.

What occurred in a homicide may be determined from the kind of injury inflicted on the victim. Trauma is the medical term for bodily injuries produced by sudden physical force—penetrating, blunt, or sharp. A bullet, a bludgeon and a sharp weapon produce visibly different injuries. If the pathologist is able to state with some certainty what kind of weapon was used, the investigator can search for it along the paths the perpetrator may have taken in fleeing the crime scene. When a suspect is developed, his or her home, garage and automobile can be searched for the weapon. The search and seizure laws must always be kept in mind, otherwise, the evidence may not be admissible. This could materially damage a case since a weapon can serve to link an offender to the crime.

Gunshot wounds

Gunshot wounds are of particular interest; from them it may be possible to determine how and what occurred. They are an important source of information which the forensic scientist interprets for the homicide detective. A gunshot wound is the result of the discharge from the barrel of a gun—flame, hot gases, smoke, partially burned and unburned powder particles and the projectile itself. The nature of the wound inflicted is a function of the distance between victim and muzzle at the time of discharge and of the characteristics of the weapon itself. Both entry and exit wounds can be observed on a body. Distinguishing between them may allow the crime to be reconstructed, as may any blood spatter pattern produced, especially when the victim is shot at close range.

Entry wounds: Entry wounds are of three kinds: contact, near discharge and distant discharge. A contact wound results when a small weapon is fired while in contact with the skin (a closed wound) or up to a distance of two or three inches from the body, or a large caliber weapon (or rifle) is fired up to a distance of six inches from the body. A near discharge wound is the result of firing at a distance of six to 24 inches for handguns, and six to 36 inches for rifles. In reconstructing the possibility of suicide, the near discharge distance cannot exceed the deceased's arm length. A distant discharge wound results when a weapon is fired from a distance greater than 24 to 36 inches, respectively, for handguns and rifles.

Entrance wounds: Entrance wounds are round or oval in appearance; their edges form an abrasion collar with the skin surface inverted—depressed and crater-like. Contact wounds inflicted over a thick bone structure have an irregular, stellate (star) shape; their edges are everted—pushed outward. The tearing of the tissue surrounding a contact wound results from the gases that, having entered the wound, seek to reverse direction and escape. The laceration is irregular in appearance; it may be oval-shaped with no abrasion around the edges, but it can and usually will have an abrasion.

Exit wounds: Exit wound results when a bullet, emerging from the body, splits the skin. This skin will exhibit greater tearing if the bullet emerges when it is no longer spinning on its axis—wobbling in its passage through the body. This can happen after striking a bone; if the emerging bullet carried bone splinters with it, the wound may be mistaken for a laceration caused by a blunt force. When the number of entrance and exit wounds is the same, it is evident that all bullets that entered the body exited as well. Should the entrance number be greater than the exit number, one bullet remains in the body to be retrieved as potential evidence. Whether a particular wound is an entrance or an exit wound is best determined by the pathologist. If the distinction is of significance in reconstructing the crime and expert testimony is required, a forensic pathologist must make this determination.

Cutting and stabbing wounds

A wound may appear to the casual observer or untrained police officer to be the result of cutting or stabbing. In fact, it is often difficult to determine the cause. For instance, a penetrating stab wound can be mistaken for a bullet wound, a gunshot wound may resemble a cleavage by a knife or axe: a laceration on the scalp can resemble a dull knife wound. These determinations often require the expert opinion of the forensic pathologist. Accidental deaths from cutting or stabbing are relatively rare, but examples might include: being impaled on a picket fence, sliding from a hayloft onto a pitchfork, or tripping onto the teeth of a rake. The circumstances surrounding the death as well as the practices and habits of the deceased will help the medical examiner/coroner decide.

Suicides by stabbing or cutting are more likely to involve a knife or razor, a broken bottle, glass, or other sharp-edged instrument. Seldom the result of one deft incision, usually a number of short superficial cuts, are inflicted before the wounds are fatal. These slight, often shallow cuts, known as hesitation marks, typify suicide and suicide attempts. The parts of the body usually assaulted in such attempted suicides are the wrists, the throat, and sometimes the ankles. If the attempt is successful, the victim is usually found where the act took place. In some unsuccessful suicides by cutting or stabbing, the individual may decide to seek help, leaving the scene of the initial assault and a trail of blood behind.

Often, stabbing is the cause of a homicidal wound. Since victims will instinctively try to defend themselves, the forearm may bear slash marks, or if a knife grasped in self-protection is pulled away by the attacker, the palm and fingers will be cut deeply. These are known as defence wounds. The upper parts of the body—most often the chest but also the side and back of the neck—suffer wounds that result in death. An autopsy can track the internal path of a stab wound. An upward thrust is normally indicative of homicide. It is easier to stab oneself with a downward or horizontal thrust; such a track usually points to suicide. Criminal homicide, however, cannot be ruled out; in such a case, blood will often be found scattered throughout the area of conflict.

Blunt force wounds

Blunt force wounds are the product of neither a penetrating nor a cutting instrument. Various weapons are able to produce such wounds: a hammer, a stout branch, a two-by-four, an iron pipe, a brick or large stone, or an automobile. Blunt force wounds can be caused merely by falling from a height and striking the head, or landing feet-first on a hard surface. The injuries vary from lacerations, bruises or contusions, bone fractures, internal bleeding and severe crushing wounds, most often to the head, neck, chest and abdomen. The wound may not necessarily be the same size and shape as the crushing weapon. Despite this, a forensic pathologist often can suggest the kind(s) of weapon(s) used, thereby allowing the homicide investigator to conduct a search for the weapon. If found, it might bear traces of the victim's skin, blood, hair, clothing fibres. Blunt impact weapons may also produce blood spatter which, if property interpreted, can help to reconstruct the crime and determine what happened.

Asphyxiation

Asphyxiation describes death caused by interference with the supply of oxygen to the lungs. Although the cause may be accidental, of greatest interest to the homicide investigator are deaths from smothering, strangulation, hanging, poisoning, and drowning. Some drownings that appear accidental may be attempts to cover up criminal homicide; hanging and poisoning deaths, on the other hand, often are mistaken for criminal homicide when in reality they are suicides or accidents.

Smothering

Smothering is frequently encountered in infanticide, in which it is sufficient to place a hand over the infant's mouth and nose. Adults can also be killed deliberately by smothering. The assailant in these cases is usually more powerful than the victim and uses a pillow, cloth, or plastic pressed tightly over the face. It is not uncommon to use greater-than-necessary force; thus, scratches and bruises from the struggle will remain on the body. Their interpretation, together with autopsy findings, are best left to the forensic pathologist. In most of these cases, the offender has a close relationship with the victim. A consideration of who had motive, opportunity and the nerve to follow through should lead to some possible suspects. Since in these cases the offender is not a hardened criminal, any evidence provided by the pathologist and family members that is raised during the interrogation is likely to result in an admission or confession.

Strangulation

Persons may be strangled manually or with a ligature such as a clothesline, electric lamp wire, belt, necktie, nylon stocking, scarf etc. External signs of manual strangulation on a corpse are different from those left by a ligature. However, in both types of strangulation, the internal signs are haemorrhage and damage to the interior structure of the neck, throat, and larynx.

Suicide by manual self-strangulation is virtually an impossibility; accidental throttling is also relatively rare. When the death is sudden and the injury slight and apparently unintentional, accidental strangulation is indicated. If, however, the signs of injury are obvious and severe, it is unlikely that the death was accidental. When death clearly resulted from manual strangulation, there is a strong presumption of felonious homicide.

It may be surprising to learn that the hands are not commonly used to strangle; for one reason, it is difficult to throttle a healthy adult, unless the attack is by stealth or the victim is stunned by a blow or under the influence of alcohol or drugs. Following rape or attempted rape an assailant may try to eliminate the victim/eyewitness by choking. During a quarrel, one person may seize another by the throat to stifle an outcry for help. If this causes death, the attacker's intent would be a decisive factor as to whether it is murder or manslaughter. Witnesses should be queried about any spontaneous utterances made before or during the altercation, particularly by the assailant. If the intent was to silence the victim's call for help, murder is an appropriate charge. Reconstructing some manual strangulations may reveal how they happened. The reconstructions are based on the probability that the force required to asphyxiate will leave an external pattern of fingermarks on the victim's neck. If the assault is from behind, the assailant generally uses both hands; if a frontal assault, one hand. The physical evidence may or may not square with the offender's account; if it does not, the discrepancy can be put to good use for interrogative purposes.

Strangulation deaths may sometimes caused by a broken wire, machine belt, or other ligature wrapping itself around the victim's neck. The nature of the circumstances together with eyewitness accounts of the incident should attest to its being accidental and not a crime. The intentional use of a ligature as a means of homicide is rare, but when one is committed, a horizontal groove or furrow cut by the ligature is often visible on the throat. Signs of bruising and blood congestion just above and below the furrow indicate the victim was alive when it was applied. Since attempts are made to cover up a homicide by simulating suicidal hanging, these contusions have investigative and probative significance.

Pathologists will also examine the inside of the eyelids and the facial skin for another sign of strangulation: pinhead-sized red dots that are minute haemorrhages called *petechiae*. It is also not uncommon to find that the victim has bitten the tongue. If a ligature is knotted, photographs should be taken before it is removed; and a cut made as far as possible from the knot, with the cut ends carefully and securely tied together and labelled as such. Although rather unusual as evidence, the use of an unconventional knot can suggest a vocation, and examining the victim's recent experience with anyone in that occupation may provide an investigative insight.

Hanging is another form of strangulation. The majority are intentional and thus suicidal, but occasionally there are attempts to cover up criminal homicide by making it appear that the victim committed suicide by hanging. If the autopsy is competent, this ruse should fail. Autoerotic deaths, a form of hanging, are indeed accidental. Being unfamiliar with eroticised death, the relatives and friends of the victim will almost invariably insist that the hanging was a case of murder.

When an individual engages in a solitary, sex-related activity whereby he is asphyxiated accidentally, such a type of death is called autoerotic death. There is some physiological support for the belief that oxygen deprivation to the brain intensifies sexual arousal. When there is too much oxygen deprivation, however, the person loses control of the autoerotic exercise and dies of asphyxiation by being suffocated or hanged. The body may be found with the head covered by a plastic bag or with a ligature around the neck. If male, the decedent is often nude, or sometimes dressed in women's clothing, his limbs shackled in a form of bondage with a mirror positioned for self-observation; if female, erotic paraphernalia such as an electric vibrator or dildo may be present.

Hanging is a more common effect of autoeroticism. A bit of cloth or other material is often found wrapped around the ligature; its purpose, to prevent marking of the neck which would require some explaining to inquisitive relatives or friends, should the exercise turn out as expected—providing enhanced sexual arousal with no fatality. If this was a frequent practice, parallel rope marks on an overhead pipe or top edge of a door are likely to be present. They should be looked for after any suspected autoerotic fatality. If most of the accompanying clues described are not present and the young victim is thought to be normal and well-adjusted, a ruling of accidental death rather than murder will almost certainly be incomprehensible to relatives.

Poisoning

Carbon monoxide is a gas to cause death by asphyxiation. Product of incomplete combustion of coal and hydrocarbon fuels, it is tasteless, colourless, odourless, and highly poisonous. Familiar sources are coal and gas appliances such as stoves, refrigerators, hot water heaters, furnaces, and automobiles.

The exhaust pipe fumes of an automobile are all too often seen as a convenient way to commit suicide. Defective home gas appliances are responsible for accidental deaths by carbon monoxide asphyxiation. Very small concentrations—one part per 1,000 parts of air-breathed for about an hour—cause headache, nausea, dizziness, and confusion.

Carbon monoxide accumulates in the blood, so that even smaller concentrations—one part per 10,000—have similar effects if breathed overnight. Awakened by headache and realising something is amiss, the sufferer often will try to open a window or leave the room, but disorientation makes this impossible. Frequently, the victim stumbles and hits a radiator, table corner, or other hard object, opening a head wound that bleeds profusely. The floundering will make the room look like a battle occurred.

In many cases, the victim will die before reaching fresh air and the accidental death will have signs of a felonious homicide. Young children, owing to their high metabolic activity, succumb more readily to carbon monoxide poisoning than do adults; however, it is possible for all the people sleeping at one residence to die from carbon monoxide leaking into a home with its windows sealed shut. This gas turns blood to cherry red and produces a patchy, pinkish colour in the lividity of the corpse. Armed with this knowledge, together with what can be learned from relatives and neighbours about the circumstances surrounding the death, the investigator can focus on the source of the gas and see that it is no longer a danger.

Drowning

Criminal homicide by drowning is largely limited to infants and small children, but adults can be overpowered and drowned. Attempts have been made to cover up a criminal homicide by placing the corpse in a bathtub filled with water to simulate a drowning. This ploy is called for when the connection between the victim and the killer is obvious and the latter will almost immediately be suspected. The manifestations of a true drowning and those of putting a dead body into water are sufficiently distinct to be differentiated by autopsy.

Burns

A body can be burned by fire, scalding liquids, and corrosive chemicals, and electricity. Fire is the most common cause of death from burns. Suicide by burning is quite rare in this culture; rarer still is burning a victim with the intent to kill. Accidental death resulting from burns is more common, particularly among the young and the elderly. A burned corpse may be of interest to the homicide detective because attempts have been made to cover up criminal homicides by making them appear to have been the result of smoking in bed. Hence, the question of accident versus cover-up needs to be considered whenever human remains are discovered at the scene of a fire.

Partially consumed dead body poses no problem as to its human origin. On rare occasions when all flesh has been destroyed, the skull, skeletal bones and especially the teeth, are likely to remain. The latter are most indestructible by fire; they generally can be recognised as human. The issue of the origin of a bone or bones is raised occasionally when skeletonised remains are discovered outdoors in a sparsely settled area. They may be a mix of human and animal bones, or bones of animal origin only. In some cases, the pathologist seek the opinion of a forensic anthropologist before arriving at an accurate conclusion.

There are two simple procedures which can determine if a person was dead or alive before the fire. The first is by autopsy of the air passageway to the lungs and the lungs themselves, inspecting for the smoke deposits that will be present only if the victim was breathing when the fire was started. The second method is a toxicological analysis of the blood for carbon monoxide. Since red blood cells combine preferentially with carbon monoxide, the gas will be found in the blood of a victim who was alive at the time of the fire. The absence of smoke deposits and carbon monoxide signifies that the individual was already dead, killed by another means.

While reconstructing a crime, it is important to know whether an injury was sustained before or after a death. Cover-ups have been attempted by claiming an injury occurred after death, when it was actually inflicted before death. The perpetrator's obvious intention is to corroborate the account he gave to investigators. Differentiating between an antemortem and a postmortem injury can be difficult when the injury occurred within minutes of the time of death; a longer timespan makes it easier for the pathologist to estimate when an injury was inflicted.

ROLE OF PEOPLE IN INVESTIGATION

An investigator should interview family members, close associates, co-workers and social acquaintances of the victim, to get more information about the crime. Some seek out the investigator to impart what they know and believe to be of value; others, either not realising that they have relevant information or feeling reticent about any contact with police, do not come forward. Still others, not being especially close to the victim, may refrain from becoming involved in a homicide investigation; if reassured, they might cooperate. The competent investigator will cultivate and explore all of these potential sources.

Informations elicited by interviewing a victim's associates may include:

i) Suggestion of a motive for the crime.

ii) Naming of a suspect or suspects and providing the reasons for such charges or beliefs.

iii) Describing the usual activities and habits of the deceased permits his or her movements to be traced at the time of, and just before, death.

As a tactic in the search for witnesses, canvassing is generally confined to the immediate crime scene area. In homicide investigation, the various places and locations visited by the deceased on the fatal day should also be revisited with the purpose of identifying anyone who was in contact with the victim. Follow-up will depend on all the facts generated through the canvass and other investigative efforts. To enlarge upon any hints or bits of information that might have been gleaned, it would be appropriate to place an individual under surveillance.

There are cases of homicides in which perpetrators appear to have successfully avoided detection, but after the initial fear of apprehension passes, they will relax their guard and talk, finding gratification in bragging about their exploits. At this point informants can provide what was overheard. Various factors motivate informants. They may be out for a monetary reward, currying future favours, or trying to make a deal with the police—either seeking leniency in connection with a matter currently under investigation or being prosecuted, or looking for revenge on one of the perpetrators. Follow-up measures include surveillance of the suspect; review of the physical evidence discovered at the crime scene; and ultimately, interrogation.

If a person has been named as a possible suspect but no supporting reasons are cited on mere suspicion, the proper procedure is an interview; its purpose, to learn what the individual knows about the crime and where he was at the time of death. The information must then be checked out. This might involve crosschecking with other people or require a reconstruction of the event, utilising the physical evidence at the scene.

The purpose of the interrogation is to determine what the suspect is willing to disclose about the crime and what connection exists between the suspect and the crime scene. Whether exculpatory or incriminating, a statement must still be checked against the alleged facts. This is true for all facts developed during the investigation.

RECORDS HELPING INVESTIGATION

Records are important sources of information which providing an insight into the motive for the crime, allowing the fatal weapon to be traced to its source or ownership and documenting previous activities of the victim or suspect. Special efforts must be expended to discover the existence of records, particularly those not maintained for law enforcement purposes. A person who stands to gain from a criminal homicide as the beneficiary of an insurance policy, a will, or other inheritance may become a suspect. Individuals may also become suspects if it is learned that their former friendly relations with the deceased had soured to the extent that police were called to restore peace, or the deceased filed a civil suit. A person may also become a suspect if he was very recently made a beneficiary and had the means, nerve, and opportunity to commit the crime.

If diaries or letters exist they hint at a motive for the crime, or disclose a hostile business or personal relationship. Unlike records that are routinely maintained and accessible to law enforcement, diaries or letters must be hunted down. They may be withheld by family members because of their intimate nature, or because their potential value to the investigator is not fully appreciated.

Any item of physical evidence represents an opportunity to trace its ownership. For example, the Mannlicher-Carcano rifle used to assassinate President Kennedy and found in the Dallas book depository was soon traced to Lee Harvey Oswald through business records and Oswald's post office box in that city. When it was determined that the glasses found near the body were not the victim's, the optical firm that sold them was traced through a faint, diamond-shaped mark on the lenses. The unique hinges on the eyeglass frames were a new item of manufacture dispensed to but three customers. Only the third customer—Leopold—failed to produce his pair upon request, and this brought him into the network of suspects.

Besides the files maintained routinely to aid in criminal investigation, other police and judicial records should be probed. There could be telephone calls to police complaining of a disturbance of the peace—a family quarrel or a noisy party. There will also be court records when a person is put under bond not to interfere with the victim or when a divorce petition involving the victim is on file. Such records can suggest who to interview, and may also disclose:

i) Unpaid bills
ii) Status of loans
iii) Credit problems
iv) Bank accounts
v) Employment
vi) Recent business transactions
vii) Safety deposit boxes
viii) IRS records
ix) Insurance policies
x) Wills
xi) Other records, if obtainable, should include:
   — Medical records
   — Psychiatric records
   — Military records.

Current knowledge of investigative activities within a department can be exchanged via police computer information networks. The extent of the sharing varies among departments within a state. The utility of crime information systems is enhanced when the reporting of major crimes or arrests is accurate and when it is done promptly and routinely. Thus, in a homicide investigation, useful information may be obtained through daily perusal of the computer printouts. Computer reports describing bank robbery/homicide perpetrators may help investigators recognise a potential suspect based on the *modus operandi* of a robbery pooling the information developed might help to clear more than one crime.

COVER-UP ATTEMPTS

Several means are employed to make the death appear accidental or explainable, to misdirect the efforts of investigators, or to conceal the perpetrator's own involvement.

Accidental Means

Accidental means are relatively common and are used to cover up a homicide to make the death appear accidental. The result of driving into a ditch or cleaning a gun. Not so common but worth noting are arson and poisoning.

Inspection of a motor vehicle which caused a death can determine if it has been tampered with a brake line nut loosened to allow fluid to leak with each application of the brake, or an accelerator made to stick in the feed position. Another kind of cover-up is the use of an automobile to run over the victim's bicycle or motorcycle to make it appear that the damage was caused by striking a telephone pole, curb, or other fixed object. To detect the deception in such cases, the services of a forensic scientist and a mechanic are needed.

The crime laboratory can sometimes determine muzzle-to victim distance through examination of gunpowder residue on fabric, a garment, or the body itself; then, based on a comparison with test firings of the suspect weapon at known distances, the information can be used to reconstruct the crime. The suspect's account of what happened should be checked against the laboratory finding and any discrepancy utilised later in interrogation. The detection of significant levels of barium and antimony on the back and thumb web of the firing hand, when there is little or no residue on the non-firing hand of the victim, is considered evidence that the deceased discharged a firearm.

Setting accidental fire to mattress to make it appear that the victim was careless about smoking in bed has been used as an attempt to mask criminal homicide. The use of apparent homicide to cover up insurance fraud is another twist; insurance investigators are confronting a flood of cases in which intense fire consumes the victims and makes identification difficult or impossible. Often the insured is found to be a recent arrival—sometimes from a third world country in which scant fingerprint, medical, or dental records exist. It is comparatively easy under these circumstances to substitute the body of a countryman or vagrant to serve as the victim of an accidental fire.

Poisoners, when caught, will claim that they put the poison in a medicine capsule with the intention of committing suicide, only to find that the victim took it accidentally. Rather than report the death immediately, they will hide the body and claim the person is missing; then, if it is discovered, allege they acted out of fear of not being believed.

Explainable Means

To make a crime explainable, two common cover-ups are employed: (i) simulating a felony to account for death; and (ii) claiming self-defence. Another ruse is to provide inquisitive neighbours with a plausible reason for the absence of a spouse or live-in companion. The experienced investigator is often able to recognise a poorly conceived and executed scenario. When a suspect is questioned, any nervousness or anxiety hints at a cover-up. Reconstructing the event and checking the results against the suspect's account can pay dividends if a cover-up has been attempted.

The use of a claim of self-defence to cover up a killing will be illustrated by the following case. In his statement to the police, a husband claimed he had called his estranged wife on the morning of the shooting to ask that she come to pick up her mail and sign an insurance check. He said he expected her in the late afternoon after work; instead, she showed up at midday. He also claimed that, after she had signed the check, he reached for it and the pen only to look into a pointed gun and to implore her,

"No, no, don't shoot!" He stated that he then turned sideways to reach for a gun hidden under a cushion; his wife fired once and missed, the bullet lodging in the couch; and only then did he pull the trigger of his gun, killing her.

Investigations revealed that the bullet retrieved from the couch had been fired by his weapon. The autopsy disclosed that the victim had been shot twice: once in the side of her body, once in the back of the head. The number of shots did not comport with his claim of self-defence; neither did the location of the head wound. These led the jury to convict him of second-degree murder.

Diversionary Means

Some criminals believe that if they discover or are the first to report a crime they will not be suspected—that the mere fact they came forward will be construed as showing honesty and integrity such credence is misplaced; many a criminal has come to regret this naive assumption. Therefore, recognising a potential diversionary tactic for what it may be experienced investigators customarily consider and check out the person who discovers the body or first reports the crime.

Contriving an alibi is another diversionary tactic. For example, a man murdered his wife and children at about 7:00 p.m.; at about 8.30.p.m., just after calling his brother- in-law ostensibly to discuss a matter of mutual interest, he left on a business trip. Arriving some 150 miles away, he put in a long-distance call to his home through the motel operator. Receiving no response, he surmised, presumably for the benefit of the motel operator, that his wife and children must be sound asleep. He asked to be awakened at 7.30 a.m. so he could place another call to his family. Again, his call was unanswered. Expressing concern to the operator, he asked that a call be placed to neighbours to took in on his family. It was shortly thereafter that he claimed to have first learned of the tragedy. In her contacts with the guest, the motel operator received the impression of a person who was not being straightforward and whose nervousness and anxiety were excessive. A background check on the family, the forensic pathologist's estimate of time of death and the operator's suspicions led to an interrogation and later to an indictment.

MISSING PERSONS

From the police viewpoint there are two kinds of missing persons cases, each having different consequences with regard to law enforcement follow-up. One kind is voluntary: the missing person has created circumstances suggesting an abduction, suicide, or accidental death. The other is involuntary: the missing person was abducted and is being held captive or is in fact dead, the victim of a criminal homicide. The murderer accounts for the disappearance by telling inquisitive neighbours that the victim is caring for a sick relative or friend living some distance away. The murderer may even attempt to mislead the police in this way, should pressure from family or friends precipitate official inquiries.

It is generally believed that disappearance of a relative, especially a child, is not voluntary. Some adolescents in a rebellious stage run away from home; such disappearances, of course, are voluntary, just as the reasons for a child, adolescent, or adult to suddenly vanish will vary. Conventional police wisdom on missing children cases dictates that some disappearances are not a cause for official concern; thus, a "24-hour rule" often governs the response. However, the rule is not invoked when there are signs of foul play or when a very young child abruptly vanishes. These circumstances call for an immediate, intensive search.

Although police quickly recognise the potential for harm to the very young, the basic assumption that runaways are not at risk is ill-founded. Moreover, abuse and neglect can be involved even when a child has been abducted by a parent. A linkage is believed to exist between the violence of a criminal and a childhood marred by physical, psychological, or sexual abuse. It has led to the development of a comprehensive multistate network for the exchange of information on missing or abducted children.

The National Centre for Missing and Exploited Children of US has classified the problem of missing children according to definitions provided by the Office of Juvenile Justice and Delinquency Prevention (OJJDP):

i) *Family abduction*: When a family member (i) takes a child in violation of a custody agreement or decree; or (ii) in violation of a custody agreement or decree fails to return a child at the end of a legal or agreed-upon visit, with the child being away at least overnight.

ii) *Non-family abduction:* Unauthorised taking of a child into a building, a vehicle, or a distance of more than 20 feet; the detention of a child for a period of more than an hour; or the luring of a child for the purposes of committing another crime.

Stereotypical kidnappings are non-family abductions in which (i) the child is gone overnight; (ii) is killed; (iii) is transported a distance of 50 miles or more; (iv) is ransomed; or (v) in which the perpetrator evidences an intent to keep the child permanently.

iii) *Runaways:* Children who have left home without permission and stayed away overnight, or children who are already away and refuse to return home, depending on their age and amount of time away.

iv) *Thrownaways:* Children who (i) have been directly told to leave the household; (ii) have been away from home and a caretaker refused to allow the child back; (iii) have run away but the caretaker has made no effort to recover the child or does not care whether the child returns; or (iv) have been abandoned or deserted.

v) *Lost, injured or otherwise missing:* Children, missing for various periods of time, depending on the child's age, disability, and whether the absence is due to an injury.

In child homicide cases, death can either be caused by another child or an adult. If the latter, the slaying is often sex-related. Death at the hands of another child is difficult for most people to comprehend. At one extreme, it happens almost accidentally as the outcome of child/adolescent exploration; at the other extreme, it may be the result of the pleasure derived from the excitement and thrill of killing. Within the psyche of a child-killer in the latter cases there often are pain, rage and a sense of ineffectiveness. Family and playmates usually provide the key to solving homicides committed by children. They may not volunteer a name or a motive, but interviewing them separately about various aspects of family life might produce insights.

The unexplained disappearance of an adult is a frightening experience for family and friends; in general they fear foul play. However, an adult may lawfully leave home, job, and normal haunts without notice, provided the family does not become a community burden. There are males, usually middle-aged, who disappear to take up a new life, as often as not with a younger mate. To soften the impact and account for the departure, they contrive an explanation. Some will leave evidence of apparent suicide. Missing persons cases are not always criminal homicides, but persons reported missing may indeed be homicides.

MULTIPLE DEATHS

Multiple deaths are frequently the subject of television and newspaper reports; this fuels public awareness and curiosity. Media speculation also makes this crime seem a modern phenomenon, which it is not. All the reporting, however, does have its upside; on-the-spot coverage enables law enforcement agencies to recognise similarities in homicides committed over time and in wide-ranging areas. All multiple killings are not the work of serial murderers. Other useful distinctions can be made among those responsible for multiple deaths. As a consequence, the investigation and solution of a case will differ depending on the classification into which the particular case falls. Before police agencies can coordinate their efforts, serial killings must first be recognised as the work of one individual.

Double Homicide

Double homicide often involving more than a few victims, is family slaughter by one of its own members; or the murder of all persons in a household by an intruder bent on robbery, burglary, or rape. The least frequent kind of multiple death, random mass murder, usually accounts for the greatest number of fatalities per event.

Criminal homicide followed by suicide is the most common kind of double homicide. For example, chronic ill-health or financial worry can cause a married pair to decide to end their lives together. A background check of family and friends will often provide a reason. Sometimes a note is left behind; not infrequently, there is a pact between the victims. It would be worthwhile to find out if any prerequisite steps were taken, like purchasing a weapon, medicine, or poison. Such evidence, when coupled with the medical examiner's findings, can obviate further investigative effort.

Another common double homicide is the shooting of a retail store clerk and a customer during a robbery. Here, the disposition rests on solving the robbery. From time to time, an individual is murdered merely for happening to be with the target, being an unwitting witness who must be eliminated. In such cases, the luckless bystander is peripheral to the solution of the case. If the killings are the work of mobsters, statistics suggest that even when the motive is ascertained, solution and conviction are unlikely.

Residence Murders

Residence murders occur in the victims' home. There are three kinds of perpetrators: a family member; an ex-family member-husband, or former lover or friend; or a stranger. When perpetrated by a family member, the case is usually amenable to solution, but the solution is considerably more difficult when an unknown factor such as a home invader is responsible. In family killings, an adolescent son rather than a daughter or parent is more likely to be the guilty party. The fact that there are no signs of forced entry suggests the crime was committed by someone with access to the premises. Intruders, however, can gain entry simply by ringing the doorbell and then pointing a weapon at whoever responds.

Investigative steps include a background check of all family members and a neighbourhood canvass. A psychological profile should also be considered. Disclosure of any odd behaviour or significant change in lifestyle, such as unanticipated flight or other uncharacteristic act of a family member, obviously warrants investigation. All are signals suggesting involvement, they call for a check on the whereabouts claimed by the individual at the time the crime was committed. It might be productive to inquire whether anyone would profit from the death of the victim, or whether there are hints or suspicion of interest in the occult or demonology.

Mass Murders

Generally, there are two kinds of mass murder—those resulting from a crime spree spread over a period of time, and those in which all deaths occur in one shooting event.

Cases of one random shooting event are easily handled: the offender is killed by the police in the act of mowing down his victims, commits suicide, or is taken into custody. There is also an abundance of supplementary information available, e.g., eyewitness accounts, physical evidence, records, which allows evidence to be developed with little difficulty.

Crime spree mass murder cases are generally solved: (i) when they are recognised as the product of a crime spree often motivated by robbery and rape, that results in the deaths of victims who are generally unknown to the killer; ii) when the public, becoming involved through media coverage, reports sightings of the wanted criminal. This may ultimately lead to apprehension, if police surveillance and other follow-up activities have not succeeded.

Three other types of killers are responsible for multiple deaths—serial murderers, lonely hearts killers and poisoners. The motive is usually an important factor in the solution of murder, but it contributes little to the solution of mass murders and serial killings.

Serial Murders

Since each serial murderer has the same motivation, the value of motive in solving such homicides is nullified. An added hindrance is the general lack of any previous connection between victim and killer. The serial killer is intelligent. When brains and a good appearance are combined with a beguiling charm, winning a victim's confidence is not difficult. What differentiates serial killers from other murderers, however, is that they know right from wrong; what they lack is a conscience impelling them to do right. These criminals genuinely relish their victim's terror; for them, murder is the ultimate thrill and this distinguishes them from the average killer. Not driven by conventional motives, therefore, they select their victims at random: perhaps some physical or mental attribute galvanises them into action, or they are attracted by the seductive prospect of a corpse with its promise of erotic pleasure.

Serial killers present the investigator with an additional burden in both quality and degree: their mobility, the absence of any prior association with the victim, and their use of remote burial sites all represent some of the difficult obstacles to be overcome. When a serial murderer continues to operate in the same locale, disposing of the bodies becomes a problem.

Several notorious serial murderers have been apprehended as a result of routine police work: preventive patrol; responding to a domestic disturbance involving a bizarre fire setting attempt and following through on a ticket for illegal parking; checking for required tax stamps or stolen plates on a vehicle; and following up on the last known contact of a missing teenager who disappeared after a job interview.

Most of these cases were the subject of intensive investigation; before being solved, they required sizeable resources: forensics, personnel, and computers. Cases receiving inordinate media coverage cause an equally inordinate quantity of misleading and vexatious information to pour in to the police.

Lonely Hearts Killings

Lonely hearts killers are murderers who prey on lonesome people. They examine the personal columns of newspapers and magazines with great care, select prospective victims, and then correspond with them. Starting off as penpals, they follow up with telephone calls, and eventually arrange a meeting. By means of charm, a reassuring voice and manner whatever it takes—they finally are able to learn whether the prospective victim has bank accounts or other assets. If they deem the potential reward worth the effort, attention is then lavished on the victim-to-be, with marriage or promise of marriage the ultimate bait. At this stage, they may take out an insurance policy on the life of the intended victim. Lonely hearts killers are most often males who work alone, but sometimes they work in pairs, perhaps with a female posing as a sister.

Poisonings

Homicide by poisoning is relatively rare today; those who employ it to seize their victims' assets are somewhat akin to lonely hearts killers. They befriend their prey and become live-in companions; in this way, they assure a supply of victims.

Poison is a substance which, when taken in small doses, causes an individual to sicken or die. It generally works by affecting a major organ such as liver, kidney, brain, lungs or the autonomic nervous system. Symptoms can be mistaken for those of a natural illness: acute bacterial food poisoning and acute arsenical poisoning resemble each other. Hence, if a toxicological examination is not conducted when a sudden onset of symptoms and death follow the ingestion of food or drink, a criminal homicide may not be recognised and a poisoner could go free. If several people had the same food or drink, and only one became ill but did not die, a bungled poisoning is a possibility.

Owing to inexperience, many poisoners believe that too much poison will be detected. They hold back, causing sickness but not death, then must increase the doses until the desired result is achieved. Some poisons act cumulatively: each dose precipitates acute symptoms until a lethal level is reached. Thus, if a person were to have repeated symptoms with no prior record of such symptoms and is otherwise in good health, the death should be regarded as suspicious. At the very least, a toxicological analysis of the body organs and fluids should be performed. The symptoms manifested before death are of utmost importance, as are the appearance and odour of the body after death.

Following are some situations in which a poison causes a death:

i) accidentally taking an overdose;

ii) accidentally taking the wrong medicine;

iii) deliberately taking poison.

The source and kind of substance should be determined, when poisoning is suspected. Investigative steps that should be taken are the following:

i) Interview the family, the physician, and any others who have had recent contact with the deceased.

ii) Examine the premises where the death occurred and collect all potential evidence relating to the possible substance used.

iii) Transmit the evidence to the laboratory for examination by a toxicologist.

iv) Check records of the pharmacy that filled the prescription and other possible commercial sources of the poison.

Normally, mass poisoners use substances that produce acute symptoms. Chronic symptoms of poisoning are more likely when the criminal is inexperienced and unfamiliar with the amount of poison required. Insufficient dosages are often administered since the victim must fail to detect the poison when eating or drinking.

Poisoners are usually motivated by revenge, hate, discontent, and even extortion. They often see themselves as having been unfairly treated—in life generally or in the business world particularly. If the motive can be learned, the investigation has taken a significant turn. Sometimes the poisoner will volunteer crucial information through a letter to the media or a note planted at the scene, or a public appeal will induce the poisoner to share the reasons for the discontent. Written communications obtained are valuable physical evidence; handwriting and typewriting specimens as well as finger or palm prints may tie a suspect to the crime.

In cases of suicide—an accidental overdose or prescription medicine taken by mistake—the suspected substance is generally located with little difficulty. The substance, together with any illicit drugs, hypodermic syringes, and needles that may be found, must be marked, preserved, and transmitted to the proper laboratory for analysis. The hypodermic needle requires special handling: the tip must be inserted carefully and securely into a cork stopper. For identification and security against tampering, it is important that physical evidence be handled to meet the requirements of both the lawyer and the toxicologist. The forensic pathologist should submit the appropriate organs obtained by autopsy to the toxicological laboratory.

If a prescription medicine appears to be the source of the poison—either by overdose or mistaken ingestion—the records of the dispensing pharmacy should be checked and the physician who wrote the prescription interviewed. When the medicine has been identified by the toxicologist, the results must be compared with what was ordered and dispensed. Records are sometimes kept on toxic compounds, supplying the date, to whom furnished, and the amount obtained. A follow-up inquiry can determine if the individual who bought the material performed work requiring the use of the toxic material. When a possible known source of the poison is established, a sample should be obtained to determine the trace elements present as impurities and contaminants.

Fortunately, fewer homicides are occurring in our world compared to other major offences. Investigation departments had allocated more resources to investigate homicide cases than for other cases.

REFERENCES

Adelson, Lester, *The Pathology of Homicide*, Springfield, IL: Charles C. Thomas, 1974.

Hughes, Daniel J., *Homicide Investigative Techniques,* Springfield, IL: Charles C. Thomas, 1974.

Geberth, Vernon J., *Practical Homicide Investigation: Tactics, Procedures, and Forensic Techniques,* 2nd ed. New York: Elsevier, 1990.

Killias, M., Gun Ownership, Suicide and Homicide: An International Perspective, In Alvazzi del Frate *et al., Understanding Crime*, Rome: UNICRI, 1993.

Ressler Robert K., Ann W Burgess and John Douglas E., *Sexual Homicide: Patterns and Motives*, Lexington, MA: Lexington Books, 1988.

3

Burglary—Crime Affected by a Society

Burglary is a crime that affects all strata of society. All burglaries violate someone's physical space, and for this reason even the most simple burglaries must be taken seriously, particularly those that occur in private residences. All too frequently, and particularly in the inner city, burglaries are given a short shrift by the police, who may be deluged with large numbers of violent crimes against the person. It is estimated that more than seventy per cent of all households will be burglarised at least once over a 20-year period, and almost half of all urban residences will be victimised two or more times.

Although difficult to investigate, burglary usually offers a relatively large number of clues. Research indicates that the preliminary analysis of a burglary case can provide "solvability factors" that make it possible to focus on those cases with the highest probability of being solved. Burglary investigation can bring a high degree of satisfaction to the person who is truly interested in the elements of solving a mystery.

The Model Penal Code of the American Law Institute defines burglary as: "A person is guilty of burglary if he enters a building or occupied structure, or separately secured or occupied portion thereof, with purpose to commit a crime therein, unless the premises are at the time open to the public or the actor is licensed or privileged to enter. It is an affirmative defence to prosecution for burglary that the building or structure was abandoned".

The Bureau of Justice Statistics Dictionary of Criminal Justice Terminology, Second Edition, defines burglary as: "Unlawful entry of any fixed structure, vehicle, or vessel used for regular residence, industry or business, with or without force, with the intent to commit a felony or larceny".

Burglaries take many forms and affect victims in different ways. The homeowner who loses a personal heirloom or other personal property—which may have little monetary value—may be more devastated than the business person who loses millions of dollars worth of insured goods. Understanding the type of burglary, the characteristics of the offence, and the demographic characteristics of the victim can provide insight into the suspect and his or her background. For example, burglaries of middle-class or poor residences are more likely to be committed by juveniles, and the probability increases in cases in which entry is through a broken window, and again when the search appears to have been haphazard and the property taken is varied rather than specific.

Burglaries in hotels are more likely to be committed by an older, more experienced professional. In a residential burglary, the method of entry and exit, as well as the type of search, will provide information about the suspect. The more professional burglar searches methodically; uses a specific type of tool for entry; takes only valuable property; and concentrates on wealthier victims. With the exception of the small store, most commercial or business burglaries require a greater degree of expertise and frequently more planning than a residential burglary. Nevertheless, many burglars operate with very little planning or "casing" of the target and the victim. In burglaries involving large amounts of merchandise or very valuable property there is likely to be an inside informant working with the burglar. This is especially true in businesses that have a high employee turnover; it is important to ask the victim about employment records. In addition to providing information about property stolen, the victim should be asked to review the past few weeks and recall any unusual events or the presence of individuals who seemed out of the ordinary.

Conventional wisdom holds that there are few witnesses to burglaries, in reality there are likely to be many more than one would suspect. In most cases the police make a cursory or half-hearted attempt to locate witnesses. A careful canvass of the immediate area should be made as soon as possible with a view to identifying or developing descriptions of potential suspects. If some time has passed since the burglary occurred, it may be worthwhile to interview persons who might have been on the scene at or near the time of the burglary. One should also keep in mind that persons who are "out of place", such as juveniles during school hours, or "strange" vehicles and unusual activity at the burglary site may not be thought important by witnesses at first.

In addition to witnesses at the scene, there will also be witnesses at the point where the property is disposed of. Although these witnesses are not likely to be cooperative, pointing out that linking the stolen goods to the burglary could result in a charge of receiving stolen property will frequently elicit their cooperation. Of course, without adequate property identification this avenue is less hopeful. Informants or petty criminals on the fringe of illegal activity in a neighbourhood also can be a source of information.

Most good burglary detectives have a good informant network, and are tied in with other sources of information, such as beat patrol officers, bartenders, truant officers, playground attendants, and other individuals who pick up information on illegal activities. Cultivating such sources is an important component of the investigator's work.

Professional burglaries represent different challenges. When large amounts of merchandise or warehouse goods are taken, identification of the truck or other vehicle used is important. Witnesses may have seen the truck at or near the scene. The vehicle may even have received a traffic citation. Witnesses should be asked about vehicles that were out of place, such as a van where tractor trailers usually park, or whether there was an inordinate number of people on the truck. Usually, a truck only has a driver and loader on it. A sympathetic and unhurried approach to questioning the victim is important, not only because it helps alleviate much of the stress associated with victimisation, but also because details provided about what has been stolen, the *modus operandi* of the burglar, or other aspects of the case may become critical as the investigation proceeds.

Stolen items overlooked in the initial report may provide the link that helps solve the case, items with serial numbers or individual marks, custom-made jewellery, or original artwork, documents such as cheque books or stocks, and even keys or personal tools taken by the burglar may be recovered later. In most cases the burglar will dispose of stolen items through a fence or even directly on the street, but some items may be kept for personal use. In addition to stealing property, the offender may do things at the scene of the crime that can help identify or link him or her to the scene of the crime at a later date.

One burglar thought it clever to leave disparaging notes on the walls of his victims' homes. When he was eventually apprehended he was surprised to learn that handwriting analysis helped add several years to his sentence because the prosecution was able to charge him with multiple crimes. Other burglars may take food from the refrigerator, use the victim's facilities, or display other forms of aberrational behaviour that help establish a *modus operandi*.

Some common techniques used by burglars to gain entry are the following:

— *Prying*: The use of a jimmy, screwdriver, tire iron, pry bar, or knife to force a door, window, or lock. The perpetrator may leave tool impressions on the point of entry.

— *Picking*: Using a knife or professional locksmith's picks to open the cylinder of a lock.

— *Pulling*: Using an auto body repair tool called a dent puller or "slap hammer" to pull the cylinder out.

— *Smash and crash*: Simply breaking a window to gain entry, and in the case of a store, reaching in and grabbing articles on display.

— *Cutting glass*: Using a glass cutter to make a hole in order to reach in and open a lock or unfasten the latch. A small suction cup may be used, such as a toy dart, to keep the glass from falling inside and making noise. After the cut is made around the suction cup, the burglar simply pulls the glass out.

— *Slipping lock or loiding*: Originally celluloid strips were used, hence the term loiding, but they are frequently replaced now by credit cards and pocket knives (the knife may be filed down to make it narrower) or other thin objects, such as nail files, that are less identifiable as a burglar's tools. The card is slipped between the lock and the door jamb where there is no "dead bolt" or other latch.

— *Brute force*: kicking, breaking, or forcing a door with the body or an instrument. Where a door has been kicked in, the perpetrator may leave shoe or sneaker impressions.

— *Removing door panel*: Kicking in or breaking the door panel, or unscrewing the panel on an aluminium door.

— *Skylight entry*: Shattering skylight and lowering oneself by rope into the premises.

— *Transom entry*: Breaking or removing the air conditioner and climbing through a transom.

— *Window/door entry*: Simply passing through an open door or window. Surprisingly, this is one of the most common forms of entry in a burglary.

— *Key entry*: Locating a key hidden by owner or using a duplicate key made on a previous visit (a technique commonly used in hotels that have not upgraded to more modern card or lock change technology), or duplicating a key that has been left with garage attendant, or using a key taken in a purse snatching.

— *Lock-in*: Entering the facility before closing and hiding in the premises until after closing.
— *Removing hinge pins*: Interior doors, and some exterior doors, are installed in a way that makes it possible to remove the hinge pins and pry the door out.
— *Spreading door jamb*: Using an automobile jack or similar instrument to push the door away from jamb.
— *Cutting wall*: Sawing, chiselling, chopping through wall of adjoining apartment, building, or hallway to gain entry.
— *Cutting screens and locks*: By knife or hacksaw
— *Partying*: Entering a residence where a barbecue, pool, or interior party is being held and stealing fur coats or other loose items.
— *Fishing*: Breaking a hole in a window and reaching in by hand or with a pole to remove items.
— *Safecracking*: A very specialised form of burglary that may involve burning, blasting, punching, chopping ripping, cutting, or peeling a safe.

In addition to such techniques, a burglary typology can serve as a frame of reference for the investigator. In burglaries of businesses, particularly where entry may have been gained through an adjoining wall or over a roof, it is likely that the perpetrator cased the location on a prior occasion. Employees should be asked about persons who either acted strangely, or asked questions about the building, or lingered for a long time. In questioning burglary witnesses it is difficult to develop good physical descriptions unless the burglar had a distinguishing facial feature, such as a moustache.

Most witnesses will probably not be able to identify the suspects, this effort may serve mainly to develop general descriptions or other items of information. In such cases, the smallest details put together over several burglaries may help to develop a composite that leads to identification of the suspect.

CONDUCTING THE INVESTIGATION

Repetition is a predominant characteristic of burglary. Burglaries are generally committed over and over again until eventually the suspect is caught. Unfortunately, in most cases, very little information from one burglary to another is exchanged by investigators, which makes it difficult to clear cases. One of the best sources of information on prior cases is the patrol force. Officers collect a great deal of information, but even over a relatively small geographical area there may be five or more officers working during a seven-day period.

When one considers the number of officers in a city or county, it becomes clear that much information is lost for lack of collation or analysis. Few burglary reports are designed to collect the unique elements of information that make it possible for the investigator to link prior cases. Fortunately, there has been significant progress over the past decade in this area. A number of forms now collect information that can help solve the crime rather than simply report it. The value of a report is only as good as the information collected. Patrol officers should be trained and supervised properly, and proper credit should be given to them when they provide information that helps solve a case. Since the vast majority of burglaries are residential, and because research suggests that many of these are committed by juveniles, a good deal of information may be found on the street. In addition to the patrol force, juvenile courts, youth squads, and other youth service agencies may be of assistance.

Investigation of large professional burglaries, which may involve multiple jurisdictions, requires communication with other agencies. Major case squads will frequently be established and information on their activities and sources of contact should be available. In some jurisdictions, such units meet periodically to discuss ongoing or unusual cases. Professional associations and business groups, particularly those affiliated with the insurance industry, also can be valuable to the burglary investigator. In addition to providing information on specific groups, such associations can provide the investigator with other helpful information—such as burglary techniques being used, types of property most frequently attacked, and kinds of merchandise in greatest demand.

Research on burglary and burglars provides some information that will help the burglary investigator to better understand the dynamics and career patterns of the crime. Generally, burglary offenders begin their careers at a young age, acting with other juveniles in break-ins or burglaries. However, according to police statistics, the average age of arrest in 1985 was 22 years. Some offenders turn to more violent forms of crime, but career burglary patterns usually emerge, and some individuals develop specialities in certain types of acts, such as safe or art burglaries. Juvenile burglars commonly operate with an accomplice, and are even more likely to work in groups of three or more. More sophisticated burglars may operate in pairs, but research on them is inconclusive. The professional burglar will frequently operate with a lookout, and may use walkie-talkies to communicate.

Most burglaries are not well planned. The choice of target is likely to be based on whether the perpetrator views it as an easy mark. An easy mark would be a place such as an unlighted residence, or one with high hedges, old windows, or easily opened doors. A small percentage of thrill-seeking perpetrators, commonly called "cat burglars", enter homes when residents are present, usually at night, and try to accomplish the crime without arousing the occupants. In recent years there has been an increase in home invasions, in which a residence is entered while an individual or a family is present. These are usually carried out by groups or gangs, who may often commit crimes such as robbery, assault, rape, or murder. The viciousness of these crimes often defies imagination, and makes home invasions a highly investigative priority.

For the most part, though, burglars are looking for quick cash or goods they can fence. Tracking stolen property offers another avenue of investigation. Many burglars are drug addicts who can frequently be identified by the types of property they take. They turn to robbery (the taking of property from a person by force) as they get older. Relatively few become professional burglars, but those who do develop a high level of expertise in planning and carrying out their crimes.

For the purposes of identifying perpetrators and making a case that will hold up in court, a wealth of physical evidence is usually available. Unfortunately, for a variety of reasons, crime scene searches are conducted in only a few cases, usually only where there has been a large loss, or where another serious crime such as assault, rape, or homicide is involved. Research indicates that most crime scenes contain much more physical evidence than is discovered. Fingerprints are the most common form of evidence sought in a crime scene search, and other items of trace evidence and materials are often overlooked. Trace evidence can establish a link between the perpetrator and the crime scene. Blood, saliva, footprints, hair, and fibres may be present. The suspect may also leave behind items such as cigarettes, matchboxes, tools, clothing, or handwriting. Successful crime scene processing begins with the initial officer on the scene. Even though a decision may be made not to call in an evidence technician, a crime scene search can and should be conducted. Bear in mind that what may seem trivial at first may later prove to be a key piece of evidence.

The search for physical evidence at a burglary scene will frequently require the assistance of the victim, who can be very helpful in identifying what has been moved or what does not belong. Oftenoverlooked are tool marks, personal items such as discarded cigarettes and matchboxes, and footprints outside the house. One of the more promising advances in scientific criminal investigation has been the Automated Fingerprint Identification System (AFIS), which makes it possible to search criminal records for a single latent print! This technological breakthrough is of particular value to burglary investigations, in which latent prints generally represent the most common form of physical evidence available. AFIS technology is based on the ability to electronically scan and identify fingerprint characteristics and store them in digital form in a computer. Using ridge endings and bifurcations it is possible to create a digitised representation of the print, which can be stored in the computer.

On a rolled inked print, usually obtained from a prior arrest, it is possible to find 90 or more points on each finger, making the print distinguishable from all other single digit prints. When a latent (partial) print is recovered at the crime scene, it can be run through the system for a match. Even a poorly developed partial print may provide enough information to conduct a successful search. It takes just minutes to accomplish a 10-print search in, a file of about 5,000 records, although it may take a half-hour or longer to search for a match to a partial, single print. The ability of the investigator to provide the names or record numbers of potential suspects can help reduce the search time. Although frequently overlooked, latent fingerprints represent a potential source of information that should not be ignored. Unlike for most other crimes, the suspect is usually in the house for some period of time and, because he is looking for things, objects are touched.

The uniqueness of burglary investigation rests in large measure on the use of records and information about the stolen property. In even the smallest burglary there is likely to be something taken that has a number or mark that individualises it for identification purposes. In the age of computers and other forms of technology, it is much easier to track items, to communicate and cooperate with other agencies, and to work closely with companies and businesses that may be able to assist.

Obviously, police records will contain information on possible suspects, reports leading to the recognition of crime patterns and MO, and property data. The key here is in knowing how to use department records to search for information. External information from manufacturers, businesses, and trade associations may also provide valuable assistance. For example, most manufacturers include identification numbers and other information on merchandise, such as where it was sold and additional details that may facilitate identification. Sometimes the investigator will have a load of stolen merchandise but will not have a victim. Tracing its sales point may indicate where, and possibly to whom, it was sold.

Some of the sources with which the investigator should be familiar include:

— The National Crime Record Bureau (NCRB) comprises all the crime data which in turn helps in tracing criminals, in investigation and predicting crime trends.

— The National Crime Information Centre (NCIC), a national database that is particularly useful in tracing weapons and items with serial numbers.

— The National Auto Theft Bureau (NATB), which provides information not only on stolen vehicles, but also on property taken from trucks.

— Credit card companies, which can provide information on the use of stolen credit cards, thus providing clues to a suspect's movements, sometimes helping to produce eyewitness descriptions by sales clerks (when the burglar has used the card).

— Chambers of commerce, which may assist in the investigation of certain types of crimes against businesses.

Using scanners and bar codes, it is also possible to more clearly identify merchandise. It is now possible for police departments to scan reports into the computer, making it much easier to retrieve information about specific items of property. Further, more sophisticated databases allow investigators to search for information using strings (groups of characters entered for computer searches), thereby making it easy to look for records of stolen property that cannot be identified by numbers.

The investigation of burglary involves: investigating the crime scene and collecting and preserving any available physical evidence; interviewing potential witnesses; using informants, examining records, tracing property; and identifying suspects. The successful conclusion of a case will frequently depend on the investigator's ability to handle a large amount of seemingly unrelated pieces of information in an analytical way.

Most burglars are known to the police. Most have prior arrests, and a large percentage are drug users. Most are young males. Generally, burglars must commit a relatively large number of crimes in order to meet their needs. They usually operate within a specific geographic area, but there are some signs that this is changing. Many burglars steal cars to carry out the crime. Distinguishing marks—such as method of entry, type of property taken, or method of search—are often left behind. All of these factors tend themselves to crime analysis.

Computers, if used properly, are an important investigative tool. Even in large cities, where burglaries are relatively common, the investigator or crime analyst can frequently "sort out" burglaries committed by one or more individuals. The computer also can be used in tracing property. The initial and follow-up reports must be as specific as possible in the identification of property. Brand names, specific marks, and serial numbers are important.

Burglary investigations can generate a vast amount of information. Information overload can be avoided if one handles the information effectively. Since computers are not readily available to most investigators, and the case load of the burglary detective is usually high, there must be an effort to screen and sort information and cases in the most efficient way possible. Some investigators use only 3×5 cards; even more rely on memory. Under ideal conditions, some form of case screening will help. With a case screening approach, individual investigators are assigned cases with common characteristics; some will work on residential, others on business—some on juveniles, others on professional jobs, etc.

Another effective but seldom used approach is the daily or weekly case review in which investigators meet to describe their cases and to identify common characteristics of burglaries and burglary suspects. In one major city, a string of burglaries was solved when an investigator attended a regional training seminar where he spoke to a colleague about a peculiar cat burglar who always drank a glass of milk at the scene and then washed the glass. The colleague named the suspect immediately. The burglar had moved from one jurisdiction to another after he was released from prison. Unfortunately, most cases are not solved that easily. Put luck and the prepared mind factor into it, and investigators help make their own breaks. Having mastered the information concerning burglary types and career patterns, the investigator has taken a long stride toward developing expertise. Putting the aforementioned information together with an investigative plan is the initial step.

A short description prepared for the case report should emphasise the differences in burglaries. It should begin with the type of burglary and proceed to include the finer details. The investigator can now ask the juvenile courts for a records check. Although it is unlikely that the television set will turn up as fenced property, the investigator can add this to his or her list of items when checking pawn shops, informants, or other outlets for stolen goods. There are enough individual items in the report to assist in the continuing investigation. By keeping the case "alive", it is possible that a break will come. "Filing" it will mean less likelihood that it will be remembered.

If a suspect is turned in—either through records, informants, or other information—there is physical evidence that may be brought into play. Although this is a relatively simple case, it is not an uncommon one. For a more sophisticated burglary, a similar, although more detailed, investigative plan may be developed. The plan need not be written out for each case, but it should be considered, used as a guide, and referred to especially when a case stalls.

Time management is a critical factor in the investigation because most investigators may be working on dozens of cases at one time. Keeping a written summary is important. "Solvability factors" have been adopted by a number of police departments as a means of screening cases to identify those with the highest probability of solution. The approach represented a major breakthrough in burglary investigation which, when combined with advances in computer technology, should move the field even further forward.

REFERENCES

Applied Criminology Group, "Evaluation Report of the Boggart Hill Anti-burglary Initiative", *Report to the Multi-Agency Panel,* University of Huddersfield, UK, 1997.

Cromwell, Paul E., James N. Olson and D. Aunn Wester Avary, *Breaking and Entering: An Ethnographic Analysis of Burglary,* Newbury Park: Sage Publications, 1991.

Ekblom, P. H., Law and M. Sutton, *Safer Cities and Domestic Burglary Schemes,* London: Home Office, 1996.

Harry, O'Reilly, *Practical Burglary investigation,* Chicago: Office of Security Programs, University of Illinois at Chicago, 1991.

Waller, I., "What Reduces Residential Burglary: Action and Research in Seattle and Toronto", In H.J. Schneider (ed.), *Victim in International Perspective,* New York: de Gruyter, 1982.

4

Robbery—A Crime Affected by Physical Emotions

Robberies have considerable impact on the community. They engender fear and reduce the quality of life in a neighbourhood, and political pressure is often brought to bear on the police department to solve them. For these reasons, supervisors will, if possible, assign their most trusted and capable investigators to robbery cases. Victimisation studies indicate that slightly more than half of all robberies were reported to the police.

In almost 90 per cent of robberies the suspects are male. Not surprisingly, most robberies occur in metropolitan areas. Black males tend to be robbed at twice the rate of black females and at two and a half times the rate of white males. In more than half the cases the suspects use weapons, with guns being the weapon of choice in more than 40 per cent of the cases. Statistics also indicate that offenders using guns have a higher probability of carrying out the robbery than those using other weapons. These statistics provide a background for the investigator and a frame of reference as the investigation proceeds. Most robberies (81.8 per cent) were committed by a stranger—about half by more than one offender.

Most armed robberies and assaults occur on the street after dark. Most victims do not perceive that they are about to be robbed. The actual event takes place in a relatively short period of time. In such cases the victim may tend to perceive things that did not occur, and care should be taken to walk the victim through a reconstruction of events. This may prove helpful in developing an MO and in searching through files for similar cases. The investigator should be aware that victimisation studies indicate that a significant number of robberies are never reported to the police. This fact can be important because the investigator may want to use the media and other community resources to ask victims who have not reported the crime to come forward in order to develop information about suspects and their description.

Robbery involves the taking of property from a person by the use or the fear of force. The Model Penal Code offers the following definition: A person is guilty of robbery if, in the course of committing a theft, she/he: inflicts serious bodily harm upon another; or threatens another with or purposely puts him in fear of serious bodily injury; or commits or threatens to commit any felony of the first or second degree. An act shall be deemed "in the course of committing a theft" if it occurs in an attempt to commit theft or in flight after the attempt or commission.

Robbery is generally defined for statistical purposes as The unlawful taking or attempted taking of property that is in the immediate possession of another, is by force or threat of force. Since theft or attempted theft is an important element of robbery, the investigator should be familiar with the definitions of theft and related offences. The definitions from the Model Penal Code provide general information. However, the investigator must be thoroughly familiar with the definitions of the jurisdiction in which he works.

Robbery victims come from all walks of life. Robbers run the gamut from unsophisticated juveniles to experienced career criminals. Males are victimised more than twice as often as females; persons between the ages of 12 and 24 have a higher probability of victimisation than those who are older. Blacks are victimised almost three times more than whites, and Hispanics twice as frequently as whites. The majority of victims are unemployed, and people making less than $10,000 are victimised more than twice as much as those making over

$50,000. Types of robberies include street robberies; residential robberies (usually termed "home invasions"); robberies in schools; bank and armoured car robberies; and other commercial robberies. The most common commercial robberies involve convenience stores, gas stations, liquor stores, drug stores, cab drivers, and other businesses or activities that frequently operate during evening hours and involve cash transactions.

The probability of victimisation is related in large measure to where individuals live, their occupation, and their "availability" as targets. Most victims do not make good witnesses because the incident occurs quickly, a high degree of stress is involved, it is often dark—at least in street robberies—and the suspects often wear masks. Facial identification is frequently difficult for this reason.

A good investigator working carefully can elicit information that may be buried in the victim's subconscious. Police artists, various identification kits, and more recently, computer imaging systems can be used to help create a drawing of the suspect. The investigator should be aware that facial identification, while important, is not the only source of information. Clothing, physical marks (e.g., a scar) or characteristics (e.g., a limp), type of weapon, and words (i.e., "tale") used by the perpetrator to convey that robbery is intended can be invaluable. The robber's tale is extremely important in establishing an MO. Since most robberies are committed by juveniles, it is likely that they will continue to wear the clothing they used in the robbery and use the weapon again.

Determining where and when the robbery took place also can be important in developing a profile and for crime pattern analysis. Keeping in mind that the victim is likely to be traumatised by the event, the investigator should take care in conducting the interview. Initially, interviews should be conducted individually when there is more than one victim. The victim should first be asked to describe in his or her own words what actually took place. The investigator should attempt to obtain answers for the questions: who, what, when, where, how, and why. During this stage careful notes of the specifics should be taken. After the victim has explained what happened, the investigator should begin to work carefully through specific items of information.

Some departments provide a checklist that is useful in obtaining specific information. The investigator should recognise that victims are prone to inadvertently giving inaccurate information; for example, height and weight are difficult to estimate accurately and are often reported incorrectly.

Robberies fall into categories based on the kind of force or threat employed. Armed robbery involves the use of a weapon such as a firearm, knife, or other dangerous weapon. Other terms for this include: holdup, stick-up and hijacking. Strong-arm robbery involves the use of physical force to commit the robbery. Other expressions for this include: mugging and muscle job.

There may be more than one victim and one suspect. In more spectacular robberies involving some degree of planning—such as a bank or armoured car robbery—there usually will be witnesses, and every effort must be made to locate them. The detective handling a robbery investigation must isolate the victim and witnesses and then interview them separately. He also must quickly identify and protect the crime scene. This aspect of the investigation is frequently overlooked or handled poorly, largely because the crime scene may actually be in more than one place.

There is also a tendency to want to interview witnesses too quickly, which may result in a loss of information or varied accounts based on misconceptions. In many instances the initial phase of the investigation is handled by the patrol force and there is a desire to broadcast a physical description of the robbers and vehicle as soon as possible, and even to remove the victim from the scene to accompany patrol officers in a search for the suspect. Such actions, though understandable, can complicate the investigation. In some cases it is almost impossible to preserve the crime scene because so many curious bystanders have entered the area. If not kept separated, witnesses too may influence each other in providing descriptive and other information.

Robbery investigations depend on the ability to reconstruct the event, to develop physical descriptions and, perhaps most important, to establish the *modus operandi*. Since individuals are creatures of habit, they are likely to say or do similar things in different acts. The ability of the investigator to identify these "calling cards" can go a long way toward solution of the crime. The investigator who bases a case solely on eyewitness testimony is endangering the case and the possibility of a conviction.

The investigator should carefully develop an interview plan, both in terms of the sequence of individuals involved and the sequence of questions asked. All too often investigators "feed" information to individuals being interviewed. Victims and witnesses generally fall into categories based on physical and emotional/psychological factors. These categories help determine the interview plan, the validity of the information, and the direction in which the investigation will head. The physical factors are age, sex, race, stature, eyesight or other physical infirmities and injury. Emotional/psychological factors include degree of distress, whether or not a prior victim, ego, attitude toward police and attitude toward race. In addition to interviewing victims and witnesses, the investigator should remember that important information may also be gleaned from officers who arrived on the scene, as well as secondary witnesses who, though they may have arrived after the event took place, may have seen or heard something that was overlooked in the preliminary investigation.

Individuals—including the officers who handled the preliminary investigation—should not be permitted to hear or take part in the initial interviews of others. At a later time, it may prove worthwhile to conduct group interviews, but this should be done only after everyone has been interviewed alone and after the investigator has compared notes with any partners or assistants. Ideally the victim should be interviewed first and witnesses interviewed in descending order on the basis of those who appear most reliable. A classic mistake often made during interviews is grouping individuals in the same location as they await the interview, or permitting those who have been interviewed to mingle with those who have not.

Victim and witness perceptions may vary considerably. Short individuals, for example, will likely perceive the suspect as being taller than will witnesses who are tall. Elderly witnesses may have varying perceptions of age. Young witnesses may be able to provide more information on specific types of details, such as automobile descriptions, types of clothing, and mannerisms. When a victim has been robbed before, he may be able to provide details resulting from that unique frame of reference. Sometimes victims experience ego problems because they did not act as they felt they should. Care should be taken to assure the individual that a lack of action or resistance was a wise course. In addition to information provided by victims and witnesses, the investigator should identify and gather any physical evidence. All too often there is an assumption that the rapidity of the event precludes the possibility of physical evidence being present, but such a possibility should never be ruled out.

ROBBERY SUSPECT

Younger suspects tend to operate within a geographical radius of two miles from their residence. The average age of arrest for robbery suspects is 24. Blacks and males are over-represented in robbery arrest statistics, with males making up more than 90 per cent of the offenders and blacks making up more than 60 per cent. For the most part, these offenders are also likely to commit street and commercial robberies with relatively little advance planning. They also are likely to commit multiple offences in a relatively short period of time, frequently under the influence of alcohol or drugs. In 1994, in the US, about one-fourth of all robberies were cleared. Sixty-four per cent of those arrested were under the age of 25, and 91 per cent were males. Adult arrests declined by seven per cent. Over the five-year period 1990-1994, juvenile arrests increased by 32 per cent and female arrests were up nine per cent.

Most robberies involve more than one offender operating against a single victim. About one-third of robberies involve three or more offenders. The number of offenders is usually age-related. Young robbers tend to act in groups, whereas older robbers frequently operate alone or with a partner. Investigation of youthful robbers will focus largely on patterns and *modus operandi*. Although these suspects may have prior arrest records, they may be difficult to retrieve because they were handled in a juvenile court and are unobtainable.

The frequency of events is in the investigator's favour. Information should be sought from youth investigators, informants, beat officers, neighbourhood residents, and others who have access to possible suspects. Professional robbers are more likely to be older and to have a prior arrest record. Frequently they have been convicted of a crime. Of those paroled for robbery, 64 per cent are rearrested for some crime, 45 per cent are convicted, and 40 per cent return to prison. Older offenders are more likely to plan the act, but the plan is sometimes no more than "casing" the location. Well-planned and well-executed robberies will usually be obvious to the investigator and will involve large sums of money or merchandise.

The professional robber is also much more likely to operate over a wide geographic area, in some cases across jurisdictional boundaries and even state lines. He is also more likely to use firearms, automobiles, masks or disguises, and lookouts. In some instances, professionals use hand-held radios for communication and monitor police radio frequencies. The professional robber represents a different challenge than the so-called opportunist robber who selects victims by chance. Since this type of robbery is executed less frequently and over a wider geographic area, it is much more difficult to establish a pattern or useful MO. In these cases the investigator must resort to the use of records, physical evidence, and robbery analysis techniques to be successful.

CONDUCTING THE INVESTIGATION

General crime scene protection and search measures should be observed at the robbery scene and in other key locations, such as a vehicle recovered after use in the crime. Some specific types of physical evidence should be considered at robbery scenes:

— Footprints may be present.

— Fingerprints may be left in proximate locations. For example, the suspect in a store robbery may have handled merchandise prior to carrying out the robbery; in a bar there may be fingerprints on the glass or bottle used; in a handbag snatching in which the item is recovered there may be fingerprints on the handbag or its contents, or footprints where it was recovered. There may also be fibre traces on recovered material.

— Saliva may be present on discarded facial masks.

— Body secretions, fibre evidence, or other trace materials may be present on the victim's clothing if there was a scuffle or the use of force.

— When a suspect has been identified or apprehended, trace material may be present on the suspect's clothing that will link him or her to the victim or the scene.

— Physical evidence may be available where a weapon is recovered. Blood samples, skin or tissue residue, or even "tool marks" should not be overlooked. In one robbery-homicide case the perpetrator struck the victim with a serrated hammer. The blow was struck with such force that an impression that matched the weapon was left on the skull.

— Fingerprints or trace evidence can be left on the articles recovered. A watch taken during a robbery, which was later pawned and recovered by police, produced a partial print that helped convict the suspect. In a rape/robbery, a suspect was identified more than a year later when a fingerprint recovered from the victim's handbag was run through the computerised fingerprint system known as Automatic Fingerprint Identification System (AFIS) when the suspect was arrested for another crime.

A robbery suspect will probably have a prior arrest record. The manner in which records are used may determine the success or failure of the investigation. By a process of elimination it may be possible to narrow the range of suspects considerably. In departments that use a computerised record system it may be possible to initiate "blind" searches. Some of the variables that can reduce a list of suspects include: sex, race, age, colour of hair, specific descriptors, clothing, type of weapon, geographic location, type of vehicle used, and number of subjects involved. This partial list of variables provides an indication of the ways in which a potential list of suspects can be developed and then reduced.

Most robbery suspects will commit more than one crime. If, over time, it is possible to link crimes to one person, a more accurate profile can be developed and used to plan a strategy for apprehension. In addition to police department records, consideration should be given to other records, including: court records, prison records, other law enforcement agency records, other agencies, credit card companies, and motor vehicle bureau records

Successful robbery investigations depend heavily on the ability of the investigator to recognise significant variables that can be used to research past crimes as a measure of identifying and locating suspects. When all leads have been exhausted with reference to the immediate investigation, the solution will frequently lie in past crimes.

Recognising patterns, geographical locations, the types of victims, and the number and characteristics of associates should be a high priority in the follow-up sequence of the investigation. By putting this information together it is frequently possible to add to the information about suspects. Having accomplished this, the investigator should begin to review arrest records of individuals who fit the composite *modus operandi* and physical characteristics. Where this fails, the investigator should relay information to other jurisdictions, requesting their cooperation in crimes of a similar nature, or those in which potential suspects may have been arrested.

REFERENCES

Banton, M. O., *Investigating Robbery*, Brookfield, V.T: Gower, 1986.

Clarke, R. V and G. McGrath, "Cash Reduction and Robbery Prevention in Australian Betting Shops", *Security Journal*, 1, 3, 1990.

Eck, John, *Solving Crimes: The Investigation of Burglary and Robbery*, Washington, DC: Police Executive Research Forum, 1979.

5

Arson—A Way of Fastest Crime

Arson is a fastest growing crime. Of those crimes recognised as arson, about 20 per cent result in arrest, yet the conviction rate is only one to two per cent. In many areas of the country, authority for arson investigation is in the hands of state and local fire marshals, and in some, the police have concurrent jurisdiction. A fire has to be investigated, in certain cases extensively, before there is proof that a crime was committed—that the fire was of incendiary origin. Some unusual aspects of the crime of arson contribute to the difficulty of obtaining evidence to convict. They are:

- The fire may consume all traces of its incendiary origin, especially if detecting and extinguishing it were delayed.
- Rather than remaining undisturbed until recorded properly and the physical evidence collected, the crime scene may be hosed down with powerful streams of water, or its contents moved outdoors.
- The perpetrator can use a timing device to delay the start of the fire, thus allowing an interim for an alibi.
- Falling debris or the collapse of a building may cover or destroy evidence of the fire's having been set.
- Freezing weather makes searching for evidence more difficult; if everything becomes caked with ice, search and recovery are further delayed. Extremely hot weather can evaporate volatile accelerants.

Recently, some states have included "the use of explosives to injure property"; and, rather than having to rely on a charge of "attempted arson", they added "the preparation of a building for burning" to the arson statute *per se*. The degree of arson is keyed to the endangerment to life; as deadly as any gun, arson is a weapon against people as well as property The fire started at night is considered more life-threatening than one set when most people are awake or unlikely to be present.

The *corpus delicti* of arson has three elements:

i) That a fire or burning occurred in a structure or property protected by law. To meet this requirement, the case law of a particular jurisdiction must be consulted to determine whether charring or merely scorching is sufficient to meet this requirement; or whether there must be an actual physical change in the material.
ii) That the fire or burning was intentional: neither accidental nor attributable to negligence or natural causes, but the result of a criminal act.
iii) That someone set the fire, caused it to be set, or otherwise furthered the act.

A fire is considered to be of accidental origin unless proved otherwise. But as firefighters know very well, it is not unusual to be unable to make out a case for arson, even when experience strongly suggests the fire was not accidental. Hence, when the police have the primary responsibility to investigate a fire, they should exploit the firefighters' eagerness to put their suspicions to the test; when the arson issue is raised, the first step toward proving the *corpus delicti* is taken. People are usually responsible for questioning the source of the fire. Not only the victim, but customers, tenants, and business rivals may express the belief that the fire in question was most timely or convenient.

Records are least likely to be of immediate service, but later in the investigation they may be invaluable in establishing a motive; for example, a large insurance policy taken out shortly before the fire occurred; or, over time, the same owner having several fires in different locations. Rather than prejudge any fire or explosion, the investigator should question all information until it is verified. To minimise the loss of evidence, every fire scene should be treated as a potential crime scene; any conclusion as to its incendiary or accidental cause must be based on the totality of the evidence gathered. The investigator must then sort it, form a "working hypothesis" and, testing new information against that hypothesis, modify it as needed.

The person who discovered the fire can report on which part of the building was ablaze when he first noticed it. This helps to determine the point of origin. Additional information from residents and bystanders might include observations on how quickly it spread, whether the colour and volume of smoke were unusual.

Based on past experience, firefighters are often the first to suspect arson and quick to recognise the unusual. Giving voice to their suspicions, they will note: flame height; how rapidly the fire expanded; smoke density, and any odd colour of the smoke; odour redolent of organic accelerants; fire doors that are open but should be shut; and boxed merchandise blocking passageways and doors. A failed fire alarm or sprinkler system certainly will give firefighters pause.

The owner or manager of the destroyed property may be questioned twice: first, soon after the fire and before arson is suspected; then, when evidence obtained from people, the scene, and records supports a case for arson. The second round of questioning may be an interrogation. During the first session of questioning, information should be sought concerning the interviewee's knowledge of the fire, e.g., how and why it started.

The whereabouts of the interviewee at the time the fire started should be ascertained, as well as how he learned of the blaze. Questions concerning insurance coverage are also in order and the responses should be placed in the record. Suspicion should be aroused if the individual can produce a fire insurance policy on the spot when no other policies are immediately on hand, or if he can account quite readily for his or her whereabouts at the start of the fire and cite eyewitnesses, yet remain hazy concerning the hours just prior to the fire. When a case can be made for arson, especially arson for profit, a second round of interviewing is in order.

Employees of a commercial enterprise possess potentially useful information, which will be divulged if they are interviewed properly. They may tell what they know of any recent changes in business practice or offer a perspective on the firm's financial health that differs markedly from management's. Although such information does not constitute evidence in and of itself, it can give direction to a line of inquiry that otherwise might not be pursued by the investigator. For example, the owner's reputation as a gambler or womaniser suggests a need for ready cash.

Employees should be questioned about the contents of the building: How was it distributed? Where was the stock? Where were the furnishings? They should be asked about any recent changes: Was new stock added or substituted for old stock that was moved or removed? Employees may report having observed fire hazards that management ignored.

The insurance company will be conducting a parallel investigation to protect its interests in potential civil litigation. Frequently, the company's investigator, whether in-house or independent, has much more latitude than the public sector criminal investigator, as insurance contracts generally require a building owner to allow company investigators on the site as often as they reasonably demand access.

A criminal investigator, however, must either have a search warrant or permission from the owner, who thereby waives forth amendment rights. Within the terms of the contract, the insured can be required to submit to examinations under oath, and may not refuse to answer any questions without jeopardising his or her right to collect on a claim. Hence, cooperation is feasible between the public and private sectors.

On the other hand, if an insured has invoked his or her Fifth Amendment rights with the criminal investigator, the company can be notified of this fact, and an exploration conducted under the auspices of the civil investigation.

Business competitors can provide information on the economic health of the industry in general and the arson target in particular. Spectators at the scene, neighbours and tenants of commercial buildings, news media staff, and those unearthed by neighbourhood canvassing are other potential sources of information not to be overlooked. Any spectator not dressed appropriately for that time—that is, wrapped in bedclothes, street clothes thrown over nightdress, and so on—should be asked for identification. If one is a stranger to the neighbourhood, how they came to be there should be ascertained.

Suspicious behaviour to be looked for among spectators at the scene includes: anyone making light of the situation, laughing, moving about constantly, or talking to other spectators, as well as the so-called eager beaver who provides unsought information or "helps" the firefighters with more enthusiasm than the situation warrants. Neighbours or tenants in the same building or one nearby should be questioned because they may have observed unusual activity immediately before the fire was reported.

In cases of insurance fraud, it would be the removal of such valuable merchandise as high-quality men's suits, and their replacement with suits of low quality. If the shift was made during regular business hours, it would probably be noticed by other tenants; if one was made after hours, it would be even more suspicious. In residential fires the removal of guns and electronic appliances, especially TVs, is common. Irreplaceable possessions like photographs, trophies, or certificates also are frequently removed prior to the setting of a fire.

Photographs and films taken of bystanders at recent fires should be scrutinised to determine if the same individual appears at several fires, or whether a suspect generated subsequently was a spectator. Videotapes made by professionals as well as amateurs have proved invaluable in documenting the course of large fires and the actions taken during their suppression.

INVESTIGATION

Motives for committing arson are numerous, but can be summarised as follows: profit, spite, and revenge; vandalism; and pyromania. Generally, motive is quite personal. When tentatively identified, it may send the investigator to search records, or require a surveillance, neighbourhood canvass, and/or additional interviewing of those who might confirm or dispute the motive attributed to the suspect.

Physical Evidences

The aim of examining the scene and attempting to recognise and collect physical evidence in a case of suspected arson is threefold: first, to determine where the fire started; second, to establish whether the fire was intentionally set, thereby proving an element of the crime; and third, if the fire is determined to have been set, to connect the arsonist to the crime scene. Despite this, tell-tale signs of where the fire started may remain, but the investigator must be capable of reading them. To do so, the following elementary knowledge of the chemistry and physics of fire is unavoidable.

Three components are required for fire: burnable material (a fuel); oxygen; and a heat source (which raises the temperature of the fuel to its kindling point). The relationship is expressed in the equation:

$$\text{Fuel} + \text{oxygen} + \text{heat source} = \text{combustion}$$

The temperature of the heat source must be greater than the ignition temperature of the fuel; also, the heat source must be able to raise the fuel to its ignition point by direct contact, or by transferring the heat through radiation, conduction, or convection. Since each component can play a role in proving or disproving that the fire was set intentionally, it is important to understand the function of each.

The temperature of the heat source must be higher than the fuel's ignition temperature. Most fuels are organic, as are the many products used in constructing and furnishing buildings, such as wood, paint, and fabrics used in rugs, draperies, upholstery, and bedding. When burning, carbon combines with oxygen to form carbon monoxide and carbon dioxide, releasing heat in the process:

Organic compounds + oxygen = Carbon monoxide + carbon dioxide + heat

A compound such as linseed oil (a drying oil found in paints) combines at room temperature with oxygen and releases considerable heat as part of the oxidation process. Should linseed oil be left on rags that are piled up or dropped in a heap, thereby preventing the air currents from carrying away the heat, fire can break out.

Most petroleum products—oils, greases, kerosenes, and gasolines—are not drying oils and thus do not pose a spontaneous combustion risk. When arson is employed to cover up a homicide, investigative use can be made of the fact that carbon monoxide is one of the by-products of combustion. Its absence in the blood of a dead person who apparently fell asleep while smoking in bed may unmask a cover-up attempt—a supposedly accidental death may be revealed to be a criminal homicide.

A living person breathing carbon monoxide retains it in the blood because haemoglobin forms a stronger chemical bond—about 200 times stronger—with the deadly gas than it does with oxygen. A dead person's blood is no longer circulating; accordingly, carbon monoxide is not taken up by the body even though it is exposed to it. Soot is another by-product of combustion. Its presence or absence in the respiratory passages of an alleged victim of a fire indicates whether he was alive or dead at the time of the fire. The absence of soot in the windpipe and lungs of the deceased could indicate that a death first believed accidental—from falling asleep while smoking in bed—may actually have been homicide.

The carbon dioxide produced by combustion is used by green plants and trees for the photosynthesis of organic compounds and the simultaneous release of oxygen into the atmosphere, thereby maintaining the earth's oxygen supply at the 21 per cent level. Fire requires at least 16 per cent oxygen content to continue; concentrations between 16 and 21 per cent promote heavy smoke production. Investigative interest is aroused when a fire extinguishes itself through a shortage of oxygen and by the carbon dioxide and carbon monoxide produced.

Heat sources

Circumstances are favourable—a flammable gas or vapour, or a finely divided, solid material such as kapok is present—a mere spark can be the ignition source. A spark was all it took to set fire to the ocean liner Normandie, being refitted as a troop carrier. Naturally, sabotage was suspected. An immediate investigation, however, revealed that an acetylene torch had been used in disregard of such a known fire hazard—the proximity of highly flammable kapok. The ship was quickly engulfed in flames and the volume of water ultimately needed to quench the flames sank the liner at her berth in New York harbour.

Accidental heat sources: The initial site of the fire may be determined from the physical evidence and traces remaining after it is extinguished. Whether its origins were accidental or natural, some evidence of the cause will usually be found at its source. The most common accidental causes include:

— *Heating / cooking systems*: Sparks from a fireplace, dirty chimney, overturned space heater, exploding or leaking kerosene oil stove, or overheated greasy frying pan. Radiant heat from boilers, stoves, furnaces, faulty chimneys, or overheated equipment—motors, gear boxes with dry bearings. Vents and exhaust systems that allow flames or hot gases to escape and come in contact with combustibles.

— *Electrical system (equipment and appliances):* Deterioration because of: worn insulation; misuse (overloaded circuits); improper installation (loose connections—especially with aluminium wire); defects (shorted circuits through a faulty switch, causing sparking or arcing); overheating caused by a loose connection; and any of the above coupled with neglect (grease collected in stove vents and hood filters).

— *Smoking:* Careless use or disposal of cigarettes, cigars, or pipes, especially in bed and in living areas is the cause of many fires, and the most common cause of death by fire. Ignition can be delayed up to 12 hours when smoking materials are improperly discarded.

— *Matches:* Fumes or vapours, virtually impossible to ignite with a glowing cigarette, are ignited easily with a spark from a match or a flame. Matches and lighters—with their exposed flames—probably are responsible for more fires than are the glowing embers of tobacco, if fires started by children playing with matches are counted. Though accidental fires do not result every time a child plays with matches, they can be a consequence of such activity. The investigator should look into the child's past behaviour, which is not likely to have escaped the family's notice. Asking the family if precautions were taken to keep matches safe and asking the child whether he was able to obtain them would also be appropriate.

Natural heat sources: Some of the natural causes include spontaneous combustion, which can make flammable material smoulder and then burst into flame; lightning (especially in remote areas), which can start fires in structures (such as silos or barns) but more frequently causes forest fires; and—although a rare cause—sunlight, which can be concentrated on combustible material by the lens effect of a water-filled glass container or a concave mirror.

Investigative efforts must make certain that the cause was not so simulated. Cover-up attempts are usually associated with insurance fraud, or with fires meant to conceal other crimes such as homicide or theft. Motive, especially pecuniary, can be an important factor in deciding to press on with the inquiry rather than accept the ostensible cause.

The absence of a natural cause, or an accidental cause leads to an assumption of arson. If both are eliminated after a thorough investigation by a qualified expert, one element for a charge of arson is sustainable. Additional factors to be considered include: the nature of the fuel present; its physical form; whether the suspected source could provide enough energy to ignite a fire; and whether normal ventilation was tampered with, which otherwise would have cooled off the fuel faster than it could be heated. Known as accelerants in the field of arson detection, some examples are: gasoline (or gasoline blended with diesel fuel, a precaution sometimes taken by arsonists); kerosene; lighter fluids; paint thinners (turpentine, mineral spirits, acetone); and toluene.

All carry a high potential for danger, the greatest attaching to the most common accelerant by far—gasoline. If gasoline and other extremely volatile fuels are ignited at concentrations between 1.5 and 6 per cent, gasoline vapours may produce an explosion that shatters windows, pushes out walls, and scorches the skin and clothing of the arsonist, who may be burned acutely on the back while making a hasty exit. By notifying hospitals, emergency clinics, and doctors of the need to report all cases of extensive burns, particularly back burns, the arson investigator may locate a likely suspect—certainly if the patient with severe back burns claims they resulted from having lighted a gas oven.

Sources for fire origination

There are three main sources for fire origination. The first source is provided by the burn patterns visible on partially consumed combustible material. In this age of high technology it may be surprising to learn that the prosaic shovel is a must if burn patterns are to be made visible, for a huge quantity of debris is the inevitable consequence of fighting a fire. Indeed, it is not uncommon for arson experts called to the scene to find a foot of rubble covering much of the site. The distorted shapes and other effects of intense heat on such objects as light bulbs or furniture springs are the second source of information. The third source, one that may lead to the point of origin is the observations of the person(s) who first noticed the fire.

Burn patterns

Fire usually burns upward (by convection), then outward (by radiation and conduction). By examining where things are burned and where they are not, the investigator establishes the pattern of the burning. Surfaces exposed to oncoming flames are always burned more than surfaces not exposed—protected, on the lee side. Bevelling takes place; this and the "V" pattern resulting from the flow of the fire are used to reconstruct its path.

i) *Pour patterns:* The kind of burn pattern that results from pouring an accelerant onto the floor of a room is particularly important. A pour pattern is clear, demonstrable evidence of the use of an accelerant.

ii) *Alligatoring:* The size of the alligatoring or checking is not useful to the investigator, for it is dependant on the type of wood and its cut rather than on exposure to the fire. The single exception is the flat, baked appearance caused by low intensity heating over a long time.

iii) *"V" Pattern:* When the "V" is distinct, the bottom of the cone sometimes points to where the fire started, or to where the fuel was burning. An ignition or fuel source may be found at the base of a "V" pattern. The action of interior structural fires, however, is not always this simple. Obstructions can prevent a fire from spreading; strong drafts from stairwells and elevator shafts can distort the "V"; and broken or open windows and doors can create drafts that dramatically alter the way the fire spreads and, therefore, the configuration of its burn pattern.

iv) *Charring:* The deeper the charring, the longer the fire burned at that spot. Since the longest burning time must be at the point of origin, observing the depth of char at various places can help them to trace the fire back to that point. An accelerant itself may burn more intensely than the materials on which it was splashed, leaving a darker, recognisable char pattern of its own. Heavy charring in a corner of a room, which would otherwise be difficult to fathom, may have resulted because the accelerant flowed there across an uneven floor.

The most useful facts relative to charring may be summed up as follows:

— The depth of char is proportional to the intensity of the fire and to the length of burning if the fire burns slowly for a long time;

— Those places where intensity was greatest—directly over a fire, or where ventilation or drafts "fan" it—will have deeper charring;

— The relative depth of char around a room may help locate sources of fuel or ventilation.

Heat distortion

Atmospheric heat build-up can distort objects, thereby impressing telltale signs on materials that partially melt, fuse, or crack when exposed to intense heat. Even without flames and charring, the direction of fire travel may be established through the deformation of some objects by heat.

Light bulbs: The glass housing of a light bulb can be partially melted, and the distorted form that results will point in the direction of the oncoming fire.

Spalling: The signs that indicate spalling are surface discoloration, chipping, crumbling, or a flaky, chalk-like appearance. Most often it results from exposure to radiant heat from a large, established fire. Brown black stains on the cement around the spalled area suggest the use of an accelerant, although experiments reveal it is very difficult to produce spalling with a liquid accelerant.

Crazing: A network of fine, irregular lines in glass and wood are termed craze lines. In glass and ceramic material they may be the result of rapid, intense heat, possibly because of the use of an accelerant.

Multiple low points, signifying possible multiple origins, are highly suspicious. They signal an intentionally set fire. Questionable sites include: a closet, bathroom, attic, crawl space, the area beneath stairs—since accidental fires in such locations are rare. An unusual burn is another suspicious sign: the fire burning down instead of up, or fire developing as a result of a flashover when normally there would not be enough fuel on hand for this to occur. Flashover is a phenomenon that occurs when, in the growth of a fire, all the fuel in a room is ignited and flames flash over the entire area.

Ignition sources

Flame from a match or a cigarette lighter is the most common source for an incendiary fire, but except through exclusion, the use of either will not be apparent in a case of arson. The presence of an electrical outlet or appliance near or at the point of origin requires checking out, as does the possibility that overheating, or a spark may have caused the fire. If such causes are to be eliminated, an expert is needed to perform these tasks. Although less common as an ignition source, it is important to ascertain whether any mechanical, chemical, or natural source was present at the point of origin to account for the fuel's having reached ignition temperature.

i) *Plants*: Arson investigators employ the term plant, or arson set, to describe a device that ignites the first fuel, or assists the initial flame to build in intensity. A timing mechanism may be included as part of the device.

ii) *Timing devices:* Arsonists employ timing devices to delay the start of a fire and allow them to establish an alibi. By this means, witnesses can be produced to attest to their presence in another place at the time of the blaze. The more complicated and clever the device, the fewer the people with the ability or the means to design, test, and build it.

iii) *Matches, candles, cigarettes, and other timing devices:* A simple but effective ignition and timing device involves the use of matches with a burning candle wrapped in excelsior or other readily flammable material. Generally, a candle three- quarters of an inch in diameter burns at about one inch per hour, making possible a few hours' delay. Blasting safety fuses and cannon/pyrotechnic fuses make shorter delays feasible, by burning at a predictable rate of 24 to 60 inches per minute. Another device, the road accident flare, is also easily obtained.

Phosphorus ignites upon exposure to air, has been employed to start a delayed fire. When dissolved in a solvent that evaporates slowly, combustion is postponed until it is exposed to the air after the solvent has evaporated. Alternatively, phosphorus may be coated with paraffin, sewn inside the shoulder pad of a garment, then sent to a dry cleaner where the cleaning fluid dissolves the paraffin, exposing the phosphorus to the air.

Lighted cigarette dropped accidentally or placed deliberately between upholstered chair cushions may smoulder and incubate for three-quarters of an hour to four hours before bursting into flame. A fire started within an upholstered chair will heavily char the chair's insides as well as the floor. The chair's coil springs will usually collapse, then be hardened by rapid cooling from the water doused on them. A fire started from the outside and engulfing the same chair would do more exterior than interior damage; the springs and floor underneath may remain virtually undamaged. Other more esoteric devices have been constructed. Electronic timers, alarm clocks, and other mechanical devices are also used, and can be set off by remote control—telephone or radio signal.

iv) *Trailers:* Trailers are used to extend the fire from the plant to other parts of the structure. Sometimes they lead from the starter plant to one or more secondary plants from which other trailers emanate. A wide variety of materials can be utilised for this purpose: newspapers, waxed paper, toilet paper, rags twisted into rope and doused with accelerant, gunpowder, certain motion picture film, and such flammable liquids as a mix of kerosene and gasoline, or a mix of gasoline and fireplace ashes.

The amateur arsonist might not make allowances for the replacement of oxygen in a relatively air-tight building that has no source of ventilation to restore the oxygen consumed by the fire. This causes the carbon dioxide and carbon monoxide to snuff out the fire. Left behind is visible evidence of the streamers and plants, photographs of which should convince a jury that arson was intended.

Accelerants

Gasoline is the most common accelerant. Turpentine and kerosene are readily identified by their distinctive odours. When searching the crime scene for an accelerant, a shovelful of debris—ashes, wood flooring, carpeting, or upholstery, for instance—must be lifted, then sniffed. The sense of smell, however, is easily fatigued or dulled; it is not always reliable. The distinctive odours of many accelerants come from the impurities remaining after petroleum, pine tree wood, or other natural products are distilled. With care and some expense, they can be removed. Accelerants can sometimes be detected at the scene of a suspected arson by visual inspection, by odour, or by means of instrumental devices.

Use of an accelerant can be found when heat intensity is sufficient to melt, twist, or oxidise metals used in the construction of a building or piece of furniture. A few people are capable of recognising one part of gasoline in 10 million parts of air; the majority require a concentration of about 10 parts per million. Trained dogs have been successful in detecting gasoline at fire scenes; their sensitivity also is on the order of one part per million. Chemical dyes and instrumental means also can establish the presence of a flammable hydrocarbon in the debris at a crime scene.

Dyes soluble only in organic solvents can change to red or another colour (depending on the dye). They are easy to use and low in cost. But just as dyes are the least sensitive detection method, they are the least specific: they may turn colour even when no accelerant is present. Their low cost does make detection of odourless accelerants feasible. Thus, samples should be collected for the crime laboratory in which sophisticated equipment is available for analysis.

Instrumental devices are available for the detection of accelerants. They vary widely in price as well as sensitivity, specificity, and portability. Underlying their operation is a broad range of scientific principles—from flame ionisation and gas chromatography to infrared spectrophotometry and catalytic combustion/resistance analysis. Specificity to hydrocarbon accelerants being impossible with field devices, some false positive results will occur; therefore, any positive reading must be confirmed by collecting and submitting samples for further laboratory analysis.

Volatility of accelerants requires that crime scene debris suspected of harbouring flammable material be sealed tightly in new, quart- to gallon-sized metal paint cans or glass jars. Polyethylene or polystyrene containers are unsuitable for collecting accelerants; they are deteriorated by, or are permeable to petroleum products. The cans or jars should be filled until they are 80 to 90 per cent full. They should not be exposed to the heat of the sun or left in a closed automobile or trunk during hot weather. A fresh cellulose sponge, gauze, or cotton batting can be used to soak up small quantities of liquid, and then stored in a small, tightly covered glass jar or can. Flour, diatomaceous earth, or calcium carbonate can be spread on a wet concrete surface to absorb traces of gasoline or other petroleum distillate.

Motivations

Since the nature of a fire can provide clues to motive, the following discussion is designed to enhance the investigator's understanding and skill in dealing with this crime.

Financial gain

When a business or person gains financially, for example, by eliminating competition, through insurance fraud, or through welfare fraud, arson may occur. Obviously, the greatest benefit accrues from swindling an insurance company.

— *Elimination of competition*: A strategically timed fire can undoubtedly benefit a surviving firm when its competitor is forced out of business by arson. For example, many companies rely on Christmas buying to ensure adequate annual profits. If, as the season is launched, its inventory is received and then destroyed by a set fire, the business may be hard put to survive.

  Arson is intimidating at any time, but especially so for a struggling new business. When arson is suspected or proved, the victim more likely than not is able to suggest who might benefit. Since fire setters are often hired professionals, a list of the calls—local, and particularly long distance—charged to a suspect's business and residence telephones can be very useful to the investigator. If the records of several months prior to and following the fire are studied, a particular number may be noted that appears abruptly, then vanishes.

Next, a background check on the recipient may turn up an individual with an arrest record or reputation as a fire setter. Since professionals usually demand ready money, cash is the most likely form of payment; therefore, an investigator's failure to examine bank statements for cash withdrawals and checks written is inexcusable.

— *Insurance fraud*: Liquidating a large inventory of unsold or obsolete merchandise—"selling" it to the insurance company by means of a set fire—is most likely when the goods are seasonal or produced by an industry that has suffered a severe downturn. Other scenarios include the need for: extensive renovation to meet new safety standards; costly retooling, or replacing of an outmoded plant, in order to remain competitive; capital that is tied up. In cases in which insurance fraud is suspected, the careful inspection of business, personal, and especially financial records is an obvious first step.

— *Resettlement allowance*: For the middle class a home fire is regarded as a calamity, the emotional impact of which is partially offset by insurance coverage. For the poor a fire may be seen as a way out. Possessions good for the junk heap can be replaced and the rundown house left behind. With the homeless given priority for public housing, and charitable organisations helping families to resettle, arson is sometimes seen as a viable option.

Intimidation

Arson may be used to instill fear regarding the safety of one's person or family; threaten economic loss; or effect a desired change in government or business policy.

— *Fear of safety*: Witnesses may be threatened with the torching of their home or business should they come forth with testimony in an upcoming criminal trial. Sometimes, owing to racial hostility, a home is burned when a new family moving into the neighbourhood is not welcomed by the dominant group. In the event of witness intimidation, the motive is clear after a threat has been made. Before the fire is set, surveillance of the targeted property, the suspect, and associates is an effective strategy. Although there might seem to be too many suspects in a racially tense neighbourhood, if the property and those who seem capable of disregarding the civil rights of others can be kept under surveillance, the offender(s) could be caught in the act.

— *Threatened economic loss*: Arson has been used to intimidate management in labour disputes, especially when the settlement of a strike seems unlikely. Mobsters have sometimes extorted money from business concerns by torching a company vehicle as a signal that more serious repercussions will take place should compliance not be forthcoming.

Emotional reasons

Emotional reasons such as jealousy, spite, revenge, and hatred are strong enough to cause some individuals to resort to arson to relieve the malaise produced by these emotions. In such arson cases, the victim usually is aware of the aggrieved individual and can provide the investigator with the name of the likely perpetrator.

Concealment of other crimes

Sometimes arson serves to conceal a homicide, account for an inventory shortage, destroy incriminating records, or distract police from another felony being committed simultaneously in the area. When the investigator realises that arson was put to such use, heed should be given to whoever may have had a motive to commit the other offence. A substantial fire requires the presence of the police to redirect traffic and see to it that spectators do not interfere with firefighters and are kept at a safe distance.

Pyromania

Pyromania is an irresistible impulse or compulsion to start a fire or set something on fire. Even though excitement or sensual gratification makes the motive clear, this kind of arson may be considered motiveless from an investigative viewpoint. *Modus operandi*, however, can be a telltale sign; the investigator armed with this information can take the necessary steps to apprehend the pyromaniac. The arsonist motivated by profit wants to do maximum damage by penetrating deep inside the structure to set the fire.

The pyromaniac, a creature of impulse who seldom forms any plans, must make do with material on hand: old newspapers, garbage chute refuse, the mattress from a baby carriage standing in a hallway, trash underneath a staircase, etc. In other words, the fire is set wherever the fuel is found.

Vandalism

A set fire is good for a certain amount of excitement. Sometimes gang members "graduate" to setting fires for landlords of rent-controlled properties; having driven the tenants out, the owners realise increased revenues by subdividing the large flats. Motives varying widely in these situations, it would facilitate the investigation if a suspect gang member can be turned into an informant. Churches and schools are vandalised and even torched from time to time. Often the individuals responsible are closely associated with the institution or congregation. But just as often, they are mischievous or malicious juveniles. Some are people who, feeling they have been unfairly treated, vandalise to redress a slight or recover self-esteem.

The investigator must follow all leads, even those that seem trivial. When religious property is the target, bigotry and hatred are usually the underlying motives, especially of older offenders; on the other hand, neo-Nazis, a younger group, also vandalise to express bigotry identifying the culprits can be difficult at best, unless an informant can be developed or an extensive surveillance conducted to catch them red-handed.

Investigation Records

The investigator must be diligent in following through to determine if any recorded evidence exists to support a motive for arson. Other law enforcement records to be checked out include those on recently released prisoners who were convicted of arson, with special attention paid to their *modus operandi* and the kinds of targets involved.

Fire records

A complete fire incident report should include the following information:

- — Location of the incident
- — Time and day of the week that the incident occurred
- — Name of the occupant(s) of the premises
- — Name and address of the owner of the premises
- — Source of heat-causing ignition
- — Type of material ignited
- — Damage: whether it is restricted, or extends beyond confines of the structure
- — Estimated damage in dollars.

The investigator should know that the insurance industry in this country maintains a property insurance loss register that records the prior fire loss history of individuals.

Records of ownerships

Uncovering hidden ownership or financial interest in the burned property can be a formidable task. If not set up for illegal purposes, straw ownership is lawful; however, the arrangement often seems questionable—bordering on "sharp."

or shady business practice. By seeking answers to questions such as who owns the building in which the "straw" lives?, for whom does the straw work?, what attorney, management company, notary public, contractor, or tax advisor does the straw hire? Are any of these people also hired by the straw's boss (at work) or landlord (at home)?, the real owner may be discovered.

Investigation of arson is a demanding task. The technical assistance of auditors, accountants, tax lawyers, real estate agents, and credit and financial managers will often be needed to get past the roadblocks set up to hide ownership of the property and the identity of the individual responsible. It can result from an admission that two separate fires in the premises occurred simultaneously; or from a finding that the door was locked, the occupant was present or in possession of the only key, and therefore had exclusive opportunity to start the fire.

Opportunity may be established through canvassing: the suspect might have been seen in the area about the time the fire was first noticed. Arson cases are also solved by direct evidence: the investigator observes the arsonist preparing to commit, or actually committing the crime. To accomplish this, surveillance is obviously necessary.

REFERENCES

Carroll, John R., *Physical and Technical Aspects of Fire and Arson investigation,* Springfield, IL: Charles C. Thomas, 1983.

De, Haan D., "Determining the Point of Origin-Diagnostic Signs and Laboratory Analysis," *Fire and Arson Investigator* 36, June 1986.

McCarney, William P. and Robert James Fischer, "Arson Investigation: One Means of Preventing Future Fires," in *Critical Issues in Criminal lnvestigation,* edited by Michael J. Palmiotto, Cincinnati: Anderson, 1988.

O'Connor, John J., *Practical Fire and Arson lnvestigation*, New York: Elsevier, 1986.

6

Crime against Women

Development along with its progressive changes in personal lifestyle, living standards, varied economic growth caused by urbanisation and changes in social ethos contribute to violent attitude and tendencies towards women and witness increase in crimes against women. Such incidents are a matter of serious concern and its containment is a necessity so that the women of India attain their rightful share and live in dignity, freedom, peace and freedom from crimes and aspersions.

The battle against the crimes against women has to be waged by the various sections of the society by campaigns and various programmes with social support along with legal protection, safeguards and reforms in the criminal justice system. Despite all safeguards, the women in our country continue to suffer, due to lack of awareness of their rights, illiteracy and oppressive practices and customs. The resultant consequences are many, viz., a constant fall in the sex ratio, high infant mortality rate, low literacy rate, high dropout rate of girls from education, low wage rates and so on.

The state has enacted various legislative measures intended to ensure equal rights, to counter social discrimination and various forms of violence and atrocities, and to provide support services especially to working women. Although women may be victims in any of the crimes, be it murder, robbery, cheating or any other crimes, the crimes which are directed specifically against women are characterised as 'crime against women'. These are broadly classified under two categories: crimes identified under the Indian Penal Code (IPC) and crimes identified under the special laws (SLL).

i) Crimes identified under the Indian Penal Code (IPC)
   - Rape (Sec. 376 IPC)
   - Kidnapping and abduction for different purposes (Sec. 363 - 373 IPC)
   - Homicide for dowry, dowry deaths or their attempts (Sec. 302/304-B IPC)
   - Torture, both mental and physical (Sec. 498-A IPC)
   - Molestation (Sec. 354 IPC)
   - Sexual harassment (Sec. 509 IPC)
   - Importation of girls (up to 21 years of age) (Sec. 366-B IPC)

ii) The crimes identified under the special laws (SLL)

Provisions of law affecting women have been reviewed periodically and amendments carried out to keep pace with emerging demands. The special social enactments to safeguard women and their interests, specifically are:

i) The Employees State Insurance Act, 1948
ii) The Plantation Labour Act, 1951
iii) The Family Courts Act, 1954
iv) The Special Marriage Act, 1954
v) The Hindu Marriage Act, 1955
vi) The Hindu Succession Act, 1956
vii) The Immoral Traffic (Prevention) Act, 1956
viii) The Maternity Benefit Act, 1961 (Amended in 1995)
ix) The Dowry Prohibition Act, 1961
x) The Medical Termination of Pregnancy Act, 1971
xi) The Contract Labour (Regulation and Abolition) Act, 1976
xii) The Equal Remuneration Act, 1976

xiii) The Child Marriage Restraint (Amendment) Act, 1979

xiv) The Criminal Law (Amendment) Act, 1983

xv) The Factories (Amendment) Act, 1986

xvi) The Indecent Representation of Women (Prohibition) Act, 1986

xvii) The Commission of Sati (Prevention) Act, 1987.

SEX CRIMES AND INDIAN LAW

The first Indian Law Commission was accordingly appointed to draft the Indian Penal Code. A draft Code was submitted by them on 14 October, 1837. On 26 April, 1845, another commission was appointed to revise the Code. The bill after long deliberation was presented to the Legislative Council in 1856 and was passed on 6 October, 1860. This Act XLV of 1860 superceding all rules, regulations and orders of Criminal law in India became the Indian Penal Code. The administration of criminal justice in India today traces its history to the year 1833 when Macaulay moved the House of commons to codify the whole criminal law in India with a view to bringing about unity.

The Charter Act of 1833 introduced a single legislature for Hindus and Muslims alike in Presidency towns as well as for provincial areas. Though India became independent on 15 August, 1947, the basic penal code with minor amendments has remained the same. The enactment is so wide in its objective that it has needed only a few amendments till date. The Indian Penal Code is the substantial law and the Criminal Procedure Code is the adjective law. "Mens rea", intention, motive, knowledge, mistake of law, accident are some of the mental elements that play an important part in Indian criminal law.

According to Indian Penal Code, the following are the major sex crimes:

i) Rape

ii) Outraging female modesty

iii) Unnatural offence

iv) Eve teasing

v) Adultery

vi) Obscenity

vii) Crimes concerning prostitution.

Section 375—Rape

A man is said to commit "rape" who except in the case hereinafter excepted, has sexual intercourse with a woman under circumstances falling under any of the six following descriptions:

i) Against her will.

ii) Without her consent.

iii) With her consent, when her consent has been obtained by putting her or any person in whom she is interested, in fear of death or of hurt.

iv) With her consent, when the man knows that he is not her husband and that her consent is given because she believes that he is another man to whom she is or believes herself to be lawfully married.

v) With her consent, when, at the time of giving such consent, by reason of unsoundness of mind or intoxication or the administration by him personally or through another of any stupefying or unwholesome substance, she unable to understand the nature and consequences of that to which she gives consent.

vi) With or without her consent, when she is under sixteen years of age.

Penetration is sufficient to constitute the sexual intercourse necessary to the offence of rape. Sexual intercourse by a man with his own wife, the wife not being under fifteen years of age is not rape.

Section 376—Punishment of Rape

1) Whoever, except in the cases provided for by subsection, commits rape shall be punished with imprisonment of either description for a term which shall not be less than seven years but which may be for life or for a term which may extend to ten years and shall also be liable to fine unless the woman raped is his own wife and is not under sixteen years of age in which case, he shall be punished with imprisonment of either description for a term which may extend to two years or with fine or with both: provided the court may, for adequate and special reasons to be mentioned in the judgment, impose a sentence of imprisonment for a term of less then seven years.

2) Whoever:

   a) being a police officer commits rape:

      i) Within the limits of the police station to which he is appointed; or

      ii) in the premises of any station house whether or not situated in the police station to which he is appointed; or

      iii) on a woman in his custody or in the custody of police officer subordinate to him; or

   b) being a public servant, takes advantages of his official position and commits rape on a woman in his custody as such public servant or in the custody of public servant subordinate to him; or

   c) being on the management or on the staff of a jail, remand home or other place of custody established by or under any law for the time being in force of a women's or children's institution takes advantage of his official position and commits rape on any inmate of such jail, remand home, place or institution; or

   d) being on the management or on the staff of a hospital, takes advantage of his official position and commits rape on a woman in that hospital; or

e) commits rape on a woman knowing her to be pregnant; or

f) commits rape on a woman when she is under twelve years of age; or

g) commits gang rape shall be punished with rigorous imprisonments for a term which shall not be less than ten years but which may be for life and shall also be liable to fine.

Provided that the court may, for adequate and special reasons to be mentioned in the judgment, impose a sentence of imprisonment of either description for a term of less than ten years. Where a woman is raped by one or more a group of persons in furtherance of their common intention, each of the persons shall be deemed to have committed gang rape within the meaning of this sub-section. "Women's or children's institutions" means an institution, whether called an orphanage or a home for neglected women or children or widow's home or by any other name, which is established and maintained for the reception and care of women or children. "Hospital" means the precincts of the hospital and includes the precincts of any institution for the reception and treatment of persons during convalescence or of persons requiring medical attention or rehabilitation.

Consent given by a woman of unsound mind is of no avail. Where, therefore, a man had carnal knowledge of a girl of imbecile mind and the jury found that it was without her consent she being incapable of giving consent from defect of understanding, it was held that his act amounted to rape. Similarly, consent given by an intoxicated woman is no consent. Where the accused made a girl of thirteen years drunk and whilst she was insensible, violated her person, he was held to have committed rape. If a girl does not resist intercourse in consequence of misapprehension, this will not amount to a consent on her part. Where a medical man, to whom a girl of fourteen years of age was sent for professional advice, had carnal connection with her, she making no resistance from a *bona fide* belief that he was treating her medically, it was held that he could be convicted of rape. There is a distinction between vulval penetration and vaginal penetration. In order to constitute rape, the statute merely requires medical evidence of penetration, and this may occur and the hymen remain intact. Seminal emission is not necessary to establish rape. What is necessary is that there must be penetration.

Section 354—Assault or Criminal Force to Woman with Intent to Outrage her Modesty

Whoever assaults or uses criminal force to any woman, intending to outrage or knowing it to be likely that he will thereby outrage her modesty, shall be punished with imprisonment of either description for a term which may extend to two years or with fine, or with both. The supreme court of India has held that when any act done to or in the presence of a woman is clearly suggestive of sex that act will fall within this section. The essence of a woman's modesty is her sex. The culpable intention of the accused is the crux of the matter.

Section 377—Unnatural Offence

Whoever voluntarily has carnal intercourse against the order of nature with any man, woman or animal, shall be punished with imprisonment for life, or with imprisonment of either description for a term which may extend to ten years and shall also be liable to fine. Penetration is sufficient to constitute the carnal intercourse.

Bestiality, sodomy, buggery as also lesbianism are also dealt with under this section. Cases of bestiality do occur among young and vigorous villagers, who go out to graze cattle in fields far away from the gaze of the human eye. Owing to loneliness and proximity of the animals they are excited to commit this abominable crime. Some of these men have mental abnormalities. The crime of bestiality is also seen in some ignorant men, who have a superstitious belief that they are cured of gonorrhoea by committing sexual intercourse with a she-ass.

Section 509—Word, Gesture or Act Intended to Insult the Modesty of a Woman

Whoever, intending to insult the modesty of any woman, utters any word, makes any sound or gesture, or exhibits any object, intending that such word or sound shall be heard, or that such gesture or object shall be seen, by such woman or intrudes upon the privacy of such woman, shall be punished with simple imprisonment for a term which may extend to one year or with fine or with both.There must be some individual woman or women whose modesty, has been outraged. It does not require the woman, whose modesty it is intended to insult, to have either heard the word or seen the action. The intention of the offender that she should see or hear is all that is required.

If a man attempts to attract the attention of a woman persistently and publicly and by unusual methods thereby causing resentment and annoyance, he is very close upon insulting the woman. If man, intending to outrage the modesty of a woman, exposes his person indecently to her, or uses obscene words intending that she would hear them or exhibits to her obscene articles, he commits this offence. If such an act is done in a public place it will amount to public nuisance. If it amounts to an assault it will be punishable under Section 354. Exhibitionism is also dealt with under this section. The act may consist of the indecent exposure of the genital organ in public mostly by males to women and girls. It is often accompanied by lewd gestures and even masturbation may be indulged in.

Section 372—Selling Minor for Purposes of Prostitution

Whoever sells, lets to hire, or otherwise disposes of any person under the age of eighteen years with intent that such person shall at any age be employed or used for the purpose of prostitution or illicit intercourse with a person or for any unlawful and immoral purpose, or knowing it to be likely that such person will at any age be employed or used for any such purpose, shall be punished with imprisonment of either description for a term which may extend to ten years and shall also be liable to fine.

When a female under the age of eighteen years is sold, let for hire, or otherwise disposed of to a prostitute or to any person who keeps or manages a brothel, the person so disposing of such female shall until the contrary is proved, be presumed to have shall be used for the disposed of her with the intent that she purpose of prostitution. For the purposes of this section "illicit intercourse" means sexual intercourse between persons not united by marriage or by any union or tie which though not amounting to a marriage is recognised by the personal law or custom of the community to which they belong or where they belong to different communities of both such communities, as constituting between them a quasimarital relation.

Section 373: Buying Minors for Purchases of Prostitution, etc.

Whoever buys, hires or otherwise obtains possession of any person under the age of eighteen years with the intent that such person shall at any age be employed or used for the purpose of prostitution or illicit intercourse with any person for any unlawful and immoral purpose, or knowing it to be likely that such person will at any age be employed or used for any such purpose, shall be punished with imprisonment of either description for a term which may extend to ten years and shall also be liable to fine.

Any prostitute or any person keeping or managing a brothel, who buys, hires or otherwise obtains possession of a female under the age of eighteen years shall, until the contrary is proved, be presumed to have obtained possession of such female with the intent that she shall be used for the purpose of prostitution.

Section 497—Adultery

Whoever has sexual intercourse with a person who is and whom he knows or has reason to believe to be the wife of another man without the consent or connivance of that man, such sexual intercourse not amounting to the offence of rape, is guilty of the offence of adultery and shall be punished with imprisonment of either description for a term which may extend to five years or with fine or with both. In such case the wife shall not be punishable as an abettor.

Section 498—Enticing or Taking away or Detaining with Criminal Intent a Married Woman

Whoever takes or entices away any woman who is and whom he knows or has reason to believe to be the wife of any other man, from that man, or from any person having the care of her on behalf of that man, with intent that she may have illicit intercourse with any person, or conceals or detains with that intent any such woman, shall be punished with imprisonment of either description for a term which may extend to two years or with fine or with both.

The essence of the offence under this section comprises depriving the husband of his control over his wife for the purpose of illicit intercourse. Any deposition or consent or willingness on the part of the wife is absolutely immaterial to the guilt of the accused.

Section 292—Sale, etc., of Obscene Books, etc.

1) For the purposes of subsection.
2) A book, pamphlet, paper, writing, drawing, painting, representation, figure or any other subject, shall be

deemed to be obscene if it is lascivious or appeals to the prurient interest or if its effect, or (where it comprises two or more distinct items) the effect of any one of its items, is, if taken as a whole, is such as to tend to deprave and corrupt persons who are likely, having regard to all relevant circumstances, to read, see or hear the matter contained or embodied in it.

Whoever:

a) sells, lets to hire, distributes, publicly exhibits or in any manner puts into circulation, as for purposes of sale, hire, distribution, public exhibition or circulation, makes, produces or has in possession any obscene book, pamphlet, paper, drawing, painting, representation or figure or any other obscene object whatsoever, or

b) imports, exports or conveys any obscene object for any of the purposes aforesaid or knowing or having reason to believe that such object will be sold, let to hire, distributed or publicly exhibited or in any manner put into circulation, or

c) takes part in or receives profits from any business in the course of which he knows or has reason to believe that any such obscene objects are, for any of the purposes aforesaid, made, produced, purchased, kept, imported, exported, conveyed, publicly exhibited or in any manner put into circulation.

d) advertises or makes known by any means whatsoever that any person is engaged or is ready to engage in any act which is an offence under this section, or that any such obscene object can be procured from or through any person, or

e) offers or attempts to do any act which is an offence under this section,

shall be punished on first conviction with imprisonment of either description for a term which may extend to two years, and with fine which may extend to two thousand rupees, and in the event of a second or subsequent conviction, with imprisonment of either description for a term which may extend to five years and also with fine which may extend to five thousand rupees.

This section does not extend to:

a) any book, pamphlet, paper, writing, drawing, painting, representation or figure:

   i) the publication of which is proved to be justified as being for the public good on the ground that such book, pamphlet, paper, writing, drawing, painting, representation or figure is in the interest of science, literature, art or learning or other objects of general concern, or

   ii) which is kept or used for bona fide religious purposes;

b) any representation sculptured, engraved, painted or otherwise represented on or in

   i) any ancient monument within the meaning of the Ancient Monuments and Archaeological Sites and Remains Act, 1958 (24 of 1958), or

   ii) any temple, or on any carriage for the conveyance of idols or kept or used for any religious purposes.

In addition, the following provisions in Minor Acts also deal with obscenity and pornography.

i) Section 3(c) of the Dramatic Performances Act, 1876. It prohibits any dramatic performance, play, etc., in a public place which is likely to deprave and corrupt persons present at the performance.

ii) Sections 3 to 6 of the Drugs and Magic Remedies (objectionable advertisement) Act, 1954. It prohibits objectionable advertisement relating to magic cure, specially of sex ailments like improvement in the capacity of human being for sexual pleasure.

iii) Section 11(c) of the Customs Act, 1962. It prohibits the import and export of obscene goods.

iv) The Sea Customs Act, 1878. It prohibits the import of any obscene book, pamphlet, paper, etc., into India.

v) Section 9(2)(a) of the Indian Telegraph Act, 1885. It lays down that rules can be framed for imposing restrictions on transmission of messages of obscene nature.

vi) Section 20 of the Indian post Office Act, 1898. It prohibits the transmission of any indecent or obscene printed matter, painting, photograph, etc., by post.

vii) Section 22 gives powers to postpone despatch.

viii) Section 3 of the Press (Objectionable Matters) Act, 1951. It prohibits the publication of objectionable matter which includes grossly indecent and obscene publication in the definition in section 3(vi).

xi) The Cinematograph Act, 1952. It gives powers to control films for public exhibition and lays down that these shall not be certified or approved in case the film or any part thereof is repugnant to the rules of decency.

ix) Section 3 of the young persons (Harmful publication) Act, 1956. It prohibits the sale, distribution, etc., of harmful publications consisting of stories told with or without the help of pictures portraying wholly or mainly the commission of offences or acts of violence or incidents or repulsive or horrible nature, etc.

The word "obscenity" is described differently at different places. Dictionary defines "obscenity" as something "offensive to chastity or modesty, expressing or presenting to the mind or view, something that delicacy, purity and decency forbid to be expressed".

i) Any book "treating sex in a manner appealing to the carnal side of human nature or having that tendency" would be obscene.

ii) The extent of such appeal is a matter for consideration in each individual case.

iii) The constitutional protection of free speech would be available if prepondering social purpose or benefit is shown.

The list of the judgment as pointed out by Justice Hidayatullah was that "law seeks to protect not only those who can protect themselves but also those whose prurient minds take delight in secret sexual pleasure from erotic writings". In order to demarcate an obscenity it must be seen if an is so preponderant as to throw the obscenity in shadow. Anything without a prepondering social purpose cannot have the constitutional protection of free release.

Brothel Keeping

The offence of brothel keeping and the acts connected therewith are made punishable under the Suppression of Immoral Traffic in Women and Girls Act, 1956 (as amended by Act no 44 of 1986).

Section: 3

Of the act provides punishment for persons who keep or manage or act or assist in the keeping or management of a brothel.

Section: 4

Penalises a person above the age of eighteen years who knowingly lives, wholly or in pan on the earnings of prostitution of a woman or girl.

Section: 5

Penalises a person who procures or attempts to procure a woman or girl whether with or without her consent for the purpose of prostitution or intent that she may for the purpose of prostitution become the inmate or frequent a brothel or takes or attempts to take a woman or girl or causes a woman or girl to be taken from one place to another to carry on prostitution.

Section: 6

Prohibits the detaining of a woman or girl in the premises where prostitution is carried on.

Section: 7

Provides punishment for prostitution in a public place. The solicitation can be by words, gestures, wilful exposure of person otherwise by tempting or endeavouring to attract the attention of any person. For all these offences, enhanced sentence is provided for the repeaters. There is a provision of special police officers to deal with the offences under this act. Such officers are appointed by the state government. The state governments have appointed the city superintendents of police in some districts to perform the duties of special police officers in their respective districts.

ANALYSIS OF IPC CRIMES

The year 1999 showed a mixed trends in all crime cases against women reported. A detailed analysis of crime incidence against women reported in India during the year 1999 is presented in tables given in the following pages.

Madhya Pradesh reported the highest incidence (12.6 per cent) of these crimes followed by Uttar Pradesh (12. 5 per cent) and Maharashtra (10.0 per cent). In contrast, Delhi, which accounted for only 1. 8 per cent of total crimes and shared only 1.3 per cent of population in the country reported the second highest rate of such crime at 17.9 after Rajasthan 24.5.

Rape

During 1999, 15, 031 (states total) rape cases were reported. Madhya Pradesh alone reported 23. 0 per cent of total rape cases in the country. Delhi, which represented only 2.6 per cent cases reported third highest rate at 3.0 after Mizoram (7.6) and Madhya Pradesh (4.5).

Kidnapping and Abduction

Uttar Pradesh and Rajasthan reported highest rates of kidnapping and abduction cases at national level, 17.2 per cent and 16.6 per cent respectively, followed by Delhi with share of 6.2 per cent cases reported highest rate at 7.3.

Dowry Deaths

Of the total 6, 564 reported cases of dowry deaths occurred in Indian states, during 1999, Uttar Pradesh share 31. 2 per cent alone (2, 088) followed by Bihar with 15.2 per cent (1, 021). Among the union territories, Delhi reported highest incidence of dowry death cases (122) with 1.8 per cent.

Molestation

During 1999, 3, 1640 molestation cases (states total) were reported in the country. Nearly 24. 9 per cent of total such cases were reported from Madhya Pradesh which also reported significantly higher rate (10.2) than National Average rate (3.3). Among union territories Delhi reported the highest number of such incidence 588 (1.8 per cent).

Sexual Harassment

A total (states) of 8, 673 sexual harassment cases were reported in 1999. Uttar Pradesh (2, 255) Tamil Nadu (1 776) and Karnataka (1, 763) reported highest rates of such cases with 25.5 per cent, 20.0 per cent and 19.9 per cent respectively.

ANALYSIS OF SLL CRIMES

Cases Under Immoral Traffic (Prevention) Act

Under Immoral Traffic (Prevention) Act 9, 223 cases were reported during 1999. More than half of the cases (69.0 per cent) were from the Tamil Nadu only. This should be construed as an indicator of better policing by Tamil Nadu police in this area.

Cases Under Indecent Representation of Women (Prohibition) Act

A remarkable decline was noticed for cases under this Act as compared to cases reported in 1998. Nearly 66.2 per cent cases were reported from Maharashtra alone.

Cases Under Dowry Prohibition Act

Of cases Under Dowry Prohibition Act, a sizable proportion (39.5 per cent) were reported from Bihar, followed by Karnataka with 11.8 per cent and Orissa with 11.4 per cent.

Table 6. 1.

Incidence of crimes committed against women in Indian states during 1999.

State	*Est-mid year population*	*Rape*			*Kidnapping & Abduction*			*Dowry Deaths*			*Cruelty by Husband and relatives*			*Molestation*		
		I	R	P	I	R	P	I	R	P	I	R	P	I	R	P
(1)	(2)		(3)			(4)			(5)			(6)			(7)	
Andhra Pradesh	750.1	895	1.2	5.8	708	0.9	4.4	452	0.6	6.7	4666	6.2	10.6	3238	4.3	10.0
Arunachal P.	11.7	39	3.3	0.3	40	3.4	0.3	0	0.0	0.0	5	0.4	0.0	65	5.6	0.2
Assam	259.8	703	2.7	4.5	1149	4.4	7.2	40	0.2	0.6	843	3.2	1.9	720	2.8	2.2
Bihar	987.3	1447	1.5	9.4	939	1.0	5.9	1021	1.0	15.2	1423	1.4	3.2	547	0.6	1.7
Goa	15.6	18	1.2	0.1	7	0.4	0.0	2	0.1	0.0	15	1.0	0.0	26	1.7	0.1
Gujarat	477.9	331	0.7	2.1	1074	2.2	6.7	94	0.2	1.4	3886	8.1	8.9	1083	2.3	3.4
Haryana	196.4	372	1.9	2.4	350	1.8	2.2	288	1.5	4.3	1369	7.0	3.1	553	2.8	1.7
H.P.	66.0	109	1.7	0.7	89	1.3	0.6	5	0.1	0.1	258	3.9	0.6	297	4.5	0.9
J&K	97.9	170	1.7	1.1	473	4.8	3.0	6	0.1	0.1	39	0.4	0.1	507	5.2	1.6
Karnataka	516.5	301	0.6	1.9	320	0.6	2.0	217	0.4	3.2	1560	3.0	3.6	1501	2.9	4.6
Kerala	320.8	423	1.3	2.7	123	0.4	0.8	31	0.1	0.5	2488	7.8	16.0	1643	5.1	5.1
M.P.	788.1	3561	4.5	23.0	942	1.2	5.9	584	0.7	8.7	3012	3.8	6.9	8054	10.2	24.9
Maharastra	904.5	1320	1.5	8.5	727	0.8	4.6	395	0.4	5.9	7026	7.8	16.0	2766	31.	8.6
Manipur	24.7	12	0.5	0.1	38	1.5	0.2	0	0.0	0.0	2	0.1	0.0	13	0.5	0.0

(Table 6.1. contd...)

State	*Est-mid year population*	*Rape*			*Kidnapping & Abduction*			*Dowry Deaths*			*Cruelty by Husband and relatives*			*Molestation*		
		I	R	P	I	R	P	I	R	P	I	R	P	I	R	P
(1)	(2)		(3)			(4)			(5)			(6)			(7)	
Meghalaya	23.8	27	1.1	0.2	10	0.4	0.1	0	0.0	0.0	0	0.0	0.0	17	0.7	0.1
Mizoram	9.3	71	7.6	0.5	0	0.0	0.0	0	0.0	0.0	0	0.0	0.0	74	8.0	0.2
Nagaland	16.5	11	0.7	0.1	5	0.3	0.0	0	0.0	0.0	0	0.0	0.0	3	0.2	0.0
Orissa	356.4	820	2.3	5.3	431	1.2	2.7	234	0.7	3.5	1208	3.4	2.8	1494	4.2	4.6
Punjab	233.7	282	1.2	1.8	280	1.2	1.8	193	0.8	2.9	562	2.4	1.3	198	0.8	0.6
Rajasthan	529.4	1198	2.3	7.7	2652	5.0	16.6	443	0.8	6.6	5425	10.2	12.4	3109	5.9	9.6
Sikkim	5.5	7	1.3	0.0	0	0.0	0.0	0	0.0	0.0	0	0.0	0.0	21	3.8	0.1
Tamil Nadu	614.3	430	0.7	2.8	1000	1.6	6.3	197	0.3	2.9	620	1.0	1.4	1959	3.2	6.1
Tripura	37.0	72	1.9	0.5	27	0.7	0.2	17	0.5	0.3	113	3.1	0.3	71	1.9	0.2
Uttar Pradesh	1676.6	1593	1.0	10.3	2746	1.6	17.2	2088	1.2	31.2	5372	3.2	12.3	2481	1.5	7.7
West Bengal	783.2	819	1.0	5.3	804	1.0	5.0	257	0.3	3.8	3777	4.8	8.6	1200	1.5	3.7
Total States	**9703.0**	**15031**	**1.5**	**97.2**	**14934**	**1.5**	**93.6**	**6564**	**0.7**	**98.0**	**43669**	**4.5**	**99.6**	**31640**	**3.3**	**97.9**

(Table 6.1. contd...)

State	Sexual harassment			Important of girls			Sati Prev. Act (P) Act			Immoral Traffic women (P) Act			Ind. Rep. of Proh. Act			Dowry Proh. Act			Total		
	I	R	P	I	R	P	I	R	P	I	R	P	I	R	P	I	R	P	I	R	P
	(8)			(9)			(10)			(11)			(12)			(13)			(14)		
Andhra Pradesh	1763	2.4	19.9	0	0.0	0.0	0	0.0	0.0	737	1.0	7.9	15	0.0	6.8	28	2	0.4	1276	17	9.4
Arunachal Pradesh	1	0.1	0.0	0	0.0	0.0	0	0.0	0.0	1	0.1	0.0	0	0.0	0.0	0	0.0	0.0	151	12.9	0.1
Assam	21	0.1	0.2	0	0.0	0.0	0	0.0	0.0	5	0.0	0.1	0	0.0	0.0	23	0.1	0.8	3504	13.5	2.6
Bihar	55	0.1	0.6	0	0.0	0.0	0	0.0	0.0	38	0.0	0.4	25	0.0	11.3	1211	1.2	39.5	6706	6.8	4.9
Goa	7	0.4	0.1	0	0.0	0.0	0	0.0	0.0	28	1.8	0.3	0	0.0	0.0	0	0.0	0.0	103	6.6	0.1
Gujarat	172	0.4	1.9	0	0.0	0.0	0	0.0	0.0	40	0.1	0.4	1	0.0	0.5	13	0.0	0.4	6694	14.0	4.9
Haryana	0	0.0	0	0.0	0.0	0	0.0	0.0	14	0.1	0.1	0	0	0.0	0.0	2	0.0	0.1	3248	16.5	2.4
Himachal Pradesh	23	0.3	1.7	0	0.0	0.0	0	0.0	0.0	0	0.0	0.0	0	0.0	0.0	3	0.0	0.1	784	11.9	0.6
j&K	341	3.5	3.8	0	0.0	0.0	0	0.0	0.0	4	0.0	0.0	0	0.0	0.0	2	0.0	0.1	1542	15.8	1.1
Karnataka	147	0.3	1.7	0	0.0	0.0	0	0.0	0.0	1225	2.4	13.1	1	0.0	0.5	361	0.7	11.8	5633	10.9	4.1
Kerala	50	0.2	0.6	0	0.0	0.0	0	0.0	0.0	62	0.2	0.7	9	0.0	4.1	9	0.0	0.3	4838	15.1	3.6
Madhya Pradesh	693	0.9	7.8	0	0.0	0.0	0	0.0	0.0	33	0.0	0.4	0	0.0	0.0	197	0.2	6.4	17076	21.7	12.6
Maharashtra	825	0.9	9.3	0	0.0	0.0	0	0.0	0.0	390	0.4	4.2	147	0.2	66.2	14	9.0	0.5	13610	15.0	10.0
Manipur	0	0.0	0.0	0	0.0	0.0	0	0.0	0.0	0	0.0	0.0	0	0.0	0.0	0	0.0	0.0	65	2.6	0.0

(Table 6.1. contd...)

State	*Sexual harassment*			*Important of girls*			*Sati Prev. Act (P) Act*			*Immporal Traffic women (P) Act*			*Ind. Rep. of Proh. Act*			*Dowry Proh. Act*			*Total*		
	I	*R*	*P*	*I*	*R*	*P*	*I*	*R*	*P*	*I*	*R*	*P*	*I*	*R*	*P*	*I*	*R*	*P*	*I*	*R*	*P*
	(8)			(9)			(10)			(11)			(12)			(13)			(14)		
Maghalaya	0	0.0	0.0	0	0.0	0.0	0	0.0	0.0	0	0.0	0.0	0	0.0	0.0	0	0.0	0.0	54	2.3	0.0
Mizoram	0	0.0	0.0	0	0.0	0.0	0	0.0	0.0	0	0.0	0.0	0	0.0	0.0	0	0.0	0.0	145	15.6	0.1
Nagaland	0	0.0	0.0	0	0.0	0.0	0	0.0	0.0	0	0.0	0.0	0	0.0	0.0	0	0.0	0.0	19	1.2	0.0
Orissa	158	0.4	1.8	0	0.0	0.0	0	0.0	0.0	22	0.1	0.2	0	0.0	0.0	349	1.0	11.4	4716	13.2	3.5
Punjab	2	0.0	0.0	0	0.0	0.0	0	0.0	0.0	14	0.1	0.1	0	0.0	0.0	7	0.0	0.2	1538	6.6	1.1
Rajastan	51	0.1	0.6	0	0.0	0.0	0	0.0	0.0	85	0.2	0.9	8	0.0	3.6	3	0.0	0.1	12974	24.5	9.6
Sikkim	0	0.0	0.0	NR	-		0	0.0	0.0	0	0.0	0.0	0	0.0	0.0	0	0.0	0.0	28	5.1	0.0
Tamil Nadu	1776	2.9	20.0	0	0.0	0.0	0	0.0	0.0	6462	10.5	69.0	0	0.0	0.0	226	0.4	7.4	12670	20.6	9.3
Tripura	0	0.0	0.0	0	0.0	0.0	0	0.0	0.0	0	0.0	0.0	0	0.0	0.0	0	0.0	0.0	300	8.1	0.2
Uttar Pradesh	2255	1.3	25.5	0	0.0	0.0	0	0.0	0.0	24	0.0	0.3	6	0.0	2.7	347	0.2	11.3	16912	10.1	12.5
West Bengal	33	0.0	0.4	1	0.0	0.0	0	0.0	0.0	39	0.0	0.4	0	0.0	0.0	1	0.0	0.0	6931	8.8	5.1
Total (states)	**8673**	**0.9**	**97.9**	**1**	**0.0**	**0.0**	**0**	**0.0**	**0.0**	**9223**	**1.0**	**98.5**	**212**	**0.0**	**95.5**	**3050**	**0.3**	**99.5**	**132997**	**13.7**	**98.0**

Table 6. 2.

Incidence of crimes committed against women in union territories during 1999.

UT	*Est-mid year population*	*Rape*			*Kidnapping & Abduction*			*Dowry Deaths*			*Cruelty by Husband and relatives*			*Molestation*		
		I	R	P	I	R	P	I	R	P	I	R	P	I	R	P
(1)	(2)		(3)			(4)			(5)			(6)			(7)	
A& N Islands	3.8	6	1.6	0.0	2	0.5	0.0	0	0.0	0.0	8	2.1	0.0	13	3.4	0.0
Chandigarh	8.7	16	1.8	0.1	36	4.1	0.2	7	0.8	0.1	42	4.8	0.1	26	3.0	0.1
D&N Haveli	1.9	3	1.6	0.0	0	0.0	0.0	2	1.1	0.0	5	2.6	0.0	8	4.2	0.0
Daman & Diu	1.4	4	2.9	0.0	2	1.4	0.0	0	0.0	0.0	5	3.6	0.0	0	0.0	0.0
Delhi	136.0	402	3.0	2.6	986	7.3	6.2	122	0.9	1.8	88	0.6	0.2	588	4.3	1.8
Lakshadweep	0.7	0	0.0	0.0	0	0.0	0.0	0	0.0	0.0	0	0.0	0.0	0	0.0	0.0
Pondicherry	10.9	6	0.6	0.0	2	0.2	0.0	4	0.4	0.1	6	0.6	0.0	36	3.3	0.1
Total (UTs)	163.4	437	2.7	2.8	1028	6.3	6.4	135	0.8	2.0	154	0.9	0.4	671	4.1	2.1
Total	**9866.4**	**15468**	**1.6**	**100.0**	**15962**	**1.6**	**100.0**	**6699**	**0.7**	**100.0**	**43823**	**4.4**	**100.0**	**32311**	**3.3**	**100.0**

(Table 6.2. contd...)

UT	Sexual harassment			Important of girls			Sati Prev. Act (P) Act			Immporal Traffic women (P) Act			Ind. Rep. of Proh. Act			Dowry Proh. Act			Total		
	I	R	P	I	R	P	I	R	P	I	R	P	I	R	P	I	R	P	I	R	P
	(8)			(9)			(10)			(11)			(12)			(13)			(14)		
A&N Islands	2	0.5	0.0	0	0.0	0.0	0	0.0	0.0	5	1.3	0.1	0	0.0	0.0	0	0.0	0.0	36	9.5	0.0
Chandigarh	18	2.1	0.2	0	0.0	0.0	0	0.0	0.0	7	0.8	0.1	0	0.0	0.0	0	0.0	0.0	152	17.5	0.1
D&N Haveli	0	0.0	0.0	0	0.0	0.0	0	0.0	0.0	0	0.0	0.0	0	0.0	0.0	0	0.0	0.0	18	9.5	0.0
Daman&Diu	0	0.0	0.0	0	0.0	0.0	0	0.0	0.0	0	0.0	0.0	0	0.0	0.0	0	0.0	0.0	11	7.9	0.0
Delhi	146	1.1	1.6	0	0.0	0.0	0	0.0	0.0	78	0.6	0.8	10	0.1	4.5	8	0.1	0.3	2428	17.9	1.8
Lakshadweep	0	0.0	0.0	0	0.0	0.0	0	0.0	0.0	0	0.0	0.0	0	0.0	0.0	0	0.0	0.0	0	0.0	0.0
Pondicherry	19	1.7	0.2	0	0.0	0.0	0	0.0	0.0	50	4.6	0.5	0	0.0	0.0	0	0.0	0.0	129	11.8	0.1
Total (UTs)	185	1.1	2.1	0	0.0	0.0	0	0.0	0.0	140	0.9	1.5	10	0.1	4.5	14	0.1	0.5	2774	17.0	2.0
Total (All India)	**8858**	**0.9**	**100**	**1**	**0.0**	**100**	**0**	**0.0**	**0.0**	**9363**	**0.9**	**100.0**	**222**	**0.0**	**100.0**	**3064**	**0.3**	**100**	**135771**	**13.8**	**100**

Table 6. 3.

Incidence of crimes committed against women in Indian cities during 1999.

Cities	*Est-mid year population*	*Rape*			*Kidnapping & Abduction*			*Dowry Deaths*			*Cruelty by Husband and relatives*			*Molestation*		
		I	R	P	I	R	P	I	R	P	I	R	P	I	R	P
(1)	(2)		(3)			(4)			(5)			(6)			(7)	
Ahmedabad	41.2	14	0.3	1.4	118	2.9	6.1	6	0.1	1.1	524	12.7	12.6	30	0.7	1.5
Bangalore	55.1	29	0.5	2.9	65	1.2	3.4	49	0.9	9.0	198	3.6	4.8	219	4.0	010.6
Bhopal	16.1	42	2.6	4.2	33	2.0	1.7	10	0.6	1.8	65	4.0	1.6	92	5.7	4.5
Calcutta	128.2	24	0.2	2.4	93	0.7	4.8	5	0.0	0.9	159	1.2	3.8	199	1.6	9.7
Chennai	65.9	27	0.4	2.7	12	0.2	0.6	22	0.3	4.0	55	0.8	1.3	40	0.6	1.9
Coimbatore	12.8	4	0.3	0.4	14	1.1	0.7	11	0.9	2.0	18	1.4	0.4	25	2.0	1.2
Delhi (City)	116.0	332	2.9	32.9	837	7.2	43.2	95	0.8	17.4	58	0.5	1.4	480	4.1	23.3
Hyderabad	67.8	48	0.7	4.8	43	0.6	2.2	19	0.3	3.5	808	11.9	19.4	86	1.3	4.2
Indore	14.1	29	2.1	2.9	29	2.1	1.5	23	1.6	4.2	128	9.1	3.1	71	5.0	3.4
Jaipur	21.2	38	1.8	3.8	154	7.3	7.9	26	1.2	4.8	337	15.9	8.1	115	5.4	5.6
Kanpur	24.3	34	1.4	3.4	147	6.0	7.6	75	3.1	13.7	287	11.8	6.9	58	2.4	2.8
Kochi	17.4	9	0.5	0.9	4	0.2	0.2	0	0.0	0.0	57	3.3	1.4	44	1.7	2.1
Lucknow	25.4	28	1.1	2.8	94	3.7	4.8	34	1.3	6.2	211	8.3	5.1	44	1.7	2.1

(Table 6. 3 contd...)

Cities	Est-mid year population	Rape			Kidnapping & Abduction			Dowry Deaths			Cruelty by Husband and relatives			Molestation		
		I	R	P	I	R	P	I	R	P	I	R	P	I	R	P
(1)	(2)		(3)			(4)			(5)			(6)			(7)	
Ludhiana	16.4	38	2.3	3.8	35	2.1	1.8	14	0.9	2.6	146	8.9	3.5	5	0.3	0.2
Madurai	12.6	6	0.5	0.6	15	1.2	0.8	5	0.4	0.9	34	2.7	0.8	10	0.8	0.5
Mumbai	179.3	141	0.8	14.0	30	0.2	1.5	60	0.3	11.0	237	1.3	5.7	243	1.4	11.8
Nagpur	20.4	42	2.1	4.2	56	2.7	2.9	4	0.2	0.7	189	9.3	4.5	112	5.5	5.4
Patna	12.8	18	1.4	1.8	11	0.9	0.6	39	3.0	7.1	66	5.2	1.6	22	1.7	1.1
Pune	34.6	51	1.5	5.1	37	1.1	1.9	0	0.0	0.0	89	2.6	2.1	76	2.2	3.7
Surat	23.2	17	0.7	1.7	39	1.7	2.0	28	1.2	5.1	121	5.2	2.9	20	0.9	1.0
Vadodara	15.9	10	0.6	1.0	53	3.3	2.7	0	0.0	0.0	162	10.2	3.9	30	1.9	1.5
Varanasi	12.8	10	0.8	1.0	11	0.9	0.6	14	1.1	2.6	39	3.0	0.9	7	0.5	0.3
Vishakhapatnam	16.9	17	1.0	1.7	9	0.5	0.5	8	0.5	1.5	168	9.9	4.0	31	1.8	1.5
Total (cities)	**950.4**	**1008**	**1.1**	**100.0**	**1939**	**2.0**	**100.0**	**547**	**0.6**	**100.0**	**4156**	**4.4**	**100.0**	**2059**	**2.2**	**100.0**

(Table 6 .3. contd...)

Cities	Sexual harassment			Important of girls			Sati Prev. Act (P) Act			Immporal Traffic women (P) Act			Ind. Rep. of Proh. Act			Dowry Proh. Act			Total		
	I	R	P	I	R	P	I	R	P	I	R	P	I	R	P	I	R	P	I	R	P
	(8)			(9)			(10)			(11)			(12)			(13)			(14)		
Ahemedabad	29	0.7	1.6	0	0.0	0.0	0	0.0	0.0	7	0.2	0.1	0	0.0	0.0	0	0.0	0.0	728	17.7	4.3
Banglore	52	0.9	2.8	0	0.0	0.0	0	0.0	0.0	292	5.3	6.2	0	0.0	0.0	266	4.8	64.1	1170	21.2	7.0
Bhopal	16	1.0	0.9	0	0.0	0.0	0	0.0	0.0	0	0.0	0.0	0	0.0	0.0	0	0.0	0.0	258	16.0	1.5
Culcutta	28	0.2	1.5	1	0.0	0.0	0	0.0	0.0	38	0.3	0.8	0	0.0	0.0	0	0.0	0.0	547	4.3	3.3
Chennai	0	0.0	0.0	0	0.0	0.0	0	0.0	0.0	3349	50.8	71.5	0	0.0	0.0	55	0.8	13.3	3560	54.0	21.2
Coimbatore	100	7.8	5.4	0	0.0	0.0	0	0.0	0.0	223	17.4	4.8	0	0.0	0.0	0	0.0	0.0	395	30.9	2.4
Delhi	126	1.1	6.8	0	0.0	0.0	0	0.0	0.0	76	0.7	1.6	10	0.1	6.5	8	0.1	1.9	2022	17.4	12.0
Hyderabad	10	0.1	0.5	0	0.0	0.0	0	0.0	0.0	9	0.1	0.2	0	0.0	0.0	2	0.0	0.5	1025	15.1	6.1
Indore	9	0.6	0.5	0	0.0	0.0	0	0.0	0.0	5	0.4	0.1	0	0.0	0.0	2	0.1	0.5	296	21.0	1.8
Jaipur	2	0.1	0.1	0	0.0	0.0	0	0.0	0.0	24	1.1	0.5	0	0.0	0.0	0	0.0	0.0	696	32.8	4.1
Kanpur	238	9.8	12.9	0	0.0	0.0	0	0.0	0.0	1	0.0	0.0	0	0.0	0.0	21	0.9	5.1	861	35.4	5.1
Kochi	4	0.2	0.2	0	0.0	0.0	0	0.0	0.0	5	0.3	0.1	0	0.0	0.0	0	0.0	0.0	123	7.1	0.7

(Table 6 .3. contd...)

UT	Sexual harassment			Important of girls			Sati Prev. Act (P) Act			Immporal Traffic women (P) Act			Ind. Rep. of Proh. Act			Dowry Proh. Act			Total		
	I	*R*	*P*	*I*	*R*	*P*	*I*	*R*	*P*	*I*	*R*	*P*	*I*	*R*	*P*	*I*	*R*	*P*	*I*	*R*	*P*
	(8)			(9)			(10)			(11)			(12)			(13)			(14)		
Luknow	227	8.9	12.3	0	0.0	0.0	0	0.0	0.0	6	0.2	0.1	0	0.0	0.0	0	0.0	0.0	644	25.4	3.8
Ludhiana	0	0.0	0.0	0	0.0	0.0	0	0.0	0.0	4	0.2	0.1	0	0.0	0.0	0	0.0	0.0	242	14.8	1.4
Madurai	100	7.9	5.4	0	0.0	0.0	0	0.0	0.0	208	16.5	4.4	0	0.0	0.0	0	0.0	0.0	378	30.0	2.2
Mumbai	36	0.2	2.0	0	0.0	0.0	0	0.0	0.0	362	2.0	7.7	144	0.8	93.5	0	0.0	0.0	1253	7.0	7.5
Nagpur	52	2.5	2.8	0	0.0	0.0	0	0.0	0.0	3	0.1	0.1	0	0.0	0.0	0	0.0	0.0	458	22.5	2.7
Patna	1	0.1	0.1	0	0.0	0.0	0	0.0	0.0	2	0.2	0.0	0	0.0	0.0	0	0.0	0.0	197	15.4	1.2
Puna	104	3.0	5.6	0	0.0	0.0	0	0.0	0.0	3	0.1	0.1	0	0.0	0.0	0	0.0	0.0	360	10.4	2.1
Surat	4	0.2	0.2	0	0.0	0.0	0	0.0	0.0	29	1.3	0.6	0	0.0	0.0	0	0.0	0.0	258	11.1	1.5
Vadodara	14	0.9	0.8	0	0.0	0.0	0	0.0	0.0	1	0.1	0.0	0	0.0	0.0	0	0.0	0.0	270	17.0	1.6
Varanasi	36	2.8	2.0	0	0.0	0.0	0	0.0	0.0	4	0.3	0.1	0	0.0	0.0	14	1.1	3.4	135	10.5	0.8
Vishakhapatnam	657	38.9	35.6	0	0.0	0.0	0	0.0	0.0	32	1.9	0.7	0	0.0	0.0	9	0.5	2.2	931	55.1	5.5
Total (cities)	**1845**	**1.9**	**100.0**	**1**	**0.0**	**100.0**	**0**	**0.0**	**0.0**	**4683**	**4.9**	**100.0**	**154**	**0.2**	**100.0**	**415**	**0.4**	**100.0**	**16807**	**17.7**	**100**

INVESTIGATION OF SEX-RELATED CRIMES

The nature of proof in sex offences, unlike most other crimes, traditionally has required some corroboration other than the victim's testimony. Sex crimes also arouse the concern of the community, and there is likely to be political and public pressure on the police to solve the case. If not handled properly, this pressure can contribute to a faulty and hasty investigation. Statistically, we know that most rapes are committed by a single individual acting alone; almost one- third occur in or near the home; almost three-fourths occur between 6:00 pm. and 6:00 a.m. and more than half of the victims are under the age of 25. According to victimisation surveys, a large percentage of rapes are never reported. Statistically, lower-income women are more likely to be raped. Location makes little difference in rape statistics; urban, suburban, and rural locations account for approximately the same number of rapes per 1,000 residents. Rape offenders are more likely to be young, between the ages of 14 and 19; individuals between 25 and 34 represent the second largest grouping.

The issue of mutual consent is frequently a key defence contention. However, it should be noted at the outset that the concept of mutual consent is not well defined in the law, and what may be perceived as consent may not in fact be the case. Minor children cannot generally give consent. Plus, the phenomenon known as "date rape" has generated new case law. Within the rubric of mutual consent lies a number of acts that may involve full consent between the parties, but that nevertheless are illegal within a particular jurisdiction. Examples of these include prostitution, adultery, homosexual acts, and other sex acts, such as anal intercourse. The most serious sex-connected crime from the perception of the public is forcible rape or sodomy, coupled with murder. It is important to recognise, though, that all rapes and serious sexual assaults must have a high priority in the investigative universe.

The legal definition of rape generally involves the following elements:

— Sexual penetration, however slight, of the victim's vulva;
— By a person or persons without the victim's consent;
— Or with a minor child.

Sex crimes include other forms of aberrant behaviour with which the investigator should be familiar. These include: sexual assault, child abuse and molestation, also known as pedophilia, some forms of pornography, indecent exposure, incest, stalking.

Two types of stalkers have been identified by New York homicide detective Vernon Geberth: the Psychopathic Personality Stalker, and the Psychotic Personality Stalker. Stalking may involve telephone calls, notes or letters, confrontations, and following a person or persons.

Understanding the reasons for stalking behaviour is a critical part of the investigation. He often may be known in the case of celebrity stalkers. In the absence of letters, phone calls, or other warnings, the victim may tell the investigator that he "feels" they are being watched. When telephone calls are being made, a pen register may be placed on the phone with the cooperation of the telephone company. This identifies the phone from which a call is being made.

In the case of mail, leads may be developed by looking at postmarks to determine where the letter was posted. In the case of love-scorned stalkers, while they do not usually intend to murder the victim, they do have a propensity for violence, and many of these cases have resulted in a murder.

There are two aspects of sex crime investigation must receive priority handling. The first is seeing that the victim receives proper medical attention and a physical examination that can establish rape or sexual assault.

The second is protection of the crime scene and, if a suspect is apprehended immediately or shortly thereafter, the collection and protection of his clothing—particularly undergarments. The attitude and demeanour of the investigator is crucial during these initial stages. A progressive law enforcement agency will have developed relationships with hospital emergency rooms and victim support groups that can be of great assistance.

The medical practitioner conducting a rape examination is expected to follow a set of standard procedures that are a part of the case during its investigative and trial stages. In rape cases there may be more than one crime scene requiring protection. For example, the victim may have been abducted and taken by car to another location and held there, or assaulted in one location and then taken to yet another location where she was released. It is necessary to establish an evidentiary link between the perpetrator and the victim that will serve to corroborate the victim's allegation. For example, the presence of semen in the vagina may be used to refute an allegation that intercourse did not take place; and trace or fingerprint evidence may be used to show that the suspect was at a location where he denied being, such as the bedroom.

After the victim has received medical attention, a follow- up interview should be conducted. In many jurisdictions this interview is conducted by a female investigator if one is available. Under ideal circumstances it is prudent to have a psychologist who is familiar with sex crimes advise the investigator as questioning proceeds (this is not usually done in the presence of the victim). The psychologist should not take part in the interview, although in some cases it may be advisable to permit a representative from a victim support group to be present.

The first officer on the scene will likely conduct a preliminary interview. These interviews are critical; patrol officers should be trained in handling them. Also, the time, manner, and nature of the interview may be affected if considerable time passes before medical authorities permit the victim to be interviewed by the investigator. For example, if there is serious physical or emotional trauma, the doctor may not permit an immediate interview. In such a case, the investigator must depend on the information from the initial interview.

The interview should be conducted in private, preferably with an impartial observer such as a nurse or female officer. Generally, the officer with the most experience should conduct the interview. However, circumstances may dictate otherwise—for example, if the victim is more comfortable with a female officer with less experience. If the victim alleges a rape, the officer should assume that one has occurred and operate on this assumption. If time permits, the next stage of the interview should attempt to build on the victim's statements, taking care not to challenge or question statements. The interview should take into account such factors as age, psychological state, willingness to co-operate, and special circumstances. This involves an ability to "size up the situation".

The officer should avoid leading questions and should respond to statements by nodding or asking, "Then what happened?" Confusion, disorientation, or fear may create inconsistencies in statements. Inconsistencies do not mean that the victim is lying. She may be avoiding certain items of information because she is psychologically traumatised, embarrassed, or worried about the reactions of a spouse, boyfriend, or some family member.

The goal of the preliminary interview should be to establish:

- — a physical description of the offender or offenders;
- — the location or locations where the crime took place;
- — the identification of possible witnesses;
- — specific actions of the offender that are volunteered by the victim;
- — circumstances leading up to the attack;
- — information on any weapon or vehicle that may have been used;
- — specific information on the actual location of the assault (bedroom, back of a vehicle, etc.).

The officer must take care to be supportive and understanding during the preliminary interview. This is as important for female officers as it is for males. It is not unusual, subconsciously, to provide the victim with visual cues that indicate scepticism, disbelief, disapproval, or even hostility. Unless there are very unusual circumstances, the interview should never be conducted in the presence of the husband, boyfriend, or other family member.

This generally should be avoided unless a determination has been made that this will aid in the interview process. The officer should refrain from telling individuals that the victim does not want them present; instead he should politely tell them that their presence is not advisable at this point and assure them that they will have an opportunity to speak to the victim as soon as possible.

An effort must be made by the investigator to be present, if at all possible, when the victim first meets with persons close to her after the assault.

A trained rape counsellor with experience in handling and counselling rape victims can be of assistance in reassuring the victim. The use of counsellors should be countenanced by department policy. Ground rules should be established for their utilisation. The task of a counsellor is not to conduct the interview; it is rather to lend support. Generally, the police station is to be avoided.

The interview should be conducted with only the necessary people present—the investigator, the victim assistance counsellor or psychologist, and perhaps the prosecutor. In some cases a stenographer may be needed. Doctors, nurses, police supervisors, and of course, reporters are excluded; the fewer people the better. The investigator should ask the victim to tell her story from the beginning, apologise for having her repeat it, and explain that some questions may be asked again—not because the investigator does not believe her but because it will help later in conducting the investigation, arresting the perpetrator and, most importantly, gaining a conviction.

The investigator should explain that the more information the police have, the greater the likelihood that the case may not have to come to trial. The defendant is likely to plead guilty in cases where the prosecutor has a lot of information. The victim should be allowed to tell the story in her own words with minimal interruptions while the investigator makes notes of the areas in which more information is needed.

The investigator should establish the basic points of information: who, what, when, where, how, and why. The elements of the crime must be established. Taking care not to "lead" the witness, the investigator should move from the general to the specific. Many victims will have difficulty explaining certain sex acts. Questioning will be governed in large measure on the experience and comfort of the victim in providing graphic details. While taking care not to appear like a voyeur, the investigator should exhibit a sense of comfort in discussing the case. The investigator must not assume that the victim understands what has been said to her just because she nods agreement or says yes. She should explain what happened in her own words. If there are multiple acts, they should be identified and categorised in chronological order.

The actions of the perpetrator and the victim, including statements made and physical actions taken at that time, must be ascertained. The psychological state of the victim may have prompted her to acquiesce out of fear even though on the surface it may not appear that a threat was present. The victim's actions and words may be crucial to a conviction and must be carefully recorded. Some victims may be reluctant to use profanity and may hesitate to repeat the words an offender used. Even some novice investigators have been known to omit profanity from reports even though it was used in a verbatim account of the crime. The so-called "experience" or moral character of the victim may also be used against the victim during a trial, and the investigator should establish in detail what in the victim's mind constituted a lack of consent, and how or why the victim may have acquiesced.

In the first case the victim, who had been drinking, had sexual intercourse with one individual willingly, after which his friend entered the room and held her down and copulated with her, despite her protests and physical attempts to stop him. In recent years "date rape" has come to be a serious problem, one frequently ignored by authorities in the past. Greater recognition and sensitivity to this issue in society has prompted concern and action by law enforcement.

The exact statements of the victim, witnesses, and the suspect may be crucial for prosecution. For this reason, it is important to try to record interviews. The actions of the suspect after the act should also be determined if possible. The victim may be able to provide other information that makes it possible to collect physical evidence linking the suspect to the scene. The investigator should make every effort to have the victim identify distinguishing marks or characteristics such as scars or tattoos—particularly those that are normally not visible.

The investigator should ask if the offender was circumcised, and should be sure that the victim understands what circumcision is and what it looks like. Interviews with the victim should be kept to a minimum; repeated interviews can cause trauma. On the other hand, the investigator must feel confident that all the necessary information has been collected. This may mean holding two or more sessions. Interviews of witnesses in rape cases fall into two categories:

i) those who can testify that the offender was with the victim, and
ii) those who may be able to testify to specific acts.

Hostile witnesses may claim that the victim gave her consent; others may be ashamed at what they saw and might not want to cooperate. With hostile witnesses efforts should be made to gather as much detail as possible. What they perceive as acquiescence may not be. Also, if they are lying to help a friend, it may be possible to develop conflicting statements or descriptions of the actions. Such witnesses should be handled carefully; the investigator must not lead them in their responses.

The investigator must keep in mind that the child may have been victimised by a parent. It is important to maintain eye contact, and to observe physical movements and the relationship between parent and child. The preliminary interview may involve parents who have discovered that a crime has taken place. Often the suspect is known. In most cases where such an allegation is made, the reporting officer need not conduct an interview immediately.

The child should be allowed to explain what happened in his or her own words. The investigator should try to secure an identification or physical description of the offender. Trained investigators, children's advocates, or counsellors who are familiar with this type of investigation should be summoned immediately.

Physical Evidence

The investigator must be aware that the lives of victims, as well as alleged suspects, can be ruined through carelessness. The crime scene and the collection of physical evidence represent an important part of the initial phase of the investigation.

The collection of physical evidence in rape and sexual abuse cases should follow the recommendations outlined. A sex crimes investigation kit should also be available to the investigator. The investigator should recognise that sex crimes may occur in multiple locations. Care should be taken to quickly identify multiple crime scenes and immediate steps should be taken to protect them. The goal of the crime scene search is to locate evidence that will:

- link the victim and the offender to the crime scene:
- establish that sexual relations took place;
- establish that force was used; and
- establish the offender's role or activity.

Establishing a link between the victim, offender, and crime scene may be necessary in cases where the offender denies being present or claims that the victim was not present. This link has great investigative and probative significance. In order to establish rape it is necessary to prove that penetration, however slight, took place. This is usually accomplished through a medical examination, which may show that intercourse took place.

However, laboratory analyses may be hampered if the victim has taken a shower or douche. Analysis also can be impeded if the victim had intercourse with another individual prior to the rape, or was attacked by more than one person. In one case a victim had sexual intercourse with her boyfriend willingly, but awoke later to find that one of his "friends" had entered her room after her boyfriend left to force her to have sexual relations. The offender maintained that he had not had sexual intercourse, but instead merely had sat on the bed, propositioned the woman, and been refused.

A crime scene search produced the victim's undergarments, which contained traces of semen. When examined to determine its blood group, the blood group found matched that of the accused, but differed from that of the victim and the boyfriend. When confronted with this evidence the man confessed.

Modern DNA technology is even more helpful than blood grouping in resolving such an issue. The use of force can be established through the recovery of weapons or material used to tie the victim down, or by showing the marks left through the use of force in restraining the victim.

How the physical evidence is used will depend on the various elements of the case as it is being prepared. For example, fingernail scrapings from the victim may be used to tie the offender to the victim. Scrapings from the suspect may be used to place the suspect in a particular location as well as link him to the victim. Blood can be grouped and examined for its DNA pattern.

The following considerations play important roles in the use of physical evidence both in investigation and prosecution:

— *Blood*: The development of a new technique for blood testing makes it possible for the laboratory to provide much more information than in the past. Using this technique it may be possible to individualise the sample. Known as DNA analysis, it determines the genetic code that is unique to that individual; only identical twins will have the same genetic codes. Care must be taken in the collection of blood samples; efforts should be made to ensure that there is no mixing of body fluids.

— *Semen*: Microscopic examination of semen may help determine if the sexual activity was recent. In most cases the crime laboratory deals with dead sperm because of the passage of time prior to examination. For this reason, if possible, a microscopic examination of a sample should be conducted as soon as possible. This is usually done in the hospital by a physician or trained medical microscopist. Semen can also provide evidence of blood type. More recent research indicates that it may be possible to identify an individual's genetic code by examining semen. Collecting semen samples from the victim will generally be handled at the hospital where rape "kits" should be available for use by a physician or nurse. The investigator or crime scene technician should collect the clothing of the victim and the suspect whenever possible. Each item should be handled as a separate piece of evidence; under no circumstances should the garments be put in the same container. Care should also be taken with garments containing dried semen samples so that it does not flake off. They should not be folded as the semen sample may then crumble and be lost. In searching for semen samples it is common to use ultraviolet light because semen fluoresces.

— *Saliva*: Saliva samples may be used to identify blood group and can also be used to identify genetic codes. It is found less frequently than blood and semen; the properties of it make it look like water. It may be possible to obtain a saliva sample from cigarettes, food, chewing gum, or bed sheets. It also may be present in bite marks on the victim. In collection, care should be taken not to touch the saliva directly as secretions on the fingers can contaminate it.

— *Hair*: Hair can be taken from the head, chest, legs, or pubic area. Facial hair is less likely to be present unless the individual has a beard or moustache. An individual's DNA can be determined from a hair if the root is present.

— *Fibres*: Fibres obtained from the suspect's clothing or from other material, such as rope or cord used to tie the victim, may be useful evidentiary material. Here again, it is important to note that each collection should be handled separately and clearly identified as to location.

— *Markings:* Tool or weapon markings may be used to link the weapon or tool to the scene or victim, particularly if it is recovered in the possession of the suspect.

When collecting or identifying physical evidence at the scene, particular care should be taken to note clearly where each piece of evidence is located. Do not rely on memory: use sketches, photographs, and notes.

Sources of Information

Records and information in sex crimes cases follows the general pattern. However, a number of additional sources of information should be pursued. The initial inquiry should be addressed either to the records department or crime analysis unit. A sex offender may have a prior arrest record, although not necessarily for rape.

Computerised record system can assist the investigator in identifying possible suspects based on physical description, prior arrests, or MO. The crime analysis unit may help by recognising similar cases that can be compared to the present one. The sex offence may have a "specific" motive known only to the perpetrator. Do not assume that it was solely for sexual gratification. Rape is rarely associated with sexual gratification, and is more likely associated with a need for power. The nature of the attack may also provide valuable clues.

The type of weapon, geographical location, time of day, and the suspect's actions can all link him to other crimes or to past activities. In addition to law enforcement records, the investigator may want to explore other sources. In recent years emphasis has been placed on the development of rape offender profiles. The methodology employed by the FBI in profiling violent offenders through the VICAP programme involves information collected from police departments, interviews with convicted offenders, and research results published by social scientists. The FBI will assist local agencies on request.

Police departments are asked to complete the VICAP forms on offenders, which are then computerised at Quantico. The rape offender profile is based on the theory that an individual displays unique characteristics in personality, crime scene behaviour, and method of operation. The investigator should be aware that many of the commonly held assumptions about rape and rapists are inaccurate.

On the other hand, there are likely to be clues in the crime itself that can assist the investigator and that are believed to be subject to profiling. The majority of rape offenders are not psychotic, but virtually all of them have deeply rooted psychological problems. According to A. Nicholas Groth, a psychologist who specialises in the study of sexual assault:

> Some men who ordinarily would never commit a sexual assault commit rape under very extraordinary circumstances, such as in wartime, but the likelihood of such a person's being a repetitive offender is very low. There are other men, however, who find it very difficult to meet the ordinary or unusual demands of life, and the stresses that we all learn to tolerate are unendurable and overwhelming to these individuals. The extent to which

> they find most life demands frustrating, coupled with their inability to tolerate frustration and their reliance on sex as the way of overcoming their distress, make the likelihood of their being a repetitive offender very high. Furthermore, they constitute an immediate and ongoing threat to the safety of the community.

The investigator may find that a profile of the offender will assist in reducing or narrowing the range of potential suspects through identification of age, and social and demographic characteristics. In a study of 170 men who were convicted of sexually assaulting adults and 178 who were convicted of sexually assaulting children, Groth identified the following patterns for various types of rape:

— *Gang rape:* In nine per cent of the cases in the study the sexual offence involved more than one assailant. Most of these cases (90 per cent) involved one victim; 77 per cent involved offenders between the ages 17 and 27.

— *Elderly rape:* In 18 per cent of the cases the suspect sexually assaulted a woman who was significantly older; in 12 per cent women over the age of 50 were attacked. All of the offenders showed life adjustment difficulties beginning with adolescence.

— *Child rape:* The individual who rapes children is likely to come from a disadvantaged background. He is usually relatively young and is rarely beyond age 40. Rape of children appears to be more class-related, the act is frequently devoid of a sexual or emotional involvement, and the suspect attacks different victims.

In sex-related homicides there is a good possibility that the offender will strike again, or that he has committed other crimes. Although the techniques for investigating a sex-related homicide are similar to those in any homicide investigation, this type of crime has unique characteristics that should be considered. The motivation of the offender may or may not have been homicide, but in most cases the perpetrator set out to commit a sexual assault. An exception to this is a sex-related homicide during a burglary or robbery in which the offender rapes and kills merely because a victim is present.

The longer he is there, the higher the probability of leaving trace evidence and other information that may assist in developing background information. Also, because the offender is likely to commit more than one attack, it is possible to bring together information from other crimes to develop a composite database.

A sympathetic understanding of the trauma of the victim should be combined with an unemotional attitude toward the suspect. The investigator should not judge or let personal emotions interfere with the investigation. However, the emotional factors involved in such investigations create a greater probability of making mistakes. The investigator should carefully check out the alibi and any other items of information that might serve to support the suspect's statements.

However, the investigator should recognise that eyewitness identification frequently is flawed. For this reason, identification through sketches, photographs, or even lineups should be considered with caution. All too often there is a tendency to couple an eyewitness identification with a prior record as a basis for prosecution. Such evidence, though valu-able, should be combined with a thorough investigation that endeavours to tie the suspect to the crime scene.

In many cases the offender will say that the victim actually induced the crime. Such claims may be difficult to prove in court; it is the investigator's responsibility, however, to explore all contentions, keeping in mind that the victim's background or reputation does not have any bearing on whether she was assaulted. Although interviews are an important part of this phase of the investigation, there are other ways in which an individual's statements can be verified or disproved. Contradictory statements, errors of fact, and descriptive comments should be explored during interrogation. For this reason it is important to keep good notes and to record statements if possible. As the case progresses and more information becomes available, the investigator should maintain a set of cross-referenced files for ease of access and comparison.

REFERENCES

Ahuja, R., *Crime Against Women*, Rawat, Jaipur, 1986.

Carrillo, Roxanna, *Battered Dreams: Violence Against Women as an Obstacle to Development,* 1992.

Indian Evidence Act, Section 113-A, A presumption has also been incorporated in the Indian Evidence Act to enable the court to draw an inference of abetment of suicide when the question is whether the commission of suicide by a woman was abetted by her husband or any relative, the complainant has been freed from that onus to prove that the accused had indeed abetted the offence.

Law Commission of India, *Eighty-fourth Report on Rape and Allied Offences,* 1980.

Singh, *Indian Women: The Captured Beings*, Intellectual, New Delhi, 1900.

The Criminal Law (Amendment) Act of 1983, among others, increased punishment for rape; distinguished gang rape and Custodial rape and laid down stiffer penalties; distinguished rape on a pregnant woman and reversed the burden of proof in case of gang rape, custodial rape, rape on a pregnant woman.

The Dowry Prohibition (Amendment) Act, 1966, Section 8-B.

The Dowry Prohibition Act, 1961, is applicable to whole of India except the State of Jammu & Kashmir where the State legislature had enacted the Dowry Restraint Act, *1960,* (Act No. XXXVI of 1960) consisting of eight sections.

7

Crime against Children and Juvenile Delinquency

There is a need for a clear definition for 'child' in the statutes of law. The Juvenile Justice Act of 1986 defines a girl-child as one who is below 18 years of age. The 'Child Marriage Restraint Act' of 1928 also specifies 18 years as the cut-off mark for restraining child marriage. For the purpose of Section 375(IPC) the crucial age in case of wife is 15 years. But in Section 376(IPC) a distinction has been made on the basis of wife below 12 years of age. These give rise to conflicting interpretations in the status of the child. There is need for harmonising these inconsistencies along with those existing in 'Special/Local Laws'.

The offences committed against the children or the crimes in which children were the victims are considered as crime against children. The general penal code of this country and the various protective and preventive 'Special and Local Laws' specifically mention the offences wherein children are known to be victims. Issues relating to child victims and crimes, committed against children, call for a human approach. Various social organisations along with the government support have been collectively addressing this menace.

Efforts are afoot to prevent and save children from the vulnerabilities and exploitations to which they are subjected by the law enforcement agencies. Such crimes are viewed as social evil and bad, the reported incidents of such crimes continue to rise in magnitude. This calls for greater involvement by the society with greater awareness and attitudes towards such crimes to fight and contain this menace. The present legislative support through various enactments, legislations which were enacted from time to time safeguard the victimisation of children against abuse, violence and inhuman treatment, have come a long way in protecting and securing children from various crimes perpetrated against them.

The following are the important specific legislation, to protect the children from the clutches of violence and abuse meted out to them:

i) The Factories Act (Amended), 1954.
ii) Hindu Adoption and Maintenance Act, 1956.
iii) Hindu Minority and Guardianship Act, 1956.
iv) The Orphanages and Other Charitable Homes (Supervision and Control) Act, 1960.
v) Probation of Offenders Act, 1958.
vi) The Child Marriage Restraint Act (Amended), 1979.
vii) The Child Labour (Prohibition and Regulation) Act, 1986.
viii) The Infant Milk Substitute, Feeding Bottles and Infant Foods (Regulation of Production, Supply and Distribution) Act, 1992.
ix) The Pre-Natal Diagnostic Technique (Regulation, Prevention and Misuse) Act, 1994.
x) The Persons with Disabilities (Equal Opportunities, Protection of Rights and Full Participation) Act, 1996.

Cases in which the children are victimised and abused can be categorised under two broad sections: (i) Crimes committed against Children which are punishable under the Indian Penal Code (IPC); (ii)Crimes reported against children which are punishable under Special and Local Laws (SLL).

i) *Crimes committed against Children which are punishable under the Indian Penal Code (IPC).*

a) Foeticides (Crime against being born) (Section 315 and 316 IPC).

b) Infanticides (Crime against unborn child) (Section 315 IPC).

c) Abetment of suicide (Abetment by other persons for commitment of suicide by children) (Section 305 IPC).

d) Exposure and abandonment (Crime against children by parents or others to expose or to leave them with the intention of abandonment): (Section 317 IPC).

e) Kidnapping and abduction:

— kidnapping for exporting (Section 360 IPC).

— kidnapping from lawful guardianship (Section 361 IPC).

— kidnapping for ransom (Section 363 read with Section 384 IPC).

— kidnapping for camel racing, etc. (Section 363 IPC).

— kidnapping for begging (Section 363-A IPC).

— kidnapping to compel for marriage (Section 366 IPC).

— kidnapping for slavery etc. (Section 367 IPC).

— kidnapping for stealing from its person (under 10 years of age only) (Section 369 IPC).

f) Procuration of minor girls (for inducement to force or seduce, to illicit intercourse) (Section 366-A IPC).

g) Selling of girls for prostitution (Section 372 IPC).

h) Buying of girls for prostitution (Section 373 IPC).

i) Rape.

j) Unnatural offences.

ii) Crimes reported against children which are punishable under Special and Local Laws (SLL).

a) Immoral Traffic Prevention Act (where minors are abused in prostitution).

b) Child Marriage Restraint Act.

c) Child Labour (Prevention) Act.

ANALYSIS OF IPC CRIMES

Cases of crime against children continues to be reported significantly from various states and union territories. Tables given in the follwoing pages provide detailed information about the crime committed against children during the years 1999.

During 1999, 4, 957 incidence of crime against children were reported in India. These cases were higher in states of Madhya Pradesh (952), Maharashtra (750), Uttar Pradesh (369), Gujarat (317), Andhra Pradesh (271) Bihar (205), West Bengal (188), and Delhi (UT) (403).

Child Rape

The cases of child rape below the age of 16 years were 3, 153 during the year 1999. The states of Madhya Pradesh (760), Maharashtra (359), Uttar Pradesh (344), Andhra Pradesh (202), and Delhi (223) reported significant number of cases of child rape.

Kidnapping and Abduction

Incidence of kidnapping and abduction cases of children share a significant percentage of the crimes committed against children. Delhi (156) Gujarat (106) and Haryana (92) reported higher such incidents in 1999.

Other Offences

Incidence of infanticide, child marriage restraint case, procuration of minor girls and buying of girls for prostitution reported decline during 1999 in comparison to previous years.

Incidence of buying of girls for prostitution were reported from West Bengal (3) and Maharastra (2).

Cases where girls being sold for prostitution were reported from West Bengal (7) and Maharashtra (3).

Higher number procuration of minor girls cases were reported from the states of Bihar (42), Maharashtra (31) Assam (29) Madhya Pradesh (16) and Karnatataka (12).

The number of incidence of infanticide were higher in Madhya Pradesh (16), Maharashtra (14) Punjab (11) Andra Pradesh (10) and Bihar (7).

The cases of foeticide were more from the states of Madhya Pradesh (17), Maharashtra (13) Haryana (9) and Gujarat (7).

Cases of children being abandoned and exposed were more from the states of Maharashtra (249), Madhya Pradesh (104) and Gujarat (73).

ANALYSIS OF SLL CRIMES

Cases under Child Marriage Restraint Act

Of the 581 cases reported under Child Marriage Restraint Act in the country, 31 cases were reported from Gujarat followed by Himachal Pradesh (7) and Haryana (2).

Table 7. 1.

Incidence of crimes committed against children in Indian states during 1999.

State	*Rape below16 years*		*Infanticide*		*Fieticide*		*Abetment of suicide*		*Exposure & abetment*	
	I	*P*	*I*	*P*	*I*	*P*	*I*	*P*	*I*	*P*
	(1)		(2)		(3)		(4)		(5)	
Andhra Pradesh	202	6.4	10	11.5	3	4.9	7	29.2	16	2.7
Arunchal Pradesh	9	0.3	2	2.3	0	0.0	0	0.0	1	0.2
Assam	119	3.8	5	5.7	0	0.0	0	0.0	1	0.2
Bihar	78	2.5	7	8.0	4	6.6	1	4.2	4	0.7
Goa	11	0.3	1	1.1	0	0.0	0	0.0	4	0.7
Gujarat	92	2.9	0	0.0	7	11.5	2	8.3	73	12.3
Haryana	88	2.8	4	4.6	9	14.8	0	0.0	9	1.5
Himachal Pradesh	29	0.9	0	0.0	1	1.6	0	0.0	13	2.2
J& K	12	0.4	1	1.1	1	1.6	5	20.8	3	0.5
Karnataka	70	2.2	2	2.3	0	0.0	5	0.0	23	3.9
Kerala	121	3.8	0	0.0	0	0.0	0	0.0	7	1.2
Madhya Pradesh	760	24.1	16	18.4	17	27.9	4	16.7	104	17.5
Maharashtra	359	11.4	14	16.1	13	21.3	3	12.5	249	42.0
Manipur	4	0.1	0	0.0	0	0.0	0	0.0	0	0.0

(Table 7.1. contd...)

State	*Rape below16 years*		*Infanticide*		*Fieticide*		*Abetment of suicide*		*Exposure & abetment*	
	I	*P*	*I*	*P*	*I*	*P*	*I*	*P*	*I*	*P*
	(1)		(2)		(3)		(4)		(5)	
Meghalaya	4	0.1	0	0.0	0	0.0	0	0.0	0	0.0
Orissa	128	4.1	2	2.3	0	0.0	0	0.0	0	0.0
Punjab	115	3.6	11	12.6	3	4.9	0	0.0	3	0.5
Rajasthan	137	4.3	6	6.9	3	4.9	0	0.0	54	9.1
Sikkim	2	0.1	2	2.3	0	0.0	0	0.0	0	0.0
Tamil Nadu	88	2.8	0	0.0	0	0.0	0	0.0	0	0.0
Tripura	6	0.2	0	0.0	0	0.0	0	0.0	0	0.0
Uttar Pradesh	344	10.9	0	0.0	0	0.0	0	0.0	3	0.5
West Bengal	84	2.7	1	1.1	0	0.0	0	0.0	0	0.0
Total (States)	**2916**	**92.5**	**84**	**96.6**	**61**	**100.0**	**22**	**91.7**	**567**	**95.6**

(Table 7.1. contd...)

State	*Kidnapping and abduction*		*Procuration of minor girls*		*Selling of girls for prostitutuion*		*Buying of girls for prostitutuion*		*Child Marriage Restraint Act*		*Total*	
	I	*P*	*I*	*P*	*I*	*P*	*I*	*P*	*I*	*P*	*I*	*P*
	(6)		(7)		(8)		(9)		(10)		(11)	
Andhra Pradesh	26	3.3	6	3.5	0	0.0	0	0.0	1	1.7	271	5.5
Arunchal Pradesh	3	0.4	0	0.0	0	0.0	0	0.0	0	0.0	15	0.3
Assam	8	1.0	29	16.9	0	0.0	0	0.0	0	0.0	162	3.3
Bihar	66	8.3	42	24.4	0	0.0	0	0.0	3	5.2	205	4.1
Goa	3	0.4	0	0.0	0	0.0	0	0.0	0	0.0	19	0.4
Gujarat	106	13.4	6	3.5	0	0.0	0	0.0	31	53.4	317	6.4
Haryana	92	11.6	7	4.1	0	0.0	0	0.0	2	3.4	211	4.3
Himachal Pradesh	2	0.3	0	0.0	0	0.0	0	0.0	7	12.1	52	1.0
J& K	0	0.0	0	0.0	0	0.0	0	0.0	0	0.0	22	0.4
Karnataka	51	6.4	12	7.0	1	7.7	0	0.0	0	0.0	159	3.2
Kerala	5	0.6	5	2.9	0	0.0	0	0.0	0	0.0	140	2.8
Madhya Pradesh	35	4.4	16	9.3	0	0.0	0	0.0	0	0.0	952	19.2
Maharashtra	74	9.4	31	18.0	3	23.1	2	40.0	2	3.4	750	15.1
Manipur	0	0.0	0	0.0	0	0.0	0	0.0	0	0.0	4	0.1

(Table 7.1. contd...)

State abduction	*Kidnapping and of minor girls*		*Procuration for prostitutuion*		*Selling of girls for prostitutuion*		*Buying of girls Restraint Act*		*Child Marriage*		*Total*	
	I	*P*	*I*	*P*	*I*	*P*	*I*	*P*	*I*	*P*	*I*	*P*
	(6)		(7)		(8)		(9)		(10)		(11)	
Meghalaya	0	0.0	0	0.0	0	0.0	0	0.0	0	0.0	4	0.1
Mizoram	0	0.0	0	0.0	1	7.7	0	0.0	0	0.0	53	1.1
Nagaland	0	0.0	0	0.0	0	0.0	0	0.0	0	0.0	2	0.0
Orissa	17	2.1	2	1.2	0	0.0	0	0.0	0	0.0	149	3.0
Punjab	12	1.5	2	1.2	0	0.0	0	0.0	2	3.4	148	3.0
Rajasthan	8	1.0	0	0.0	0	0.0	0	0.0	6	10.3	214	4.3
Sikkim	0	1.0	0	0.0	0	0.0	0	0.0	0	0.0	4	0.1
Tamil Nadu	4	0.5	4	2.3	0	0.0	0	0.0	0	0.0	96	1.9
Tripura	0	0.0	0	0.0	0	0.0	0	0.0	0	0.0	6	0.1
Uttar Pradesh	18	1.3	3	1.7	0	0.0	0	0.0	1	1.7	369	7.4
West Bengal	87	11.0	6	3.5	7	53.8	3	60.0	0	0.0	188	3.8
Total (States)	**617**	**78.0**	**171**	**99.4**	**12**	**92.3**	**5**	**100.0**	**57**	**98.3**	**4512**	**91.0**

Table 7. 2.

Incidence of crimes committed against children in union territories during 1999

UT	*Rape below16 years*		*Infanticide*		*Fieticide*		*Abetment of suicide*		*Exposure & abetment*	
	I	*P*	*I*	*P*	*I*	*P*	*I*	*P*	*I*	*P*
	(1)		(2)		(3)		(4)		(5)	
A & N Islands	4	0.1	0	0.0	0	0.0	0	0.0	0	0.0
Chandigarh	5	0.2	0	0.0	0	0.0	1	4.2	5	0.8
D&N Haveli	1	0.0	0	0.0	0	0.0	0	0.0	0	0.0
Daman &Diu	3	0.1	0	0.0	0	0.0	1	4.2	1	0.2
Delhi	223	7.1	3	3.4	0	0.0	0	0.0	20	3.4
Lakshadweep	0	0.0	0	0.0	0	0.0	0	0.0	0	0.0
Pondicherry	1	0.0	0	0.0	0	0.0	0	0.0	0	0.0
Total (UTs)	237	7.5	3	3.4	0	0.0	2	8.3	26	4.4
Total (All-India)	**3153**	**100.0**	**87**	**100.0**	**61**	**100.0**	**24**	**100.0**	**593**	**100.0**

(Table 7.2. contd...)

UT	Kidnapping and		Procuration abduction		Selling of girls of minor girls		Buying of girls for prostitutuion		Child Marriage for prostitutuion		Total Restraint Act	
	I	P	I	P	I	P	I	P	I	P	I	P
	(6)		(7)		(8)		(9)		(10)		(11)	
A& N Islands	0.	0.0	0	0.0	0	0.0	0	0.0	1	1.7	5	0.1
Chandigarh	17	2.1	1	0.6	0	0.0	0	0.0	0	0.0	29	0.6
D&N Haveli	0	0.0	0	0.0	0	0.0	0	0.0	0	0.0	1	0.0
Daman & Diu	0	0.0	0	0.0	0	0.0	0	0.0	0	0.0	5	0.1
Delhi	156	19.7	0	0.0	1	7.7	0	0.0	0	0.0	403	8.1
Lakshadweep	0	0.0	0	0.0	0	0.0	0	0.0	0	0.0	0	0.0
Pondicherry	1	0.1	0	0.0	0	0.0	0	0.0	0	0.0	2	0.0
Total (UTs)	174	22.0	1	0.6	1	7.7	0	0.0	1	1.7	445	9.0
Total (All-India)	**791**	**100.0**	**172**	**100.0**	**13**	**100.0**	**5**	**100.0**	**58**	**100.0**	**4957**	**100.0**

JUVENILE DELINQUENCY

The juvenile are highly vulnerable groups to fall a prey to temptations, inducement and mechanisations by vested groups to embark on a path of criminality. Crimes committed by juveniles may range from petty ones to heinous ones. The nature of juvenile sensitivity is such that it necessitates a treatment or dealing apart, by way of counselling special care and rehabilitation through special legal provisions.

The Juvenile Justice Act 1986 defines a juvenile as male below 16 years of age and female below 18 years of age. The act takes good care for adjudication and rehabilitation of juvenile delinquents.

The share of offences committed by the juveniles to the total IPC crimes reported in the country has shown a declining trend since 1988, not withstanding the fact that there is an appreciable increase in the population of the country.

During 1999, a total of 8, 574 IPC cases were registered against juvenilesin Indian states including murder cases: 241 attempt to murder cases: 168, kidnapping and abduction cases: 74, dacoity cases: 25, robbery cases: 63, riot cases: 508 and cheating cases: 26, sexual harassment cases: 26, arson cases: 40 not amounting to murder cases: 20, dowry death cases: 51 and molestation cases: 108, theft cases: 2044 hurt cases: 1452 and burglary cases: 1302. The detailed information on juvenile delinquency ocuured in Indian states during 1999 are given in table 7.3., 7.4., and 7.5.

Madhya Pradesh (2380) and Maharashtra (1848) reported high incidence of juvenile crimes under IPC. Of the 241 cases of murder registered against juveniles, Madhya Pradesh and Maharastra reported 72 and 48 cases respectively. Similarly, cases of attempt to murder (53) and rape (75) were the highest from Madhya Pradesh. Maharashtra reported the highest cases of theft (539)against juveniles.

Among the union territories, Delhi had major share of juvenile crimes committed in all union territories taken together.

More juvenile girls than boys were involved in cases related to kidnapping and abduction, dowry death, cruelty by husband or his relatives, Prohibition Act, Immoral Traffic (Prevention) Act, Dowry Prohibition Act and SC/ST (Prevention of Atrocities) Act.

The states which apprehended the largest juveniles in specific SLL cases were: Assam in Indian Passport Act; Bihar in Explosive and Explosives Substances Act; Haryana in Excise Act, Maharashtra in Prohibition Act, Karnataka in Immoral Traffic (Prevention) Act.

ANALYSIS OF IPC CRIMES

During 1999, a total of 8, 574 IPC cases were registered against juveniles. Madhya Pradesh (2, 380) and Maharashtra (1, 848) reported high incidence of juvenile crimes under IPC.

Cases of theft (2, 044), hurt (1, 452) and burglary (1, 302) constituted the major part of total juvenile IPC crimes. Of the 241 cases of murder registered against juveniles, Madhya Pradesh and Maharashtra reported 72 and 48 cases respectively.

Cases of attempt to murder (168) and rape (148) were reported during 1999. highest number of all these cases were reported from Madhya Pradesh. Maharashtra reported the highest cases (529) of theft against juveniles.

Among the union territories, Delhi had major share (288) of juvenile crimes committed in all union territories (314) taken together.

Table 7. 3.

Juvenile delinquency under different crime heads (IPC) in states during 1999.

State	Murder	Attempt to murder	C.H. not amounting to murder	Rape	Kidnapping abduction			Dacoity	Preparation for dacoity	Robbery	Burglary
					Total	of women	of girls				
	(1)	(2)	(3)	(4)	(5)	(6)	(7)	(8)	(9)	(10)	(11)
Andhra Pradesh	20	4	1	14	3	3	0	0	1	2	120
Arunchal Pradesh	0	0	0	2	0	0	0	1	0	1	10
Assam	5	0	0	0	1	0	1	0	0	0	37
Bihar	14	38	10	4	1	0	1	5	0	9	29
Goa	0	1	0	1	0	0	0	0	0	1	7
Gujarat	17	19	0	7	31	31	0	3	0	3	111
Haryana	11	4	0	4	7	4	3	0	0	3	16
Himachal Pradesh	5	0	0	4	1	0	1	0	0	1	8
Jammu & Kashmir	0	0	0	0	0	0	0	0	0	0	0
Karnataka	8	7	0	0	0	0	0	1	0	4	57
Kerala	2	1	0	2	0	0	0	0	0	1	7
Madhya Pradesh	72	53	4	75	9	8	1	2	0	17	309
Maharastra	48	24	0	20	10	5	5	13	1	11	359
Manipur	0	0	0	0	0	0	0	0	0	0	0
Meghalaya	1	0	0	2	0	0	0	0	0	0	0

(Table 7.3 contd...)

State	*Murder*	*Attempt to murder*	*C.H. not amounting to murder*	*Rape*	*Kidnapping abduction*			*Dacoity*	*Preparation for dacoity*	*Robbery*	*Burglary*
					Total	*of women*	*of girls*				
	(1)	(2)	(3)	(4)	(5)	(6)	(7)	(8)	(9)	(10)	(11)
Mizoram	0	0	0	0	0	0	0	0	0	0	1
Nagaland	0	0	0	0	0	0	0	0	0	0	0
Orissa	15	2	0	2	0	0	0	0	0	0	37
Punjab	1	2	1	1	2	1	1	0	0	0	2
Rajasthan	17	13	0	8	3	2	1	0	0	7	97
Sikkim	0	0	0	0	0	0	0	0	0	0	1
Tamil Nadu	2	0	4	1	0	0	0	0	0	2	84
Tripura	2	0	0	0	0	0	0	0	0	0	10
Uttar Pradesh	1	0	0	0	0	0	0	0	0	0	0
West Bengal	0	0	0	1	6	6	0	0	0	1	0
Total	**241**	**168**	**20**	**148**	**74**	**60**	**14**	**25**	**1**	**63**	**1302**

(Table 7.3. contd...)

State	Theft Total	Auto Theft	Other Theft	Riot	Criminal breach of trust	Cheating	Counterfeiting	Arson	Hurt	Dowry death	Molestation	Sexual harassment	Cruelty by husband and relatives	Importation of girls	Other IPC crimes	Total
	(12)	(13)	(14)	(15)	(16)	(17)	(18)	(19)	(20)	(21)	(22)	(23)	(24)	(25)	(26)	(27)
Andhra Pradesh	264	6	258	11	0	2	0	1	74	1	3	1	15	0	53	590
Arunachal Pradesh	12	0	12	2	0	0	0	0	7	0	1	0	0	0	6	42
Assam	83	0	83	16	0	0	0	2	17	0	2	0	4	0	15	182
Bihar	74	6	68	39	1	2	0	0	7	5	1	0	4	0	139	382
Goa	6	2	4	2	0	0	0	0	1	0	0	0	0	0	2	21
Gujarat	233	38	195	71	7	6	1	7	189	2	9	4	51	0	304	1075
Haryana	40	4	36	27	0	1	0	0	88	8	7	5	31	0	48	300
Himachal Pradesh	9	0	9	4	0	0	0	0	8	0	1	1	1	0	4	47
Jammu & Kashmir	0	0	0	0	0	0	0	0	0	0	0	0	0	0	0	0
Karnataka	72	3	69	47	0	0	0	1	53	0	1	0	10	0	25	286
Kerala	21	0	21	5	0	0	0	1	3	0	0	0	0	0	8	51
Madhya Pradesh	273	10	263	55	2	5	0	7	528	4	51	9	26	0	879	2380
Maharastra	529	30	499	100	0	7	0	18	377	17	20	5	90	0	199	1848
Manipur	0	0	0	0	0	0	0	0	0	0	0	0	0	0	0	0
Meghalaya	11	0	11	0	0	0	0	0	0	0	0	0	0	0	1	15
Mizoram	8	0	8	0	0	0	0	0	0	0	0	0	0	0	2	11
Nagaland	0	0	0	0	0	0	0	0	0	0	0	0	0	0	0	0
Orissa	81	1	80	1	0	2	0	0	0	0	3	0	3	0	49	195
Punjab	4	0	4	0	0	1	0	0	1	1	0	0	0	0	4	20

(Table 7.3. contd...)

State	Theft			Riot	Criminal breach of trust	Cheating	Counterfeiting	Arson	Hurt	Dowry death	Molestation	Sexual harassment	Cruelty by husband and relatives	Importation of girls	Other IPC crimes	Total
	Total	Auto Theft	Other Theft													
	(12)	(13)	(14)	(15)	(16)	(17)	(18)	(19)	(20)	(21)	(22)	(23)	(24)	(25)	(26)	(27
Rajasthan	103	9	94	107	2	0	6	3	66	10	7	0	30	0	195	674
Sikkim	4	NR	NR	0	0	0	0	0	1	0	0	0	0	NR	0	6
Tamil Nadu	199	20	179	20	0	0	0	0	31	1	1	1	0	0	57	403
Tripura	5	0	5	0	0	0	0	0	0	0	0	0	0	0	0	17
Uttar Pradesh	6	0	6	1	0	0	0	0	1	2	1	0	2	0	0	14
West Bengal	7	0	7	0	0	0	0	0	0	0	0	0	0	0	0	15
Total States	**2044**	**129**	**1911**	**508**	**12**	**26**	**7**	**40**	**1452**	**51**	**108**	**26**	**267**	**0**	**1990**	**8574**

Table 7. 4.

Juvenile Delinquency under different crime heads (IPC) in union territoreis during 1999.

UT	*Murder*	*Attempt to murder*	*C.H. not amounting to murder*	*Rape*		*Kidnapping abduction*		*Dacoity*	*Preparation for dacoity*	*Robbery*	*Burglary*
	(1)	(2)	(3)	(4)	(5)	(6)	(7)	(8)	(9)	(10)	(11)
A& N Islands	0	0	0	1	0	0	0	0	0	0	1
Chandigarh	0	0	0	0	0	0	0	0	0	0	2
D&N Haveli	0	0	0	0	0	0	0	0	0	0	0
Daman & Diu	0	0	0	0	0	0	0	0	0	0	0
Delhi	9	11	1	10	9	6	3	0	0	4	37
Lakshadweep	0	0	0	0	0	0	0	0	0	0	1
Pondicherry	0	0	0	0	0	0	0	0	0	1	1
Total (UTs)	9	11	1	11	9	6	3	0	0	5	42
Total (All-India)	**250**	**179**	**21**	**159**	**83**	**66**	**17**	**25**	**2**	**68**	**1344**

(Table 7.4. contd...)

UT	Theft			Riot	Criminal breach of trust	Cheating	Counterfeiting	Arson	Hurt	Dowry death	Molestation	Sexual harassment	Cruelty by husband and relatives	Importation of girls	Other IPC crimes	Total
	Total	Auto Theft	Other Theft													
	(12)	(13)	(14)	(15)	(16)	(17)	(18)	(19)	(20)	(21)	(22)	(23)	(24)	(25)	(26)	(27
A& N Islands	0	0	0	0	0	0	0	0	0	0	0	0	0	0	1	3
Chandigarh	7	2	5	0	0	0	0	0	1	0	1	0	0	0	5	16
D&N Haveli	0	0	0	0	0	0	0	0	0	0	0	0	0	0	0	0
Daman & Diu	0	0	0	0	0	0	0	0	0	0	0	0	0	0	0	0
Delhi	118	27	91	1	1	5	0	0	19	1	7	1	6	0	48	288
Lakshadweep	0	0	0	0	0	0	0	0	0	0	0	0	0	0	0	1
Pondicherry	3	0	3	0	0	0	0	0	0	0	0	0	0	0	1	6
Total (UTs)	128	29	99	1	1	5	0	0	20	1	8	1	6	0	55	314
Total (All-India)	**2172**	**158**	**2010**	**509**	**13**	**31**	**7**	**40**	**1472**	**52**	**116**	**27**	**273**	**0**	**2045**	**8888**

Table 7. 5.

Juvenile delinquency under different crime heads (IPC) in cities during 1999.

Cities	*Murder*	*Attempt to murder*	*C.H. not amounting to murder*	*Rape*		*Kidnapping abduction*		*Dacoity*	*Preparation for dacoity*	*Robbery*	*Burglary*
	(1)	(2)	(3)	(4)	(5)	(6)	(7)	(8)	(9)	(10)	(11)
Ahmedabad	4	1	0	0	15	15	0	0	0	0	22
Bangalore	2	0	0	0	0	0	0	0	0	1	21
Bhopal	0	0	0	0	0	0	0	0	0	0	0
Calcutta	0	0	0	0	0	0	0	0	0	1	0
Chennai	0	0	0	0	0	0	0	0	0	0	6
Coimbatore	0	0	0	0	0	0	0	0	0	0	1
Delhi (City)	9	11	1	10	9	6	3	0	0	4	37
Hyderabad	4	0	0	2	0	0	0	0	0	1	36
Indore	10	6	0	8	0	0	0	0	0	0	10
Jaipur	1	0	0	1	0	0	0	0	0	2	10
Kanpur	0	0	0	0	0	0	0	0	0	0	0
Kochi	0	0	0	0	0	0	0	0	0	0	0

(Table 7.5. contd...)

Cities	*Murder*	*Attempt to murder*	*C.H. not amounting to murder*	*Rape*		*Kidnapping abduction*		*Dacoity*	*Preparation for dacoity*	*Robbery*	*Burglary*
	(1)	(2)	(3)	(4)	(5)	(6)	(7)	(8)	(9)	(10)	(11)
Lucknow	0	0	0	0	0	0	0	0	0	0	0
Ludhiana	1	1	1	0	2	1	1	0	0	0	1
Madurai	0	0	0	0	0	0	0	0	0	1	3
Mumbai	8	0	0	1	0	0	0	0	0	0	38
Nagpur	1	2	0	2	0	0	0	3	0	1	86
Patna	0	2	0	0	0	0	0	0	0	2	0
Pune	1	0	0	1	2	1	1	0	1	0	15
Surat	C	1	0	1	0	0	0	0	0	0	1
Vadodara	0	1	0	0	0	0	0	0	0	0	3
Varanasi	0	0	0	0	0	0	0	0	0	0	0
Vishakhapatnam	0	0	0	0	0	0	0	0	0	0	15
Total (cities)	**41**	**25**	**2**	**26**	**28**	**23**	**5**	**4**	**1**	**13**	**305**

(Table 7.5. contd...)

Cities	Theft Total	Auto Theft	Other Theft	Riot	Criminal breach of trust	Cheating	Counterfeiting	Arson	Hurt	Dowry death	Molestation	Sexual harassment	Cruelty by husband and relatives	Importation of girls	Other IPC crimes	Total
	(12)	(13)	(14)	(15)	(16)	(17)	(18)	(19)	(20)	(21)	(22)	(23)	(24)	(25)	(26)	(27
Ahmedabad	55	11	44	11	0	0	0	0	18	0	1	0	9	0	54	190
Bangalore	35	1	34	0	0	0	0	0	4	0	0	0	0	0	3	66
Bhopal	0	0	0	0	0	0	0	0	0	0	0	0	0	0	3	3
Calcutta	2	0	2	0	0	0	0	0	0	0	0	0	0	0	0	3
Chennai	18	0	18	0	0	0	0	0	0	0	0	0	0	0	7	31
Coimbatore	8	0	8	0	0	0	0	0	0	0	0	0	0	0	0	9
Delhi (City)	118	27	91	1	1	5	0	0	19	1	7	1	6	0	48	288
Hyderabad	57	0	57	0	0	0	0	0	6	0	0	0	0	0	0	106
Indore	24	2	22	0	1	0	0	0	33	0	3	1	0	0	83	179
Jaipur	24	3	21	14	2	0	5	0	3	0	1	0	0	0	21	84
Kanpur	0	0	0	0	0	0	0	0	0	0	0	0	0	0	0	0
Kochi	0	0	0	0	0	0	0	0	0	0	0	0	0	0	0	0
Lucknow	0	0	0	0	0	0	0	0	0	0	0	0	0	0	0	0
Ludhiana	2	0	2	0	0	0	0	0	1	0	0	0	0	0	2	11

(Table 7.5. contd...)

Cities	*Theft* Total	*Theft* Auto Theft	*Theft* Other Theft	*Riot*	*Criminal breach of trust*	*Cheating*	*Counter feiting*	*Arson*	*Hurt*	*Dowry death*	*Molestation*	*Sexual harassment*	*Cruelty by husband and relatives*	*Importation of girls*	*Other IPC crimes*	*Total*
	(12)	(13)	(14)	(15)	(16)	(17)	(18)	(19)	(20)	(21)	(22)	(23)	(24)	(25)	(26)	(27
Madurai	20	0	20	1	0	0	0	0	0	0	0	0	0	0	3	28
Mumbai	53	0	53	1	0	1	0	0	37	1	4	0	0	0	14	158
Nagpur	18	0	18	3	0	0	0	13	16	0	1	1	0	0	13	160
Patna	2	1	1	1	0	2	0	0	2	1	0	0	0	0	12	26
Pune	68	22	46	7	0	0	0	0	13	0	3	0	0	0	8	119
Surat	14	8	6	4	1	0	0	0	12	0	1	0	2	0	1	39
Vadodara	28	0	28	4	0	1	0	0	8	0	0	1	1	0	37	84
Varanasi	2	0	2	0	0	0	0	0	0	0	0	0	0	0	0	2
Vishakhapatnam	43	0	43	0	0	0	0	0	4	0	0	1	0	0	0	63
Total (cities)	**591**	**75**	**516**	**47**	**5**	**9**	**5**	**13**	**176**	**3**	**21**	**5**	**20**	**0**	**309**	**1649**

REFERENCES

Saraf D. N., 'Objectives of the Seminar', in DN- Saraf (ed.) *Social Policy, Law and Protection of Weaker Sections of Society*, 3 1986.

The Govt. of India, 'Crime in India' New Delhi, *National Crime Records Bureau*, 1995, 1997, 1999.

UNICEF, "Child Abuse and Neglect in a Global Perspective", E/ICEF/1986/CRP-4.

_______________, *Early Childhood Development: The Challenge and the Opportunity*, UNICEF, New York, 1993.

_______________, The Rights of the Child, India Country Office, New Delhi, August, 1994.

_______________, *The State of the World's Children* 1989, UNICEF, New York, 1988.

_______________, *The State of the World's Children* 1997, UNICEF, New York, 1996.

8

Custodial Crimes

Individuals come under the police custody for various reasons like arrest, police remand or even where the custody *per se* is unauthorised. Most prevalent crimes in police custody are: assault of various types, rape and murder. For custodial rape, the Indian Penal Code provides special treatment aide Section 376 (2) by specifying an immediate punishment. When any person dies while in custody of the police, the law requires a mandatory enquiry by the magistrate into the cause of the death. Every custodial death may not be an offence. However, when the cases are registered for custodial death, the investigation will proceed as prescribed for in other case of culpable homicide.

Custodial crimes which include deaths in police custody have drawn attention of the public media, and the legislature over the past many years. Police, which is a primary agency for ensuring safety of women, children who are downtrodden is not forgiven by the society if they themselves get involved in rape cases, that too in police custody.

Even the human rights commission has taken serious note of such incidents. Therefore, it was decided to collect data of custodial crimes for the first time since the year 1995. From the information furnished by the states/union territories, it is seen that trials in custodial rape cases were slow and the percentage of trials completed were fluctuating around 10.0 per cent only. The information furnished hereunder, received from states/ union territories shows the details of custodial crimes.

Table 8. 1.

Deaths in police custody / lockup in India during 1999 (of persons remanded to police custody by court).

States / UTs	*Death reported*	*Autopsy conducted*	*Magesterial ordered*	*Judicial enquiry ordered*	*Cases in connection with deaths*	*Police men chargesheeted*	*Police men convicted*
States							
Andhra Pradesh	0	0	0	0	0	0	0
Arunchal Pradesh	0	0	0	0	0	0	0
Assam	4	0	1	0	2	0	0
Bihar	0	0	0	0	0	0	0
Goa	0	0	0	0	0	0	0
Gujarat	0	0	0	0	0	0	0
Haryana	0	0	0	0	0	0	0
Himachal Pradesh	1	1	1	0	1	3	0
J& K	1	0	1	1	1	0	0
Karnataka	0	0	0	0	0	0	0
Kerala	1	0	0	0.0	0	0.0	0
Madhya Pradesh	4	0	2	1	1	16	0
Maharashtra	6	5	4	1	3	0	0
Manipur	0	0	0	0	0	0	0
Meghalaya	0	0	0	0	0	0	0
Mizoram	0	0	0	0	0	0	0
Nagaland	0	0	0	0	0	0	0
Orissa	0	0	0	0	0	0	0
Punjab	0	0	0	0	0	0	0
Rajasthan	2	0	2	0	1	1	0
Sikkim	NR	NR	NR	NR	NR	NR	NR
Tamil Nadu	0	0	0	0	0	0	0
Tripura	0	0	0	0	0	0	0
Uttar Pradesh	0	0	0	0	0	0	0
West Bengal	3	3	3	1	1	0	0

Table 8.1 contd....

Union Territories							
UT	*Death reported*	*Autopsy conducted*	*Magesterial ordered*	*Judicial enquiry ordered*	*Cases in connection with deaths*	*Police men chargesheeted*	*Police men convicted*
A & N Islands	0	0	0	0	0	0	0
Chandigarh	0	0	0	0	0	0	0
D&N Haveli	0	0	0	0	0	0	0
Daman &Diu	0	0	0	0	0	0	0
Delhi	0	0	0	0	0	0	0
Lakshadweep	0	0	0	0	0	0	0
Pondicherry	0	0	0	0	0	0	0
Total (All-India)	**22**	**9**	**14**	**4**	**10**	**20**	**0**

Table 8. 2.

Deaths in police custody / lockup in India during 1999 (of persons not remanded to police custody by court).

States / UTs	*Death reported*	*Autopsy conducted*	*Magesterial ordered*	*Judicial enquiry ordered*	*Cases in connection with deaths*	*Police men chargesheeted*	*Police men convicted*
States							
Andhra Pradesh	0	0	0	0	0	0	0
Arunchal Pradesh	1	1	1	0	1	0	0
Assam	0	0	0	0	2	0	0
Bihar	1	0	0	0	0	0	0
Goa	1	1	1	0	0	0	0
Gujarat	0	0	0	0	0	0	0
Haryana	1	0	0	0	1	0	0
Himachal Pradesh	0	0	0	0	0	0	0
J& K	0	0	0	0	0	0	0

Table 8.2. contd....

States / UTs	*Death reported*	*Autopsy conducted*	*Magest-erial ordered*	*Judicial enquiry ordered*	*Cases in conne-ction with deaths*	*Police men char-gesh-eeted*	*Police men conv-icted*
States							
Karnataka	0	0	0	0	0	0	0
Kerala	4	4	0	0	4	0	0
Madhya Pradesh	5	3	5	0	3	2	2
Maharashtra	4	4	1	0	1	0	0
Manipur	0	0	0	0	0	0	0
Meghalaya	0	0	0	0	0	0	0
Mizoram	0	0	0	0	0	0	0
Nagaland	0	0	0	0	0	0	0
Orissa	0	0	0	0	0	0	0
Punjab	3	3	3	0	2	6	0
Rajasthan	0	0	0	0	0	0	0
Sikkim	NR	NR	NR	NR	NR	NR	NR
Tamil Nadu	6	6	6	0	6	0	0
Tripura	0	0	0	0	0	0	0
Uttar Pradesh	13	13	9	1	13	0	0
West Bengal	3	3	3	0	0	0	0
Union Territories							
A & N Islands	0	0	0	0	0	0	0
Chandigarh	0	0	0	0	0	0	0
D&N Haveli	0	0	0	0	0	0	0
Daman &Diu	0	0	0	0	0	0	0
Delhi	1	1	1	1	1	0	0
Lakshadweep	0	0	0	0	0	0	0
Pondicherry	0	0	0	0	0	0	0
Total (All-India)	**43**	**39**	**30**	**2**	**34**	**8**	**2**

Table 8. 3.

Deaths in police custody at the time of prodcuction / proceedings in court / journey connected with investigation in India during 1999.

States / UTs	Death reported	Autopsy conducted	Magesterial ordered	Judicial enquiry ordered	Cases in connection with deaths	Police men chargesheeted	Police men convicted
States							
Andhra Pradesh	0	0	0	0	0	0	0
Arunchal Pradesh	0	0	0	0	0	0	0
Assam	1	0	1	0	0	0	0
Bihar	0	0	0	0	0	0	0
Goa	1	1	1	0	0	0	0
Gujarat	0	0	0	0	0	0	0
Haryana	1	0	0	0	1	0	0
Himachal Pradesh	0	0	0	0	0	0	0
J & K	1	1	0	0	1	2	0
Karnataka	1	0	1	0	0	0	0
Kerala	0	0	0	0	0	0	0
Madhya Pradesh	4	0	2	1	1	16	0
Maharashtra	3	2	2	0	1	6	0
Manipur	0	0	0	0	0	0	0
Meghalaya	0	0	0	0	0	0	0
Mizoram	0	0	0	0	0	0	0
Nagaland	0	0	0	0	0	0	0
Orissa	0	0	0	0	0	0	0
Punjab	1	1	1	0	0	0	0
Rajasthan	0	0	0	0	0	0	0
Sikkim	NR	NR	NR	NR	NR	NR	NR
Tamil Nadu	2	2	2	0	2	0	0
Tripura	0	0	0	0	0	0	0
Uttar Pradesh	1	1	1	0	0	1	0
West Bengal	0	0	0	0	0	0	0

Table 8.3. contd....

States / UTs	*Death reported*	*Autopsy conducted*	*Magesterial ordered*	*Judicial enquiry ordered*	*Cases in connection with deaths*	*Police men chargesheeted*	*Police men convicted*
Union territories							
A & N Islands	0	0	0	0	0	0	0
Chandigarh	0	0	0	0	0	0	0
D&N Haveli	0	0	0	0	0	0	0
Daman &Diu	0	0	0	0	0	0	0
Delhi	0	0	0	0	0	0	0
Lakshadweep	0	0	0	0	0	0	0
Pondicherry	0	0	0	0	0	0	0
Total (All-India)	**15**	**8**	**11**	**1**	**5**	**25**	**0**

Table 8.4.

Reasons of custodial dealths in India during 1999.

States / UTs	*During Hospitalisation*	*Due to accidents*	*By mob attact / riot*	*By other criminals*	*By suicide*	*While escaping from custody*
Andhra Pradesh	3	0	0	0	2	0
Arunchal Pradesh	0	0	0	0	1	0
Assam	1	0	1	0	0	0
Bihar	3	1	0	0	0	0
Goa	0	0	0	0	1	0
Gujarat	2	1	0	0	1	0
Haryana	2	0	0	0	0	0
Himachal Pradesh	0	0	0	0	0	0
J& K	0	0	0	0	0	0
Karnataka	0	0	0	0	0	0
Kerala	0	0	0	0	0	0
Madhya Pradesh	4	0	0	0	4	0

Table 8.4. contd....

States / UTs	*During Hospitalisation*	*Due to accidents*	*By mob attact / riot*	*By other criminals*	*By suicide*	*While escaping from custody*
States						
Maharashtra	5	2	3	2	6	0
Manipur	0	0	0	0	0	0
Meghalaya	0	0	0	0	1	0
Mizoram	0	0	0	0	0	0
Nagaland	1	0	0	0	0	0
Orissa	0	0	0	0	0	0
Punjab	2	0	0	1	0	0
Rajasthan	0	0	0	0	0	0
Sikkim	NR	NR	NR	NR	NR	NR
Tamil Nadu	1	1	0	0	1	1
Tripura	0	0	0	0	0	0
Uttar Pradesh	1	0	0	0	3	11
West Bengal	20	0	0	0	3	0
Union Territores						
A & N Islands	0	0	0	0	1	0
Chandigarh	0	0	0	0	0	0
D&N Haveli	0	0	0	0	0	0
Daman &Diu	0	0	0	0	0	0
Delhi	0	0	0	0	0	0
Lakshadweep	0	0	0	0	0	0
Pondicherry	0	0	0	0	0	0
Total (All-India)	**44**	**5**	**3**	**3**	**24**	**12**

According to the information supplied by national records of crime bureau, about 22 custodial deaths were cccurred during the year 1999. The detailed account of Six of such cases were reported from Maharastra, four from Assam and Madhya Pradesh, three from West Bengal and 2 from Rajastan. Four cases of custodial deaths are under judicial enquiry. 20 police men were charge-sheeted.

Hospitalisation, accidents, mob attacks, riots, suicides etc., are found to be major reasons for custodial crimes. There are also cases of muder by other criminals.

REFERENCES

Alvazzi del Frate A., *Manual International Crime (Victim) Survey*, Rome: UNICRI, 1996.

The Govt. of India, 'Crime in India' New Delhi, *National Crime Records Bureau*, 1999.

9

Drug-related Crimes

Drug-related crimes have increased disproportionately in the last two decades when compared to other crime-related phenomena. This chapter has two main aims. The first is to delineate the relationship between drugs, drug control, crime and criminal justice. The second aim is to build an empirical picture of the influence of drugs and-drug control upon crime and criminal justice, at the global level and using a specific country or regional case studies of interest.

Victims and victimisation, guns and gun control are often drug-related. Persons charged with drug-related offences, or who have committed offences in some way related to the drug trade, are brought to justice and the resources of criminal justice systems are expended upon them. In addition, the resources of health and social services and other areas of public and private policy are also increasingly focused upon drug-related crime and drug-related issues. The end result is that a clear typology of drug-related crime does not and, perhaps, should not exist.

Illicit drug use has spread far and wide across the globe, there are relatively few solid indicators of which drugs arrived where and when. Individual accounts or anecdotal evidence are often all that is available. A simple but useful indicator of the speed and extent of the expansion of different illicit drugs across the world is a count of the number of countries seizing different types of drugs. Although this measure is imperfect, as with almost all indicators related to illicit drugs and crime, it is reasonably good because national law enforcement agencies typically record drug seizures for their own operational purposes. In contrast, there are relatively few countries that keep centralised and internationally comparable records of illicit drug consumption.

At the very least, the count of countries where law enforcement has made drug seizures shows the minimum number of countries affected by specific illicit drugs. While there are variations in the number of countries in the world as well as in law enforcement recording and reporting practices, the consistency of the trends and the fact that they concord with other more fragmentary indicators and evidence, suggests that the trends in the global spread of illicit drugs may be fairly representative of actual events.

Cannabis has long been and remains the most prevalent global illicit drug according to this indicator. Estimates of global consumption suggest that sedatives are the most prevalent illicit drug in terms of the global population, but otherwise conform roughly to the indicator used here. By 1994, around two-thirds of countries in the world had been affected by cannabis. However, the gap between cannabis and the next two most prevalent illicit drugs—heroin and cocaine—has narrowed rapidly. This measure of the global spread of illicit drugs supports indirect evidence of increases in the volume of heroin and cocaine production and consumption and suggests about half of all countries are affected by these illicit drugs in the 1990s. Though having similar levels of coverage in 1980, opium trafficking has spread at a much slower pace than heroin, as might be expected since it is a more unwieldy substance.

Both lysergic acid diethylamide (LSD) and sedatives appear to have been stable or falling in their global coverage. The global coverage of amphetamine-type stimulants (ATS) increased by about half in the decade between the mid-1980s and 1990s, though they have still infiltrated far fewer countries than cannabis, heroin and cocaine. About a quarter of countries worldwide are affected by amphetamine-type stimulants. There is ample reason to believe that the spread of ATS will continue. As stimulants, they are cheaper per "hit" and have a far longer duration than cocaine. They have a relatively benign public image, and since the drugs are often produced in developed countries, the distributors experience lower barriers to market entry than drugs from other regions.

In industrialised countries there is increasing use of indoor cannabis plots to avoid detection, and of hydroponic techniques to speed growth times. Heroin is produced in and around the main areas in which the opium poppy is growth, in South-east and South-west Asia, and increasingly in the Andean region of South America. From there it is transported to the major markets in Europe and North America by an increasingly diverse number of routes and methods. Cocoa leaf and paste are produced from cocoa bush cultivation primarily in the Andean countries of Peru, Bolivia and Colombia, though the manufacture of cocaine is disproportionately concentrated in Colombia. From here it is trafficked to North America overland and by air and ship though a range of routes including the Caribbean basin.

The number of types of illicit drugs has increased and their nature diversified in recent years. The increased manufacture and production of the amphetamine-type stimulants and synthetic and designer drugs during the last decade has been located primarily in industrialised countries. This is a marked geographical change from that of the "traditional" illicit drugs of choice. It also means that trafficking often originates within the confines of the geographical and economic boundaries of the consumer market.

Drug control law enforcement must be more diverse than sealing the borders. Increased global coverage by the illicit drug traffic has been supported by increased volume of traffic in those areas where it already existed. Seizures of different drug types around the world suggest strong increases in the volume of illicit drug trafficking.

Global illicit production of different drugs has increased greatly over the last decade according to available estimates. Estimated potential illicit opiate production more than trebled in the decade prior to 1996, mainly in the late 1980s. About a third of this is estimated to be consumed as opium, so that potential annual heroin manufacture has been around 300 tons for much of the 1990s.

About 1,000 tons of cocaine could have been produced from estimated cocoa production in 1996, the figure having remained relatively stable during the 1990s after doubling in the second half of the 1980s. These estimates are based on ground and satellite surveys of crops from which the drugs are produced.

While being imperfect estimates, they remain firmer than estimates of potential production of most other illicit drugs for which there are relatively few indicators. Seizures provide some imperfect evidence of trends in production, although the trend in production is probably less steep since seizures also reflect increased law enforcement emphasis.

Innocuous factors related to technological socioeconomic and political change and advancement have inadvertently provided opportunities for expansion of the illicit drug industry. In turn, expansion of the illicit drug industry drives the range of drug-related crime.

The process of globalisation in the late twentieth century mean that the world in which drug trafficking now takes place is quite different from that in which many of the global drug control systems were developed. The relative contributions of different factors cannot be quantified with methodological accuracy. At the same time as increasing opportunities become available to the illicit drug industry, technological developments have also improved law enforcement efforts in many ways. Those related to the illicit drug industry include remote sensing satellite technology, infrared and x-ray detection equipment, computing, weaponary and transportation.

An increasing number of countries around the world are bound by the international drug control conventions of 1961,

1971 and 1988. By 1997, over two-thirds of countries in the world were bound by the 1988 UN drug control convention. The number and proportion of countries signing and ratifying the treaties is increasing, which in time will reduce the number of havens left open to different aspects of the illegal drug trade. In essence, the conventions set broad parameters within which countries define their national drug control laws. The United Nations International Drug Control Programme (UNDCP) provides technical and legal assistance to implement the treaties, monitor and evaluate their effectiveness, and assist national drug control law enforcement agencies.

The International Narcotics Control Board (INCB) works primarily to implement, monitor and evaluate those parts of the treaties pertaining to the international trade in drugs and precursors. The most comprehensive and accessible account of the international drug control treaties, illicit drug use and types of drug control is given in the World Drug Report.

Global illicit consumption is a landmark in drug-related research. The estimates developed by UNDCP were based upon a basket of indicators including local and national user surveys, rapid assessments based on other indicators including health and social service indicators, health-related data, law enforcement seizure and arrest data, and other available sources. UNDCP estimates that, in any one year, slightly over one in 1,000 persons illicitly use heroin or other opiates, and two in 1,000 illicitly use cocaine.

Illicit use of cannabis is estimated to be seventeen times more prevalent than that of opiates, and over ten times as prevalent as that of cocaine. Sedatives are estimated to be the most prevalent illicitly used drugs, although the estimate is believed to be high. The illicit use of sedatives is concentrated in South American countries as well as countries in Southern Africa.

A small fraction of the world's population uses drugs illicitly. Prevalence rates of illicit drug use are, overall, characterised by the similarity of the rarity of use. However, when illicit drug users only are examined, variation in the prevalence of illicit drug use is apparent between drug types. Of those persons who use illicit drugs in any given year, a proportion experience drug use that is problematic in terms of health and a proportion become addicted, with the proportions varying by drug type and circumstances. Of those who become addicted, some will cease drug use at varying rates, and a proportion will turn to crime to fund their continued drug use. These addicts will also cease drug use over time, at a relatively low annual rate, and a "maturing out" of illicit drug use is apparent.

The strategies and tactics used to tackle drug-related crimes are as varied as the types of drug-related crime themselves. Measures to tackle drug supply at different levels, to tackle demand, and measures to prevent crime by drug users are the main categories. Strategies can overlap to differing degrees, so that measures to reduce demand and to treat drug users are assumed, if successful, to reduce drug-related crime indirectly. Supply reduction efforts to reduce illicit cultivation in some producer countries range from eradication to crop substitution and alternative development programmes. A recent global review of these efforts concluded that some success can be achieved in reduction of narcotic crop production.

The balloon effect, in which reduction in one area has resulted in increases in other areas, has thus far prevented production at the global level from declining in absolute terms. The effectiveness of drug demand reduction efforts has been recently reviewed at the global level. The review of demand reduction programmes suggested that primary prevention (preventing initiation) and secondary prevention (treatment and rehabilitation of drug users) were being widely supplemented by tertiary prevention (controlling health risks to users). Other treatment efforts such as medical prescription of hard drugs to users, with a view to removing the economic incentive to commit crimes to fund drug use, operate in different countries and contexts with varying degrees of success. The extensive demand reduction programme known as Drug Abuse Resistance Education (DARE) undertaken initially in schools in the United States and now elsewhere, was comprehensively evaluated in the 1990s.

Law enforcement efforts to reduce drug supply indirectly influence drug consumption. This is because, as with any economic product, a reduction in supply causes a rise in the price. When the price of a product increases, then the number of persons willing to purchase it decreases. Therefore, when law enforcement efforts reduce supply, the principal mechanism by which consumption is reduced is the price mechanism of the illicit retail market.

A universal rule of thumb long used by almost all involved in drug control was that ten per cent of illicit drugs were assumed to be intercepted and seized by law- enforcement agencies. It was based on hearsay and anecdotes, but many have served as a heuristic aid to thinking about trafficking and enforcement. Debunking the myth utilised a conceptually simple methodology: comparing annual estimates of total drug production for opium and cocaine to the total amount of those drugs seized around the world. From this, a crude measure of the proportion intercepted—termed the global interception rate (GIR)—can be estimated.

The GIR is subject to the limitations of the global estimates of production and seizures, and the rate presented here uses midpoint estimates that lie within a possible range for each year. However, if errors in production and seizures are reasonably consistent over time, then trends in the GIR can be assumed to be fairly accurate representations of what has occurred. The global rate of interception of cocaine appeared to change markedly during the 1980s, but less so for opiates.

While the rate of interception of cocaine was far below that of opiates in the early 1980s, it rose rapidly during the mid 1980s to reach levels almost double those of the opiates during the 1990s. These changes may well reflect the increased emphasis upon the interception of cocaine by law enforcement efforts across the Americas. Like most indicators related to crime and criminal justice, the GIR is partial. It gives a "success rate" in terms of interception, and suggests that positive gains have been made.

Yet as a partial indicator it does not reflect the fact that while interception rates have been stable or increasing, the amount of opiates and cocaine passing through the enforcement net has increased. This is because illicit production and manufacture has increased severalfold. The net result is that despite the improved performance of law enforcement, far larger amounts of illicit opiates and cocaine are being consumed than was the case in previous years.

A range of organised crime groups is involved in the illicit manufacture, diversion, trafficking and distribution of drugs. Organised crime is most simply defined as any ongoing criminal enterprise. Organisations vary widely in geographical scope and level of organisation, from small loose-knit networks "disorganised crime", which may include organisations and gangs in a particular town or city through national organisations perhaps with international connections, to regional, international and transnational criminal organisations. Defining characteristics suggested for the large scale organisations include their large size, wealth, political power and enforcement resistance.

The main driving force for organised crime is economic profit, but each organisation differs. In structure and scope and whether or not it is involved in a range of legal or criminal activity in addition to the illicit trade: not all organised crime is drug-related, and not all of the illicit drug trade is organised. The activities of organised crime are influenced by law enforcement activities aimed directly at the organisations but also by enforcement aimed at other aspects of the illicit drug trade.

Increased general drug enforcement, as opposed to that targeted at organised crime can give organised crime groups and networks a relative competitive advantage, because their capacity for violence and corruption helps protect them against ordinary enforcement actions. Similarly, assuming that increased enforcement succeeds in raising the costs of dealing and, consequently, the retail price of the drugs, consumption will tend to decrease. However, if prices rise and consumption increases less, in percentage terms, than prices rise, then the overall money to be made in the illicit drug market will, ironically, increase.

The key determinant is the change in consumption brought on by a change in retail price, known as the price elasticity of demand. Since some drugs, particularly the more addictive ones, exhibit low elasticity (demand falls less than proportionately compared to a price rise), then increased drug law enforcement can reduce drug assumption while at the same time increasing the profit of organised criminal groups.

Different types of drug law enforcement have different effects. Retail-level enforcement will have most effect upon the number and aggressiveness of retail drug dealers rather than on drug prices. This causes a drop in consumption, due to increased time and risk in making a purchase, producing an unambiguous reduction in the profit of organised crime. There has been a range of drug control enforcement crackdowns against organised crime involved in the drug trade. The arrest and incarceration of many key figures in the Colombian cartels was heralded as a significant success. However, the economic incentives of the illicit drug trade serve to make organised trafficking extremely durable.

The rapid replacement and substitution or of one organisation with a new one or an altered one, make preventing drug-related organised crime a different prospect than much crime prevention work. While many types of crime, even organised crime, can be prevented without much displacement, the prospect is more daunting when it comes to organised crime involved in the illicit drug trade.

From the available information, it appears that drug trafficking and possession play an increasingly important role in the later stages of the criminal justice system, particularly imprisonment. Whereas drug crimes account for less than four per cent of recorded crimes, eight per cent of suspects and prosecutions, and around nine per cent of convictions, they account for over thirteen per cent of all prison admissions. This suggests that on average in 1994, for those countries that made the information available, drug trafficking and possession cases were more likely than the average crime to proceed to each subsequent stage of the global criminal justice system and to result in a sentence of imprisonment.

Perhaps, however, it seems that drug possession offences play an increasingly greater role than drug trafficking offences at the later stages of the criminal justice system. Two main explanations may account for this. The first and most likely is that it is an artifact of the fragmentary nature of the available data. The second is that it is a real difference and the explanation lies in the workings of the various criminal justice systems. A possible partial explanation for the finding that possession is more likely to result in imprisonment than is trafficking might be found in the fact that some countries use capital punishment for drug trafficking, although this might not be expected to make a significant difference at the global level.

While the proportion of drug trafficking and possession cases appears to increase in magnitude relative to other crimes at each stage of the global criminal justice system, the number of such cases decreases in absolute magnitude. This is because some cases are dropped for various reasons between each stage. In fact, it seems that ten per cent of those originally apprehended as trafficking and possession suspects go to prison. The greatest absolute number of cases not proceeding to the next stage is between being formally processed as a suspect and being prosecuted. However, in terms of rates the picture is slightly different. Slightly less than half of all cases proceed to prosecution, and two-thirds of those prosecuted are convicted, but only one-third of those convicted are sentenced to imprisonment.

In terms of rates, the greatest attrition is at the stage of sentencing, when the available data suggests that two-thirds of cases are given a non-incarceration sentence. Combining the two elements of analysis of the criminal justice system so far, some comment can also be made on the respective roles of drug possession and trafficking cases compared to other types of crime. The two indicators have gone in different directions: only ten per cent of drug trafficking and possession suspects go to prison, but the proportion of trafficking and possession cases at each stage of the criminal justice system increases in relation to other, crimes. This implies that a drug trafficking or possession case is more likely than the average case to be retained by the criminal justice system. The analysis so far shows that trafficking and possession cases are important in the aggregate picture of criminal justice. These aggregates will mask the fact that such cases are disproportionately concentrated in some countries as opposed to others.

Drug-related arrest rates have increased rapidly in recent years in some countries to the extent that they have placed great strain upon their respective criminal justice systems. The analysis presented so far must be viewed with caution. While it is based on data for all countries which provided the relevant information, this is only a sample of the global total.

The patterns and trends might need to be revised as additional information becomes available. Having gained this snapshot of criminal justice processing of trafficking and possession cases at the global level, the following sections examine each stage of the process in more detail, and present available information relating to particular countries. Sections are presented in the sequential order of the justice system, from arrest through to prison admissions.

Comparing the number of formal suspects to the number of crimes committed would not indicate the success of law enforcement since offending, like victimisation, is highly skewed. A small proportion of offenders commits a large proportion of offences for any given crime type. However, making the large assumptions that the distribution of offending among offenders is relatively constant across countries, and that other factors are also constant, then cross-national comparison of the number of suspects arrested per crime committed could be a partial and relative performance indicator.

The two key processes on which it might shed light are the performance of law enforcement (in making arrests), or the rate of cautioning or other process which does not lead to a formal arrest being recorded. In fact, this measure is almost certainly not as indicative of actual criminal justice processes pertaining to drug trafficking and possession crimes as it is for other offences. This is because drug trafficking and possession offences are less likely to be recorded than other offences. Unlike burglaries, car crimes and other property offences that are often reported to the police for insurance purposes or personal crimes where there is a clearly definable victim, drug trafficking and possession offences are unlikely to be reported to the police.

The main source of official and quantifiable information relating to offences is from arrests made, and so the difference between the two would not be expected to be great in many instances. In what follows, countries that reported more suspects than crimes were excluded.

In general, the proportion of arrests per crime recorded was high, as might be expected. The lack of reporting of trafficking and possession cases to the police by victims may well also explain why a large number of countries appeared to report more arrests than crimes for trafficking and possession. Median and mean global arrest rates were close together, suggesting a little skew in the distribution of results across countries. All three data points relating to crimes and arrests for trafficking and possession were available for twelve countries. Sweden appeared to have unusually low numbers of suspects per crime recorded. It might have been expected that offences recorded for drug trafficking were more likely to result in a formal suspect being charged than cases recorded for possession. This did not seem to be the case. There was virtually no difference in the mean number of suspects per crime between the two types of drug-related offences.

The average rate of success of convictions across the 25 countries reporting was 62 per cent. Drug possession cases that were prosecuted appeared to have a higher likelihood of conviction at 71 per cent, although the different samples could well influence this finding. This may be connected to the possibility that a smaller proportion of possession cases reach prosecution, so that those that do are prosecuted more successfully.

There are a number of different ways of measuring and comparing cross-national imprisonment rates. One simple way of looking at the level of usage of imprisonment between countries is to see what proportion of convictions result in imprisonment. This is problematic if cases reaching sentencing are qualitatively different between countries. While this will undoubtedly be the case to some extent, it is not unreasonable to assume at least some degree of seriousness for a trafficking possession case to have passed through all the prior stages of the criminal justice system. Making this assumption, differences in the proportion of convictions resulting in imprisonment may reflect two main factors. First, since the only available data relates to an aggregate of both trafficking and possession, the proportions of each in the total may vary. If the likelihood of imprisonment varies between trafficking and possession, then this will influence the aggregate results. A second explanation is that judicial practices vary between countries in the use of a sentence of imprisonment for crimes of a similar nature.

While there is an ever expanding and improving knowledge base related to the illicit drug industry, knowledge related to other drug-related crimes, including street crimes and drug markets, remains extremely fragmented at the international level. Information relating to the progress of drug users through and in the criminal justice system is almost nonexistent, primarily because these categories of information are typically not recorded. Information relating to the drug trafficking and possession cases in the criminal justice system is extremely fragmented, almost certainly in part because of wide variation in legal definitions and recording practices between countries.

There is a need for a more systematic collation of governmental and non-governmental reports produced at the national and local levels to be used to supplement methodologically standardised data collection instruments. The global picture of the influence of drugs and drug control upon crime and criminal justice is fragmented. What is clear is that drugs and drug control have come to play all increasingly significant role in the overall picture of crime and criminal justice in recent years. The global coverage of drug-related crime has increased. The overall volume of drug-related crime has increased in those countries where it was already established.

While law enforcement activities have increased and appear to have improved in many ways, they have been faced with overwhelming odds. Relative improvements in enforcement efficiency have taken place alongside absolute reductions in effectiveness. The overall influence upon criminal justice systems of drug-related offending is not readily apparent at the global level, since only data pertaining to drug trafficking and possession cases are available. It is likely that the role of drug-using offenders has concurrently increased at each stage of the criminal justice system. The increase in drug-related crime and the increased strain placed upon criminal justice systems have seen the emergence of innovative approaches to managing the problems, including medical prescriptions for addicts, and dedicated courts for drug-related cases.

10

Urban Crimes

The urban area is generally recognised as a breeding ground for the criminals, and prone to higher incidence level of crimes compared to rural areas. Criminals brought up in such an environment are known to indulge in crimes as a way of life. The unchecked and unplanned growth of cities as well as large floating population are major contributing factors for urban crimes. Criminal propensity is also known to be higher in urban industrial areas.

Migration of poor, illiterate people having roots in a simple environment consequent to migration suffer emotional instability in the urban setting. The problem of unemployment is yet another compounding factor. They are easily lured into theft, robbery, smuggling or even terrorists activities. Crime and development, therefore are intrinsically linked.

Urban crimes are important features in mega cities but the pattern varies from city to city. India is predominantly a rural country as only 25.7 per cent of its population lives in urban areas while majority of the population lives in rural areas. Of the estimated total urban population, nearly one-third constituting 35.06 per cent live in 23 metropolitan cities. The proportion of metropolitan cities population to the national population is 9.01 per cent.

There is no demarcation between rural and urban areas as far as the crime statistics are concerned since these were not collected on this basis, but as the crimes in urban areas are peculiar and have shown a consistent rise parallel to the population increase, during the previous few decades, it has generated interest to make a study of such crime phenomenon. Worldwide, urban violence is estimated to have grown by between three and five per cent a year over the last decades, although there are large variations between nations and between different cities within nations in the scale of urban violence and in the extent of its growth. Violent crime has increased in most cities in recent years, and generally as a proportion of all crimes. It includes murder, infanticide, kidnapping/abduction, kidnapping for rasnsom, assault, rape and sexual abuse and domestic violence and it now makes up between 25 and 30 per cent of urban crimes in many countries.

One aspect of the increase in violent crime is the increase in murders. The murder rates for particular cities can be much higher than those for the national averages. In the early 1990s, Cali, Colombia's third largest city, had a murder rate of 87 per 100,000 people. Several cities in the north also had high murder rates—for instance, the murder rate in Washington DC was reported to be over 70 per 100,000 inhabitants in the early 1990s.

The combination of very large populations and high murder rates means that in several of the world's largest cities, more than 2,000 people are murdered each year. The murder rate for a whole country or for a city obscures the fact that it is particular groups who are most at risk from murder. For instance, murder rates are generally much higher for men than for women—with the rate being particularly high among men. But care is needed when making comparisons between different countries or cities, as the causes of murders and the perpetrators of the murders vary considerably. One of the main causes of murder in Maharashtra is young brides being burnt to death for not bringing enough dowry. In Bangladesh, the murder of wives by husbands accounts for a high proportion of all murders. For every murder, there are many times more non-fatal assaults. There is also a lot of crime that goes unreported, including vandalism or hooliganism. Although often considered 'petty' in the legal sense of the word, such incidents can make life very unpleasant for city dwellers.

High levels of urban crime and perhaps especially of violent crime are bringing major changes in the spatial form of many cities and of their built-up areas and public spaces. Violent crimes are more visible in cities, and they help create a sense of insecurity that generates distrust, intolerance, the withdrawal of individuals from community life, and in some instances, violent reactions. For instance, the increase in violence, insecurity and fear in Sao Paulo are changing the city's landscape and the patterns of daily life, people's movements and the use of public transport—as crime and violence discourages people from using the streets and public spaces altogether. Streets where children used to play, where neighbours used to congregate and where it was common for people to stroll are now much less used.

Increasingly, higher-income groups are living, working, shopping and taking their leisure in what are essentially fortified enclaves and are no longer making use of streets or public spaces which are abandoned to the homeless and the street children. Similar developments are evident in many cities around the world as middle- and upper-income groups journey by private automobile between apartment complexes, shopping centres or malls and office complexes each with sophisticated security systems and their own secure car parks so there is little or no necessity to walk on the streets or to use open spaces.

High levels of crime and fear of violence have helped to push shopping malls, office complexes and leisure activities to suburban areas and in some cities, this has reached the point where it is increasingly rare for middle- and upper-income groups to visit the city centre. High levels of crime can have a very serious impact on the economy of a neighbourhood or city centre.

The most common form of violence against women is domestic violence and in recent years, it has become acknowledged that in most countries, there are very serious problems with domestic violence. Surveys in a variety of countries in the south found that between a third and half (or more) of women surveyed report being beaten by their partner. It is also acknowledged that statistics collected from police records or from other official sources usually greatly underestimate the scale and the seriousness of the problem, as those who suffer domestic violence are reluctant to report the abuse. But it is not only in the domestic arena that violence against women is a serious and often growing problem. For instance, an estimate made by a US Senate Judiciary Committee suggested that at least one women in five in the United States will be sexually assaulted in her lifetime. Rape and sexual abuse are now known to be far more common than was thought a few years ago, with generally a high proportion of those who perpetrate sexual abuse being known to their victims and often with a considerable proportion of victims being 15 years of age or under.

There is a growing understanding that violence should be considered a public health problem for which there are prevention strategies. Many cities have very low levels of violence while others with high levels of violence have managed to reduce them by addressing some of the underlying causes. Urban violence is the result of many factors which affect each city depending on the specific local context—and there is considerable debate about the relative importance of different factors.

Certain specialists stress the significance of inadequate incomes which are usually combined with very poor and overcrowded housing and living conditions, and often insecure tenure, as fertile ground for the development of violence. It is also more difficult for parents living in very poor quality housing and also usually working long hours to provide children with the social support they need both at school and at home. An unsupportive home life can lead to non-adaptation at school and to a lack of personal discipline and self-esteem which increase the risk of anti-social or criminal activity. Other explanations, while not contradicting those noted above, emphasise more the contemporary urban environment in which attractive goods are continuously on display and create targets for potential criminals.

In cities, particularly in the south, the ostentatious display of luxury and prosperity (shops, cars) in certain areas, provokes those who have not accepted their unfavourable social situation, and engenders an attitude that legitimises the 'distribution of wealth' through criminal activity. In addition, police forces are usually unable to protect all individuals and businesses against theft, and the police and the judicial system do not provide sufficient deterrent with low clear-up rates for most theft and violence.

Meanwhile, insurance against theft, for those who can afford it, does not resolve the problem of prevention since it does not bait the theft itself (the breaking of the law) or its consequences. Finally, oppression in all its forms, including the destruction of original cultural identities, together with racism and discrimination, is one of the root causes of many forms of violence. It is difficult for any individual or household to identify with a culture if subjected to racism or discrimination in finding employment and in finding housing or obtaining access to social services—or for children, at school. This, in turn, inhibits their integration within schools, workplaces and neighbourhoods.

There are also many risk-factors associated with crime. There are the factors connected with the built environment itself and with the lack of a stable population within many residential areas. For instance, in many city areas such as those with a high proportion of short-term tenants or boarding houses, the constant movement of people in and out of the area inhibits the development of community actions and informal community surveillance that can deter crime or help identify the criminal. The nature and quality of street-life has a considerable influence on the incidence of crime and vandalism.

So too does the physical design of housing areas, including the extent to which public areas are subject to informal supervision and the extent to which there is a clear visual definition as to who has the right to use it and is responsible for its maintenance. The inadequate provision for or deterioration of public space and public facilities also discourages their use as well as the community-networks that they help reinforce.

Lack of opportunities, uneven distribution of incomes, diverse socio-religio cultural disparities make urban areas a breeding ground for criminal activities. Organised groups, gangsters, professional criminals, new entrants, youths, juveniles, etc., find crime a thriving vocation in their quest for an easy and good living in urban environment. Urban population of India as per the 1991 census was 21,71,77,625 accounting for 25.72 per cent of the country's total population. The definition of urban areas though remained fairly constant for several decades, it was specified for uniform application only since 1961.

There was a steady increase in the number of towns till 1951 but due to defined standards applied in 1961 to determine whether a place qualified to be treated as an urban centre or not, many urban centres were declassified and hence, the number declined from 2,843 in 1951 to 2,365 in 1961. According to the latest census (1991), the number of such towns have risen up to 3,768 (an increase of 59.3per cent over 1961). As per Section 8(1) of the Cr. PC, the state governments have the power to declare, by notification, any area in the state comprising a city or a town whose population exceeds one million (10 lakhs), as a metropolitan area. Vide Section 20(5) of the Cr.PC, the state governments can confer, under any law, for the time being in force, on a Commissioner of Police, all or any of the powers of an Executive Magistrate in relation to a metropolitan area.

After the 1991 census, the number of urban agglomeration/cities (cities having population of one million or more) increased from 12 to 23. So, for the purpose of present analysis on 'Urban

Crimes', the crime statistics of these 23 cities have been taken into consideration. Based on the prescribed standards (population size, male working population engaged in non-agricultural pursuits and density of population) these cities have been categorised as 'A-class' and 'B-class' cities, as per the following table.

Table 10. 1.
Classification of metropolitan cities.

Sl. No.	*City*	*Estimated mid-year (1995) population (in lakhs)*	*Sl. No.*	*City*	*Estimated mid-year (1995) population (in lakhs)*
(1)	(2)	(3)	(4)	(5)	(6)
1.	Ahmedabad	37.1	1.	Bhopal	13.3
2.	Bangalore	48.0	2.	Coimbatore	11.9
3.	Chennai	60.0	3.	Indore	12.6
4.	Calcutta	119.2	4.	Jaipur	18.8
5.	Delhi	99.5	5.	Kochi	14.2
6.	Hyderabad	54.8	6.	Ludhiana	13.2
7.	Kanpur	22.3	7.	Madurai	11.7
8.	Lucknow	20.8	8.	Patna	11.9
9.	Mumbai	151.4	9.	Pune	29.6
10.	Nagpur	18.5	10.	Surat	18.9
			11.	Vadodara	13.5
			12.	Varanasi	11.5
			13.	Visakhapatnam	13.5
	Total	631.6		Total	193.9

Grand Total: Metropolitan Cities: 23 Population: 825.5 lakhs

VARIOUS FORMS OF CRIMES

The prominent urban crimes that are being presently reported and recorded can be grouped under the two major categories.

(i) crimes identified under the Indian Penal Code (IPC) and (ii) crimes identified under the Special & Local Laws (SLL).

Crimes Identified Under the Indian Penal Code (IPC)

Crimes Identified under the Indian Penal Code (IPC) include:

i) Violent crimes, such as
   a) crime against life; namely, murder; its attempt and culpable homicide not amounting to murder, its attempt.
   b) kidnapping/abduction, rape,
   c) molestation, sexual harassment,
   d) dowry deaths/torture of women grouped as crime against women,
   e) riots,
   f) arson,
   g) grievous hurt.

ii) Property crimes, such as
   a) crime against property accompanied by violence, namely, dacoity, its attempt,
   b) robbery, its attempt,
   c) other crimes against property, namely, burglary and thefts of various types.

iii) Economic crimes such as criminal breach of trust, cheating, counterfeiting etc.

Crimes Identified under the Special & Local Laws

i) Crimes related to arms and explosives
ii) Terrorists and disruptive activities
iii) Drug offences/trafficking
iv) Gambling offences
v) Prohibition/excise offences

vi) Offences related to essential commodities

vii) Offences related to Railways Act

viii) Foreigners' registration and passport offences

ix) Immoral trafficking

x) Crime in art and treasures/cultural objects

xi) Dowry prohibition

xii) Civil rights protection/atrocities on SCs/STs

xiii) Child marriage

xiv) Copyright

xv) Indecent representation of women

xvi) Environmental crimes.

VIOLENT CRIMES

Incidents of violent crimes affect the law and order fabric, peace, tranquillity and the life pattern of the mainstream population. Crimes associated with violence dampen the common man's feelings regarding safety and security of the society. Repeated occurrence of heinous crimes have wider impact in people's mind. Sequel to the reported incidents of violent crimes in the day-to-day life sense of insecurity, fear and annoyance over take the community.

For the analysis of offences which are of furious, violent in nature, committed with force, fierce criminal acts, impetuous criminal attacks, criminal acts of vehemence, crimes committed with intensity and extremity have been grouped for discussion and analysis in this chapter. The following IPC crimes which are reported to the police authorities have been grouped as violent crimes for the purpose of crime analysis.

i) Violent crimes affecting life

— murder

— attempt to commit murder

— culpable homicide not amounting to murder

— Dowry deaths

— kidnapping and abduction

ii) Violent crimes affecting property

— dacoity

— preparation and assembly for dacoity

— robbery

iii) Violent crimes affecting public safety

— riots

— arson

iv) Violent crimes affecting women

— rape

During 1999 the violent crimes reported in India shared 13.7 per cent to the total IPC crimes reported. Pattern of violent crimes during 1998-1999 reveal that there has been a steady trend in the reported incidents of violent crimes in India during 1996 to 1999. During the year 238, 081 violent crimes were reported in India. The crime rate (24. 0) of violent crimes under IPC, during 1999 showed a decline over the previous year at all-India level.

Among Indian states, Uttar Pradesh reported the highest incidence with 3, 8070 cases sharing 21.9 per cent of the total violent crimes reported during 1999 in the country. The other states contributing significantly to the total violent crime at national level during 1999 were: Bihar (31,479 cases,), Rajasthan (27,564), Madhya Pradesh (18, 376), Maharashtra (17, 122, 9.6 per cent) and Tamil Nadu (12, 983).

The crime rate for violent crimes during 1999 at all-India level was 24. The highest crime rate for violent crimes (under IPC) was recorded in Rajasthan (52.1) Sikkim (40.7) Jammu and Kashmir (40.2). Assam (38.5) Arunachal Pradesh (37.6) and Tripura (30.7).

During 1999, violent crimes situation in the union territories reveals that of the total violent crimes reported in the country (238, 081), 4843 violent crime cases constituting 2 per cent were reported in the 7 union territories. The crime rate for violent crime in the union territories during 1999 was 29.7.

Out of the 4843 cases reported during 1999, in the 7 union territories 4289 incidents of violent crimes (31.5 per cent) were reported in the National Capital Territory. Though the Union Territories except NCT Delhi recorded less violent crimes by incidence, the crime rate was high above the national average in 4 territories.

The percentage share of violent crimes to the total IPC crimes reported in their respective Union Territories during 1999 show that union territories of Daman and Diu (17.8 per cent) and Dadra and Nagar Haveli ((17. 4 per cent) recorded higher percentage share of violent crimes under IPC.

ANALYSIS OF VIOLENT IPC CRIMES

The detailed account of violent crimes occurred in Indian mega cities, during the year 1999, is given in Table 10.2.

Murder

During 1999, the highest incidence (7, 850) of murder, was reported from Uttar Pradesh. Bihar also reported significantly large number (5, 116) of murder cases. The other states which reported more than 2,000 cases each were Madhya Pradesh (3, 225), Maharashtra (3, 024) and Andhra Pradesh (2, 711).

Motives behind the murder cases reveal, as in the past, the prominent motives behind murders were personnel vendetta or enmity and property dispute. The other significant causes were: love intrigues, dowry and gain.

Bihar reported the highest number of murder cases due to property dispute, dowry and gain in 1999 at all-India. Uttar

Table 10. 2.

Incidence and rate of violent crimes in Indian cities during 1999.

State	*Murder*	*Attempt to murder*	*C.H. not amounting to murder*	*Rape*	*Kidnapping abduction*	*Dacoity*	*Preparation for dacoity*	*Robbery*	*Riots*	*Arson*	*Dowry death*	*Total crime*	*Crime rate*	*% to total crime under IPC*
Ahmedabad	105	60	3	14	200	20	1	224	200	9	6	842	20.4	5.4
Bangalore	203	349	2	29	158	66	0	451	329	l	49	1643	29.8	5.9
Bhopal	44	92	0	42	37	1	0	85	57	12	10	380	23.6	4.0
Calcutta	72	148	11	24	134	24	72	157	324	0	5	971	7.6	8.5
Chennai	93	333	1	27	41	18	0	104	60	0	22	699	10.6	10.3
Coimbatore	22	28	0	4	23	0	0	17	75	8	11	188	0.9	4.9
Delhi (City)	514	509	61	332	1176	42	30	649	163	49	95	3620	31.2	6.9
Hyderabad	115	97	1	48	96	3	0	79	148	0	19	606	8.9	5.2
Indore	95	83	2	23	35	0	9	41	48	9	23	374	26.5	4.4
Jaipur	47	51	2	38	191	8	0	61	1369	24	26	1817	85.7	14.6
Kanpur	208	175	43	34	190	24	6	125	202	29	75	1111	45.7	16.3
Kochi	22	30	3	9	9	5	0	27	193	4	0	302	17.4	6.0
Lucknow	129	140	21	28	114	17	0	127	229	8	34	847	33.3	12.0

(Table 10. 2. contd...)

State	Murder	Attempt to murder	C.H. not amounting to murder	Rape	Kidnapping abduction	Dacoity	Preparation for dacoity	Robbery	Riots	Arson	Dowry death	Total crime	Crime rate	% to total crime under IPC
Ludhiana	39	34	8	38	50	6	12	4	0	5	14	210	12.8	11.2
Madurai	28	36	0	6	21	7	0	29	87	2	5	221	17.5	6.0
Mumbai	340	184	4	141	189	74	81	549	200	1	60	1823	10.2	6.2
Nagpur	135	86	1	42	68	21	63	200	135	12	39	1202	93.9	21.3
Patna	226	271	21	18	104	69	11	296	135	24	4	779	38.2	8.2
Pune	82	40	6	51	50	25	4	89	1012	10	0	1369	39.6	14.3
Surat	106	21	3	17	70	17	0	83	81	12	28	438	18.9	9.6
Vadodara	37	17	1	10	61	11	0	92	140	7	0	376	23.6	6.5
Varanasi	68	56	8	10	17	0	0	52	63	9	14	297	23.2	21.6
Vishakhapatnam	17	28	0	17	12	3	0	18	3	11	8	117	6.9	3.1
Total (cities)	**2747**	**2868**	**202**	**1008**	**3046**	**461**	**289**	**3559**	**5253**	**252**	**547**	**20232**	**21.3**	**7.9**

Pradesh reported the highest number of murders due to personnel vendetta or enmity. Murders due to casteism were high in Bihar and Tamil Nadu. Murders due to class conflict were higher in Manipur and in Bihar.

Attempt to Commit Murder

As in the case of murder, Uttar Pradesh registered the highest (7, 849) incidence of attempt to commit murder, followed by Bihar and Madhya Pradesh with 3, 818 and 3, 082 cases respectively. The states of Kerala, Orissa, Rajasthan, Tamil Nadu and Chandigarh registered more cases under this head.

Culpable Homicide

As in the cases of murder and its attempt, Uttar Pradesh recorded higher number of cases (1, 354) of culpable homicide not amounting to murder, followed by Bihar and Madhya Pradesh with 742 and 189 cases respectively. Personnel vendetta or enmity, property dispute, dowry, gain and love intrigues were the major specified motives for culpable homicide not amounting to murder.

Cities of Delhi, Kanpur, Lucknow and Patna and Calcutta reported high incidence under this category of crime.

Rape

Madhya Pradesh, Uttar Pradesh and Bihar reported a significant number of such cases, 3, 561, 1, 593, 1, 447, respectively.

Total number of persons arrested in the registered rape cases were more in the cities of Delhi, Mumbai, Bhopal and Pune. More females were arrested in Mumbai in connection with such cases. The urban cities reported higher percentage of rape victims in the age-group below 10 years and 10-16 years than the all-India average. Victims in the age-group of 16-30 years are well below the national average in urban areas. This clearly indicates that girls below 16 years of age are the vulnerable group predominantly in urban areas.

Magnitude-wise, Delhi accounted the highest victims of paedophilia followed by Mumbai.

Kidnapping and Abduction

About 21, 797 cases of kidnapping and abduction were recorded during 1999. The highest incidence (4, 158) were reported in Uttar Pradesh followed by 3, 157 cases in Rajasthan and 2, 599 cases in Bihar. The other states and UTs which reported more than 1,000 cases during 1999 were Assam (1, 440), Delhi (1, 375), Andhra Pradesh (1, 169), Gujarat (1, 336), Maharashtra (1, 125) Madhya Pradesh (1, 203) and Tamil Nadu (1, 178).

Delhi recorded the highest incidence of kidnapping and abduction among the cities. The magnitude of kidnapping and abduction of women and girls are high in the cities of Ahmedabad, Bangalore, Calcutta, Indore, Jaipur, Ludhiana, Madurai, Nagpur, Patna and Surat.

Dacoity

Bihar reported the highest dacoity incidences (2, 153) of the total cases reported during 1999 in India. Uttar Pradesh with 927 cases was the next. Delhi city recorded the highest crime rate among the mega cities in India in this year. The cities which registered the highest incidence of dacoity are Mumbai followed by Patna and Surat.

Preparation and Assembly for Dacoity

In India, about 1, 464 cases of occurrence of preparation and assembly for dacoity cases reported during the year 1999. West Bengal recorded the largest number (475) of such cases, closely followed by Bihar with 200 cases.

Robbery

The highest incidence of robbery (4, 197) were reported from Uttar Pradesh followed by Bihar (2, 691) and Maharashtra (2, 554).

Riots

During the year 1999, the highest incidence of riots (16, 598) was reported in Rajasthan, followed by 11,06 in Bihar. States which recorded higher riots cases during 1999 were Karnataka (7, 596), Kerala (6, 610), Tamil Nadu (5, 428) and Maharashtra (5, 246).

Arson

During 1999, a total of 111, 24 arson cases were reported in India. Tamil Nadu (1, 183) recorded the highest number of cases of this type. Other states which registered more than 1,000 arson cases were Madhya Pradesh (1, 145), Maharashtra (1, 234), Uttar Pradesh (1, 171), Rajasthan (1, 230) and Andhra Pradesh (1, 057).

Dowry Death

During 1999, a total of 6, 564 dowry death cases were registered in India. Uttar Pradesh reported the highest such incidents (2, 088) followed by Bihar (1, 021), Madhya Pradesh (584) and Andhra Pradesh (452).

Economic Crimes

To study economic crimes, the number of cases reported under criminal breach of trust, cheating and counterfeiting have been taken for analysis. The 23 mega cities accounted nearly 22.4 per cent criminal breach of trust cases, 26.5 per cent cheating cases and 50.0 per cent counterfeiting cases that were reported in India in 1997. White collar crimes is mainly an urban phenomenon due to prevalent higher level of economic activities.

Hurt

The mega cities contributed 9.7 per cent towards the total cases of hurt reported in India during 1997. Bombay (3,652), Bangalore (3,775) and Delhi (2,356) accounted for more cases of hurt among the mega cities. In all 22,159 cases from cities were reported, registering an increase of 9.6 per cent over 1996.

Molestation

Molestation cases were reported in the mega cities accounted for 6.8 per cent of the total cases registered at the national level during 1997. The incidence, increased by 4.2 per cent over 1996. Such cases were higher in Delhi (586), Bangalore (227) and Bombay (223). These three cities accounted for 49.7 per cent of the total cases reported in the 23 metropolitan cities.

Sexual Harassment

Share of sexual harassment cases, reported in the 23 mega cities, to the total cases reported in the country was 17.1 per cent. The cases increased by 6.3 per cent over 1996. Coimbatore and Vishakapatnam each reported more than 200 cases in the country. Coimbatore, however, reported a significant increase from 1 to 219 cases in 1997.

Cruelty by Husband or his Relatives

Cases of torture of women by husband or his relatives in the mega cities shared 9.1 per cent of the total cases reporting an increased of 13.8 per cent in India, during 1997. Such cases were higher in Hyderabad (587) and Ahmedabad (465). These two cities shared 31.5 per cent of such cases at city level.

ANALYSIS OF SLL CRIMES

The mega cities from where the details of crime statistics are collected, reported 23,36,219 cases registered as crimes under special and local laws during 1997 as compared to 23,23,839 cases during 1996 reporting a marginal increase of 0.5 per cent in 1997. The increase at national level was reported to be at 2.3 per cent. As compared to national level reporting of these crimes (46,91,439), half (50.0 per cent) of these cases were registered in the 23 mega cities. A sudden spurt 59.1 per cent was reported in 'Forest Act' cases while significant decline of 50.0 per cent was in cases reported under 'Antiquity and Art Treasure Act'. 95.1 per cent of all cases registered in the cities were categorised under 'Other SLL Crimes', comparatively this per cent at national level was lower at 78.6 per cent, signifying higher registration of cases under local laws of the state than under special laws under study.

Crimes under Arms and Explosives/Explosive Substances Act

Incidence of cases under Arms Act in cities declined by 7.0 per cent to 9650 from 10,376 in 1997. These cities reported around 13.0 per cent of the total cases reported in India in 1997 under this Act. Against the national level crime rate of 7.8, Kanpur (101.6) reported a very high crime rate relating to violation of Arms Act. Incidence-wise, after Delhi (2,714), more cases were reported from Kanpur (2,357) and Lucknow (1,479). Similar is the case with reported cases under Explosives and Explosive Substances Act. Against the national level crime rate of 0.5 only, Kanpur city (5. 1) recorded the highest crime rate in this category followed by Varanasi city (3.6).

Terrorist and Disruptive Activities

No case was reported during 1997 from any city against 16 such cases reported in India as a whole.

Drug Offences

Cases of drug offences, drug trafficking reported for cities shared 19.1 per cent at national level with reporting of 4110 cases during 1997, registering negligible declining of 0.2 per cent in cities as compared to 19 per cent. Incidence-wise, Kanpur (1056), Delhi (750) and Bombay city (604) reported higher incidences. Crime rate-wise Kanpur (45.5 per cent) and Varanasi (29.4 per cent) reported higher rates compared to national level rate of 2.3.

Gambling Offences

Offences related to Gambling Act that were reported in 1997 in the 23 mega cities accounted for 11.5 per cent of the total such offences reported at all-India level. The offences reported under this Prohibitory Act have shown a declining trend during the last 5 years. The incidence of these crimes in cities declined by 11.5 per cent in 1997 over 1996. Madras (2,728) and Bombay (1,863) continued to report high incidence which were registered under this Act. Crime rate-wise, Indore (44.5) and Madras (43.4) recorded the higher crime rates compared to 12.5 at national level.

Prohibition and Excise Offences

Enforcement of prohibition is an important regulatory duty of police in urban areas. The cases reported under Prohibition Act and Excise Act in cities shared 9.3 per cent and 6.7 per cent at national level. Surat city (15924) reported the highest incidence of prohibition Act cases. Delhi city reported the highest incidence of cases under Excise Act sharing 48.6 per cent of all cities.

Immoral Traffic Offences

Offences under immoral trafficking and their prevention is predominantly an urban specific crime demanding considerable attention of the Law Enforcement Agencies of the cities in detecting and curbing of these unlawful activities. The police in the cities of Bombay (1640) and Bangalore (394), have effectively enforced this act whereas their counterparts in other mega cities have reported less such incidence which clearly calls for greater intensification in the enforcement of this preventive law.

Offences under Registration of Foreigners Act and Passport Act

Cases registered under the Registration of Foreigners Act in the 23 mega cities amounted to 13.8 per cent of the total cases reported in India during 1997. These cases reported a decline of 17.1 per cent. Pune city alone recorded more than half of total cases (130) sharing 65.3 per cent of all cities. The incidence of offences under Passport Act was only 8.2 per cent of the total cases reporting an increase of 20.0 per cent at national level. Bombay city reported 12 such cases out of 36.

Offences under Dowry Prohibition Act

Cases in the (23) cities reported a share of 9. 1 per cent at national level. Information in respect of enforcement of Dowry Prohibition Act reveals that the cities such as Bangalore (107) and Madras (66) registered higher number of cases under this Act. Crime rate-wise Patna (4.1) recorded higher rate in 1997 among the cities for offences under Dowry Prohibition Act.

Protection of Civil Rights Act

Instances of violation of civil rights was low in urban areas with only 4.9 per cent cases of all such cases at national level. The number of cases increased by one from 70 to 71 during 1997. The cities of Bangalore (15) and Nagpur (14) reported the highest incidence of such cases.

Offences under the Copyright Act

Offences under Copyright Act are basically committed in the urban areas. The percentage contribution from the 23 mega cities was 37.6 per cent towards total such offences reported in India during 1997. The higher incidence of violation of this Act were reported from the cities of Bombay (101) and Delhi (82).

11

Economic Offences

The present decades are experiencing a major socioeconomic phenomenon called globalisation. These phenomenon were driven by vast increase in trade, more mobility, fast means of communications and technological innovations. Trafficking in narcotics, trafficking in arms and explosive, fraudulent financial deals, foreign exchange manipulations, etc., falling under the head 'Organised Crimes' are adding new dimensions to the emerging crime scenario. 'Economic Offences' are the manifestation of criminal acts done either solely or in an organised manner with or without associates or gangs with an intent to earn wealth through illegal means, and earn out-illicit activities violating the laws of land, other regulatory, statutory provisions governing the economic activities of the government and its administration. These offences by far are not different from the traditional penal offences as far as the criminality is concerned.

The categorisation of this offence as a separate class is mainly due to the facts that they differ in *modus operandi*, and such activities are continued without legality by taking advantage of the deficiencies of the laws, rules, regulations. Such operations are also conducted with precision by circumventing the prescribed rule of law with impunity until after passage of time, the consequences of such offences surface leading to *post facto* legal intervention by the enforcement authorities. The activities of the above nature indulged in by organised crime groups by adopting various strategies are to be specially dealt with by an appropriate counter strategy. To tackle such forms of crimes one of the important legal developments within the country as well as other developed countries in the world is to being under the ambit of law powers to confiscate assets acquired by illicit means.

Traditional laws to some extent deal with confiscation of assets acquired by criminal acts and these have to be supplemented by some special acts as well. Institutional supports have been developed over the years to concentrate the enforcement drives by setting up special units exclusively to deal with such forms of economic crimes.

The economic offences, the experts opine, cause irreparable damage to the economy of the country, and its impact is felt in the economy down to a common man on the street affecting the growth and development of the country. Some of the major impacts that may be caused by the economic offences illustratively are:

— increase in inflationary pressure,
— distortion of developmental work,
— uneven distribution of resources and creation of elitism,
— marginalisation of tax base,
— generation of abundant black money,
— creation of a parallel economy,
— development works/efforts are undermined,
— the country's economic equilibrium is at stake,
— the breeding ground of corruption,
— illicit business and public office corruption thrive and affect normal business activities,
— resources of financial institutions and commercial institutions are diverted and distorted,
— weakens morale and commitment of the citizens, and
— the poor/weakest continue to be poorer and are at risk.

There being a range of economic offences, some are cognisable and some non-cognisable in nature. Hence, the police alone is not directly empowered nor are they equipped adequately considering the range of specific laws to investigate and successfully arraign the offenders except in cognizable offences. None the less, regular police deal with a considerable number of economic offences falling under the broad category of 'cheating', 'counterfeiting' and 'criminal breach of trust'.

The present day range of economic offences are far too many in its range as well as levels of sophistication of commission. Considering the importance to deal with such kind of offences which undermine the economy of the country, the Government of India have established a number of enforcement agencies having the requisite skills to investigate such crimes with successful results. These enforcement agencies are specially authorised under relevant provisions of various acts as listed in the preceding paragraphs with the primary objective of dealing with economic offences falling under their respective ambits.

Mutual coordination and cooperation among different law enforcement agencies as a single point directorate exists to ensure that serious frauds and scam are effectively investigated for successful trial. The initial efforts in this direction of establishing special agencies to investigate crimes of such nature falling under the ambit of economic offences and also to deal with corruption and bribery in respect of public servants, was by a special enactment, namely, 'The Delhi Special Police Establishment Act, 1946'.

The Special Police Establishment constituted in 1946, now known as Central Bureau of Investigation since 1962, is in existence for the purpose of investigation of specified offences or classes of offences as notified under Section 3 of the same Act including the economic offences, with the concurrence of the state governments wherever necessary. This particular agency, the central police organisation, has countrywide operation on par with the regular police to deal with not only economic offences, offences relating to corruption by public servants but also normal crimes of importance by mutual consent of central as well as state governments.

A number of special laws have been enacted in the country regulate customs, excise, taxes, foreign exchange, narcotics drugs, banking, insurance, trade and commerce relating to export and import, etc. The respective laws directly empower enforcement of the laws by their respective departmental enforcement agencies created under statutory provisions. These laws provide necessary legal powers of investigation, adjudication, imposing of fines, penalties and under special circumstances arrest and detention of the persons for the offences committed by them. These officers of the enforcement agencies are also vested with powers similar to those of police to summon witnesses, search and seize goods, documents and confiscate the proceeds. The economic offences which carry the principal motive of acquiring wealth through illicit means require special strategies to counter.

The universally emerging legal recourse to combat economic crimes which is popularly getting characterised as 'money laundering' and 'dealing in proceeds of crime' is by enacting legislations bringing under its ambit powers to attach and confiscate proceeds so as to deny the monetary advantage illicitly achieved. Some of the existing legislations of the country provide for scope for confiscation of the proceeds of crime and forfeiture of assets. These include the following:

i) Criminal Law (Amendment) Ordinance, 1944
ii) Customs Act, 1962 (Sec. 119 to 122)
iii) Law of Criminal Procedure Code 1973 (Sec.452)
iv) Foreign Exchange Regulation Act, 1973 (Sec.63)
v) Smugglers and Foreign Exchange Manipulators (Forfeiture of Property) Act, 1976)
vi) Narcotic Drugs and Psychotropic Substances Act, 1985 (Sec.A to Sec.68 Y)

vii) Terrorist and Disruptive Activities (Prevention) Act, 1987 (Sec.8 to Sec.21 relating to presumption)

New legislations may be called for to plug the existing loopholes and to bring into force a comprehensive legislation to make confiscation of properties and forfeiture of assets more effective, in the light of new legislations adopted in different countries.

Information in respect of number of seizures made by the customs officials, the total value of seizures and the nature of commodities seized by the customs received from Directorate of Revenue Intelligence for the year 1991-1995 presents the gravity of the offence and tradings in the contraband goods. Over the years, there has been a steady fall in the total number of seizures conducted by the customs. During the year 1995, on an average, around 153 seizures were made in a day and the average value of the property seized in such seizure amounted to around 2.9 crores.

The nature of the commodities seized by the customs include gold, silver, diamonds, watches, synthetic fibres, electronic goods, narcotic drugs and others. Details relating to the various commodities seized and their value for the year 1991 to 1995 are given in table 11.1.

Data of the table include baggage seizures, demonstrate that there has been a fall in the smuggling of precious metals over the years since 1992. The quantity of gold smuggled has also fallen from 4946 kgs in 1991 to 1169 in 1995. Similar is the case with silver which recorded 1979 25 kgs in 1991 had dwindled to 678 kgs in 1995. 'Narcotic drugs' are, however, found to be in the priority list of smuggling in 1995 compared to the 1996. There has been a sharp increase of around 58 per cent in the value of the 'drugs' seized by the customs. Electronic goods also seem to be much sought after items for smuggling in 1995 because of perceived premium and the value of the seized articles accounting to Rs. 63.3 crores compared to Rs. 37.2 crores in 1994.

Table 11. 1.
Nature and value of commodities seized by customs.

Rs. in crores

Commodities	1991	1992	1993	1994	1995
Gold (Qty. in kgs)	4946	2889	1372	1147	1169
	(187.8)	(126.1)	(59.1)	(53.4)	(58.3)
Silver (Qty. in kgs)	197925	161060	42237	6404	678
	(138.1)	(118.2)	(25.7)	(4.5)	(0.5)
Diamonds	6.7	1.9	1.4	2.9	NA
Synthetic fibres	5.2	2.5	3.1	7.2	NA
Electronic goods	52.4	23.7	35.8	37.2	63.3
Drugs/ Narcotics	23.4	18.3	15.8	54.3	85.7
Others	361.3	211.3	248.1	347.7	854.2
Total	**774.8**	**502.1**	**389.0**	**535.2**	**1062.0**

The information provided by the directorate shows that the number of searches/raids conducted in 1995 were only 1,175 as against 1,540 in 1994. The recoveries/seizures in the money laundering cases during 1995 yielded currencies (both Indian and Foreign) to the value of 10.2 crores and 6.5 crores (Indian equivalent of foreign currencies), respectively.

Among the economic offences, tax evasion is the most illegitimate activity which is practised by suppressing the facts and manipulation of records mostly by the corporate houses, professionals and other eligible tax payees.

Information made available by Central Board of Direct Taxes reveals that though there had been a steady and continuous efforts to unearth the income tax evasion through searches. The assets seized during 1995 were to the tune of 458 crores. The undisclosed income during such searches have shown significant rise in the past four years.

The quantum of amount involved both in the assets seized and in the undisclosed income in cases of income tax evasion is far greater than the value of the smuggled commodities into the country. This huge money necessarily plays an important role in black marketing which, not only give rise to inflationary pressures but also adds to the parallel economy. A look into the prosecutions that were launched into the tax evasion reveals that conviction awarded was low for such prosecutions. During the year 1995, of the 2,158 prosecutions decided under Direct Taxes enactments, 1,592 cases were compounded, 487 cases were acquitted and only 79 cases resulted in convictions.

The Directorate General of Foreign Trade, Ministry of Commerce regulates and enforces the Export and Import (Control) Act. The cases are registered, offences are investigated and adjudicated by the departmental officers. The information received from the D.G. Foreign Trade provides information about the number of inspections conducted, the no. of cases registered, cases adjudicated and the fines levied thereon.

There had been a sharp fall in the inspections conducted during 1992 and 1993 and again increased in 1994. The cases registered showed a fall in 1992 and increased in 1993 and 1994. During 1995 such inspections were considerably lower than those in 1994. The fines imposed in the various adjudications were in the range of 34 crores in 1992 and 1993, it suddenly increased to 83 crores in 1994 but decreased to 54 crores in 1995.

Drug trafficking and illicit manufacture/cultivation of narcotics is a money-spinner in the underworld market. The government of India has made a multi-pronged anti-drug policy to curb the menace through NDPS Act, 1985 and PIT NDPS Act, 1988. These laws provide regulation in the cultivation, production and distribution of narcotic drugs and psychotropic substances, enforces the prohibition of these substances otherwise, and prevents the illicit traffic in such trade which had assumed a potential threat. The Narcotics Control Bureau (NCB) functions as a separate drug law enforcement agency and coordinates with other agencies. The information received from the Narcotics Control Bureau provides a detailed survey of the drug trafficking, enforcement and the preventive action taken.

Table 11. 2.
Quantity of drugs seized.

Quantity in Kgs

Drugs	1991	1992	1993	1994	1995
Opium	2,145	1,918	3,011	2,256	1,339
Morphine	6	35	36	51	4
Heroin	622	1,153	1,088	1,011	1,678
Ganja	52,633	64,341	98,867	187,896	121,873
Hashish	4,413	6,621	8,238	6,992	3,629
Methaqualone	4,415	7,475	15,004	45,319	20,485

The above table provides the information regarding the quantity of the various drugs that were seized in the searches conducted by the law enforcement agencies. The quantity-wise analysis of the drugs that were seized indicates that over the years a very high quantity of ganja was illicitly transported. From 52,633 kgs in 1991, ganja seizures increased to 1,21,873 kgs in 1995, which is well over 131 per cent. Similar is the case with methaqualone and heroin which recorded over 5 times and 2 times in 1995 compared to the seizures made in 1991.

The information regarding persons involved in the trafficking would indicate the number of persons involved in the offence. During 1995 a record number of 14,673 persons were arrested which included 148 foreigners. The drug trade has a thriving market and is well run as a business and the money generated from the trafficking is capitalised through various money laundering processes.

Recent incidents show drug money has created a number of neo-rich class of people who could sit on empire in legitimate business and control real estates, film production, airlines, corporate houses, etc. Their role in anti-national, smuggling, terrorist activities and clandestine trading in arms and ammunition have since recently surfaced.

TRADING IN CULTURAL PROPERTY

Trading in artifacts is another economic crime which brings in ill-gotten wealth in the mainstream of the national economy. Though the reported cases for this offence is, magnitude-wise, small it is estimated that the cultural property involved in such trafficking are priceless objects which attract very high premium and prices in the international clandestine market.

Though corruption or bribery cases of public servants fall in a different category of crime, the money power involved to seek favours from the public servants by the economic offenders through corrupt practices and paying illegal gratifications, places this type of offence on a different footing in the economic offences. Corruption, illegal gratifications, considerations which are not due, which involve a huge amount of money, valuables and their transactions not only breed black money but also generate potential ground for the vested interests for commission and expansion of the activities directed towards economic offences. Even a few millions of illegal dispensation by way of bribery is sufficient for a huge economic manipulation by billions by these offenders. The information collected from the Central Bureau of Investigation and State Vigilance Bureaus provides the nexus between the public servants and the vested interests who willingly foot a share of the future booty by way of bribery or corruptive actions.

There had been a steady trend in the incidence of cases registered under Prevention of Corruption Act by the Central Bureau of Investigation during the years 1991 to 1995. During

1995, CBI have taken 297 persons under custody for various offences under PC Act. Enforcement by the states/UTs on this account shows that the years 1992 to 1993 had seen a slight fall in the cases registered under PC Act, followed by a marginal increase in 1994. The cases reported in 1995 were less than the cases registered in 1994 but more persons were arrested (2,604) under this act in 1995.

During 1995, property worth Rs. 6.8 lakhs were seized by the CBI. The state/UT vigilance officials seized a property to the tune of 16.6 crores in the various raids, seizures connected with corruption charges. In the various cases investigated by CBI, in 1995, against 735 persons regular departmental action was taken, whereas in the state governments, regular departmental actions were initiated, against only 295 persons. The punishment awarded to various public servants in the cases handled by CBI included 27 dismissals, 11 removals, 133 major and 194 minor punishments in 1995.

A look in the profile of the public servants involved in states/UT's reveals that there were 1,114 gazetted officers (373 group 'A', 741 group 'B' officers) 1,278 NGO's and 499 privately employed involved in such cases. In state vigilance cases 295 persons were referred for regular departmental action in 1995. There were 27 dismissals, 14 removal from service, 53 major and 76 minor punishments were awarded to the public servants. Cases related to other economic offences are neither reported regularly nor detailed information on such offences are made available for making an indepth analysis and follow up the trend for such crimes. The present analysis of the economic crimes is only of illustrative and brings forth the range and enormity with the available information received in this areas. An exhaustive picture on the pattern and trend on these offences can be attempted only when the central law enforcement authorities collect and disseminate the information in entirety so that a useful analysis could be attempted for better planning and enforcement of the various laws and regulations.

12
Cyber Crime

Information technology is a double-edged sword, consistently presenting us with benefits and disadvantages. The internet is no different. The net is a powerful tool, providing the ability for global communications in a heartbeat; sharing information without boundaries; a platform for illicit and unethical shenanigans. Before three decades, when the internet was born, it was a medium used by the government and assorted academicians, primarily to perform and share research. The user community was small and mostly self-regulated. The requirements for availability and reliability were not as much a consideration then as they are now. The increasing opportunities for productivity, efficiency and worldwide communications brought additional users in droves. Today, the internet is a utility, analogous to the electric company, and '.com' is a household expression. The reliability and availability of the internet are critical operational considerations. Activities that threaten these attributes like spamming, spoofing etc., have grave impacts on its user community.

Sending unsolicited junk electronic mail, such as an advertisement, to one user or many users via a distribution list, is considered spamming. One of the most publicised spamming incidents occurred in 1994, when two attorneys from Arizona, flooded the cyberwaves, especially the usenet newsgroups, with solicitations to the immigrant communities of the US to assist them in the green card lottery process to gain citizenship. The lawyers saw the spamming as an ideal, low-cost and perfectly legitimate way to target people likely to be potential clients. Many usenet newsgroup users, however, saw things differently. The lawyers' actions resulted in quite an uproar among the internet communities primarily because the internet has had a long tradition of non-commercialism since its founding. The attorneys had already been ousted from the American Immigration Lawyers' Association for past sins, and eventually they lost their licenses to practice law. There have been several other spams since the green card lottery.

Today, threatening electronic mail messages have become pervasive in the internet space. Businesses are establishing policy to inhibit employees from using company resources to perform unethical behaviour on the internet. In an early 1999 case, a California firm agreed to pay a former employee over $100,000 after she received harassing messages on the firm's electronic bulletin board, even though the company reported the incident to authorities and launched an internal investigation. The case is a not so subtle reminder that businesses are accountable for the actions of their employees, even actions performed on electronic networks. Businesses have taken a stern position on employees surfing the web, sending inappropriate messages, and downloading pornographic materials from the internet. This is due to a negative impact on productivity, as well as the legal view that companies are liable for the actions of their employees.

Cyberstalking has becoming more prevalent, and the law has seen fit to intercede by adding computers and electronic devices to existing stalking legislation. In the first case of cyberstalking in California, a Los Angeles resident, accused of using his computer to harass a woman who rejected his romantic advances, is the first to be charged under a new cyberstalking law that went into effect in 1998. The man was accused of forging postings on the internet, on America Online (AOL) and other internet services, so that the messages appeared to come from the victim. The message provided the woman's address and other identifying information, which resulted in at least six men visiting her home uninvited. The man was charged with one count of stalking, three counts of solicitation to commit sexual assault, and one count of unauthorised access to computers. According to recent estimates, internet-based gambling has grown from about a $500 million-a-year industry in the late 1990s, to what some estimate could become a $10 billion-a-year enterprise by 2020. Currently, all states regulate in-person gambling in some manner.

Fears of invasion of privacy on the internet increased for last few years. People wanted to insist that their personal information should be stored on computer databases by government agencies and commercial entities. It is just of late that people realising that logging on to the internet and using the World Wide Web threatens their privacy as well. The Center for Democracy and Technology (CDT), a Washington, DC advocacy group, reported that only one third of federal agencies tell visitors to their web sites what information is being collected about them. A study conducted by AT&T Labs discovered that Americans are willing to surrender their e-mail address online, but not much more than that.

The internet promulgates a lack of identity. Users of the internet are virtual, because, they are not speaking with, interacting with, or responding to others, at least not face to face. They sit behind their computer terminals in the comfort of their own home, office, or school. This anonymity makes it easy to masquerade as another, since there is no way of proving or disproving who you are or who you say you are. Moreover, this anonymity lends itself to the venue of internet chat rooms.

Chat rooms are places on the net where people congregate and discuss topics common to the group, such as sports, recreation, or sexuality. Many chat rooms provide support to persons looking for answers to questions on health, bereavement, or disease and, in this manner, can be very beneficial to society. Conversely, chat rooms can be likened to sleazy bars, where malcontents go seeking prey. There have been too many occurrences of too-good-to-be-true investments that have turned out to be fraudulent.

Too many times, miscreants have struck up electronic conversations with innocent victims, masquerading as innocents themselves, only to lead them to meet in person with dire results. Unfortunately, electronic behaviour mimics conduct that has always occurred over phone lines, through the postal service, and in person. The internet only provides an additional locale for intentionally malicious and antisocial behaviour. We can only hope that advanced technology, as with telephonic caller ID, will assist law enforcement in tracking anonymous internet bad guys. Attempts at self-regulation have not been as successful as advertised, and many question whether the industry can police itself. Meanwhile, there are those within the legal and judicial systems that feel more laws are the only true answer to limiting unethical and illegal activities on the internet.

WHAT IS CYBER CRIME ?

Cyber crime can be defined as any crime with the help of computer and telecommunication technology with the purpose of influencing the functioning of computer or computer system. It is estimated that there are over 600 million users connected to the internet and e-mail by 2001. With the boom in e-commerce and e-governance, the cybercrimes are very serious threat for the information age.

TYPES OF CYBER CRIME

Computer crimes are different from conventional crimes, as they can be easily committed from distant places, difficult to detect and even harder to prove them. It is a very low risk and high reward venture. As it is evident, computer crimes do not involve violence but rather greed, pride or pay on some character weakness of the victims. It is very difficult to identify the culprit, as the net can be accessed from any part of the globe. The field is wide open for hackers. That is why cybercrimes are also called "white collar crimes".

Cyber crimes can be basically divided into three categories:

i) Cyber crime against person: e.g., cyber stalking, child pornography, impersonation, loss of privacy.

ii) Cyber crimes against property: e.g., unauthorised computer-trespassing through cyberspace, computer vandalism, harmful programme transfer, e-cash, money laundering, copy right act.

iii) Cyber crime against government: e.g., Hacking, cyber extortion, NASA website hacked, cyber-terrorism, computer viruses, counter-feiting currency and industrial espionage etc.

There are some other forms of computer crimes:

i) *Logic bomb*: A programme that causes the system to crash at a specific time.

ii) *Trap doors*: A quick way into a program bypassing security,

iii) *Spamming*: Mass mailing of unsolicited e-mail messages.

iv) *Piggibacking*: Following an authorised person through a locked door, either a physical one or a computer's security firewall.

v) *Dumpster diving*: Scavenging through materials that have been thrown away.

vi) *IP spoofing*: Unauthorised access to computers where hacker send messages to a computer with an IP (Internet Protocol) address indicating the messages is coming from a trusted sources.

vii) *Data diddling*: False data entry, changing data before or during their input into a system.

viii) *Masquerading*: Where one person uses the identity of another to gain access to a computer.

ix) *Password sniffing*: Automated guessing of phone numbers, user ID's and passwords.

x) *Trojan horse*: A method for inserting instructions into a complete programme so that the programme performs an unauthorised function while apparently performing useful one.

xi) *Viruses*: A programme that modifies other programmes so they replicate the virus.

xii) *Worms*: A stand alone programme that replicates itself on one computer and tries to infect other computers.

xiii) *Cyber-loafing*: Spreading excessive time on the internet gambling, pornography, checking stock travels, sports scores, etc.

xiv) *Salami techniques*: An unauthorised programme that causes the unnoticed debiting of small amounts of assets from large number of sources/accounts.

xv) *E-mail abuse*: Sending unwanted e-mails e.g., "I Love You", "Love Bug", etc.

PREPARATORS OF CYBER CRIMES

The cyber crime preparators could be students amateurs or members of an organised group. The cyber criminals are bright eager and highly motivated and willing to accept technological challenges. The cyber threat are from:

i) *Insiders*: The insiders are main sources of cyber crimes for many companies.

ii) *Hackers*: They crack into networks simply for the challenge of it.

iii) *Crackers*: Person who breaks security on a system.

iv) *Phreaker*: One who breaks into telephone companies networks and use them.

v) *Virus writers*: Virus writers pose serious threats to networks and systems worldwide.

vi) *Foreign intelligent services*: FIS uses cyber tools as part of their espionage activities.

vii) *Information warfare*: IW by foreign nations against critical infrastructures are the greatest potential threat to national security.

viii) *Terrorist*: Terrorist groups are using cyber networks to formulate plans, raise funds, spread propaganda etc.

ix) *Denial of service attack*: Using someone else's machine to launch bogus request on a site.

CYBER CRIME CASES REPORTED IN INDIA

i) *Paedophilic website busted by the CBI:* The CBI has busted a paedophilic (child pornography) site and arrested a Hyderabad based computer engineer, the owner of the domain, which was hosting the paedophilic site. The investigation revealed that the site, www. sweeties. arjika. com. was created by a person in Peru, under the domain (arjika.com) owned by the arrested Indian national while the server was situated in the USA. The site, featured a cartoon character—Pokeman on its homepage and listened its creator as a 15 year old girl.

ii) *Microsoft hacked*: The software giant Microsoft Corporation has been hacked into. The company reported the break-in to the US Federal Bureau of Investigation and are working with authorities to protect its intellectual property. Citing sources close to the situation, the Wall Street Journal reported that the hackers were believed to have stolen the blue prints to the latest versions of its flagship one rating system Windows and its Office software package. The company interpreted electronic logs as showing that the internal passwords were used to transfer source code outside the microsoft campus. The newspaper quoted a person familiar with the case as saying that the hackers used a programme called a 'Trojan'. Named after the Greek myth of the Trojan Horse, the hacker sends a seemingly innocuous file to an unsuspecting person. Hidden within the coding of the file is in insidious programme designed to infiltrate, the computer of the user who opens the file.

iii) *Pak-hackers deface pro-Israeli website*: Pakistan-based hackers attacked a US website belonging to a pro-Israeli lobby In early November, 2000 stealing credit card numbers and member records as, a part of on online war between Israel and Arabs. The attack, against the American-Israel Public Affairs Committee consisted of the hackers defacing its website with pro-Palestinian slogans The Pakistan Hackers Club, which consist of at least two members known as "Doctor Nuker" and "Mr. Sweet", took responsibility for the attack. The hackers wrote, "The hack is to protest against the atrocities in Palestine by the barbarian Israeli soldiers and their constant support by the US government. Instead of writing articles or putting pictures of Israeli's atrocities in Palestine, this time I've put e-mail and comments that I got from the website." In the past year, the Pakistan Hackers Club has defaced over a hundred websites.. Normally, its attacks are targeted against Indian government and business websites where they post statements and pictures supporting Pakistan's Kashmir case.

iv) *Arrest of an engineer for stealing internet hours: The* Delhi Police, in June, 2000, arrested an engineer on charges of stealing over 100 hours of Internet time. The accused, a Service Engineer employed in a South Delhi-based firm had installed the Internet connection for a retired Army Colonel who had purchased it from the Videsh Sanchar Nigam Limited. The accused allegedly sold the password to atleast 10 others in the Colonel's internet time was consumed by them.

v) *Credit card fraud through internet: The* CBI has registered a case, the first of its kind, reported in India, for the misuse of credit card number of a doctor by a miscreant. The Delhi based doctor, lodged the complaint with the CBI that he had been receiving inflated credit card bills. The scrutiny of the mail orders revealed that goods were purchased in different countries through the doctors' credit card by an unknown person who had obtained the card number.

vi) *Counterfeiting of share certificates*: Counterfeiting of 500 rupee currency note using DTP (Desk Top Publishing) systems have reported especially in North-East India.

Counterfeiting of Degree Certificates, Registration Certificates of vehicles using DTP system have been reported.

Counterfeiting of share certificates: In October 1995, Economics Offence Wing of crime branch, Mumbai seized over 22, 000 counterfeit share certificate of reputed companies worth Rs. 34.47 crores. These were illegally prepared using DTP systems.

vii) *Software engineer arrested for using the internet to harass neighbour*: In July, 2000, a software engineer was arrested by the Delhi Police for misusing the Internet to distribute the phone number of his neighbour as a contact number to reach call girls. The neighbour, a retired government official, was harassed by a flood of humiliating 4000 in 6 weeks on the telephone. Enquiries revealed that the message to the callers, had been distributed to the Airtel phone users from net-4 India—a private Internet Service, provider (ISP). The search of logs of the ISP by the police resulted in retrieving the Internet Prolocol (IP) address of the accused and the login time. The accused had routed the message, through a website.

viii) *Cyerstalking*: An engineering and management graduate, facing prosecution in a dowry harassment case, was arrested by Delhi Police for sending obscene e-mails in his wife's name to several persons.

ix) *Use of chat channels to harass women*: In June. 2000, a man was arrested by the Delhi Police for assuming the identify of his ex-employer's wife in a chat channel and encouraging others to telephone net. The victim who was getting obscene telephone calls at night from stranger made a complaint to the police. The accused was then located 'on line' in the chat room under the identity of the, victim and later traced through the telephone number used by him to access the Internet.

x) *Hijacking website:* In the first ever case, of its kind in India, a web designer has been arrested by the Delhi police, for trying to extort money from an export company, for whom he had designed a web-site. The accused had transferred the website of the company in his name illegally and had demanded money for returning it. The accused had been maintaining the website, since 1997 on a 3 year contract. His contract was terminated in December, 2000. When the company asked him to return the contents of the website, domain name, and the passwords, he refused. He had changed the ownership details of the domain in all rights of the website, in his name.

The police, upon scanning his computer database found evidence of the various e-mail instructions sent by him to the registration authorities and other correspondence done by him to hijack the site. It was also revealed that the accused had been operating his business under various names and styles, even changing his address while launching a new firm. He had changed his address more than five times in the past one year. The case was registered by the police under sections of IPC and Copy Rights Act.

PREVENTION FOR CYBER CRIMES

Present information systems are susceptible to cyber crime, because, it is inexpensive, quick and easy for anyone to launch attacks against the critical information infrastructures. The high density of information, high processing power and open connectivity of the system provide an attractive target for infiltrators for attacking information.

The new technologies for preventing cyber-crimes are:

i) *Firewall*: Firewall implemented with secure standards will not allow any intruder into the system.

ii) *Encrypted tunnelling*: An encrypted tunnel allows secure communications across internet. In this the data packets on inetrnet are encrypted and then wrapped in IP at the initiation point of the tunnel. The encrypted packets can be then be transmitted over the internet. When the packets arrive at the other end of the tunnel, they are unwrapped and decrypted.

iii) *Secure Sockets Layer (SSL) and Secure HTTP (SHTTP)* provide an encrypted TCP/IP. Pathways between two hosts on the internet (they require that both the browser and server be SSL-enabled). SSL can be used to encrypt any TCP/IP protocol (HTTP, FTP, TEL:NET), SHTTP, only can encrypt HTTP.

iv) *Secure Electronic Transform (SET)* is the new technology for credit on internet. This involves cryptographic algorithms to encrypt the credit card numbers so, it can't be seen on the internet.

v) *Digital signature:* Cryptographic technique is used so that only authorised and authenticated person can enter in the system.

vii) Employees training.

viii) Cash account security.

COMPUTER CRIME INVESTIGATION

Any illegal act, for which knowledge of computer technology is essential for its perpetration, investigation, or prosecution is known as computer crime. Computer crime investigation is more an art than a science. It is a rapidly changing field that requires knowledge in many disciplines. Computer crime investigation and computer forensics are evolving sciences which are affected by many external factors: continued advancements in technology, societal issues, legal issues, etc.

Investigation Process

The processes of computer-crime investigation ranging from reporting and containment to analysis and eradication need to be accomplished as soon as possible after the attack. An incident response plan should be formulated and a computer emergency response team should be organised prior to the attack. The incident response plan will help set the objective of the investigation and will identify each of the steps in the investigative process.

Before any investigation can take place, the system intrusion or abusive conduct must first be detected. The closer the detection is to the actual intrusion event will not only help to minimise system damage, but will also assist in the identification of potential suspects. To date, most computer crimes have either been detected by accident or through the laborious review of lengthy audit trails.

Based on the type of investigation and extent of the abuse, the victim must decide who is to conduct the investigation. This used to be a fairly straightforward decision, but high-technology crime has altered the decision-making process. Inadequate and untested laws, combined with the lack of technical training and technical understanding, has severely hampered the effectiveness of our criminal justice system when dealing with computer-related crimes. The law enforcement officers have greater search and investigative capabilities than private individuals, but they also have more restrictions than private citizens. For law enforcement to conduct a search, a warrant must first be issued. No warrant is needed if the victim or owner of compromised system gives permission to conduct the search. Issuance of the search warrant is based upon probable cause. Once probable cause has been identified, law enforcement officers have the ability to execute search warrants, subpoenas, and wire taps.

The Fourth Amendment to the Constitution of USA states that 'the right of the people to be secure in their persons, houses, papers, and effects, against unreasonable searches and seizures, shall not be violated and no warrants shall issue, but upon probable cause, supported by oath or affirmation, and particularly describing the place to be searched, and the persons or things to be seized'.

With technology changing so rapidly, most law enforcement officers lack the technical training to adequately investigate an alleged intrusion. The same problems hold true for the prosecution and the judiciary. To successfully prosecute a case, both the prosecutor and the judge must have a reasonable understanding of high-tech laws and the crime in question. Additionally, many of the current laws are woefully inadequate. Even though an action may be morally and ethically wrong, it is still possible that no law is violated. Even when there is a law that has been violated, many of these laws remain untested and lack precedence. Many recent judicial decisions have indicated that judges are lenient towards techno-criminals just as with other white-collar criminals.

Investigation plan

The goal of any investigation is to know who, what, when, where, why and how. It is important that the investigator logs all activity and accounts for all time spent on the investigation. The amount of time spent on the investigation has a direct impact on the total dollar loss for the incident. This may result in greater criminal charges and, possibly, stiffer sentencing. The money spent on investigative resources can be reimbursed as compensatory damages in a successful civil action. Once the decision is made to further investigate the incident, the next course of action for the investigative team is to establish a detailed investigative plan, including the search and seizure plan. Some informal strategy that will be employed throughout the investigation include:

i) Identification of potential suspects
ii) Identification of potential witnesses
iii) Identification of type of system to be seized
iv) Identification of search and seizure team members
v) Obtaining search warrant.

Identification of potential suspects: Type of crime and attacker will set stage for overall investigation. When an organisation plans to conduct an investigation pertaining to unauthorised access or a violation of company policy all the factors should be considered. This includes the anticipated cost and the chances of success.

Identification of potential witnesses: Selecting whom will be interviewed, and when, may have important impact on the investigation. Sources of information may be staff members, expert witnesses, associates, etc. Interviews are not the same as interrogations, and great care should go into not confusing the two. If a hostile witness does not want to be interviewed, then the process should cease immediately.

Identification of type of system: The investigator should learn as much as possible about the target computer system. If possible, obtain the configuration of the system, including the network environment, hardware, and software.

Identification of search and seizure team members: Based upon who's conducting the search, there are different rules for search and seizure Under the Fourth Amendment, law enforcement must obtain a warrant, which must be based on probable cause. Regardless of who's conducting the search and seizure, a team should be identified and should consist of the following members:

i) Lead investigator.
ii) Information security department.
iii) Legal department.
iv) Technical assistance.

Obtaining search warrant: If the suspect has crucial evidence at his home or office, then a search warrant will be required to seize the evidence. If a search warrant is going to be needed, then it should be done as quickly as possible before the intruder can do further damage.

Many times it is required to seize a disk from the suspect's computer, mirror image a copy of the disk, and then replace the original with a copy of the disk, all without the suspect knowing what is happening. This allows the investigative team to protect the evidence and continue with the investigation, while retaining secrecy of the investigation. Enter the area slowly so as not to disturb or destroy evidence. Evaluate the entire situation. In no other type of investigation can evidence be destroyed more quickly. Do not touch the keyboard as this may invoke a Trojan Horse or some other rogue or malicious programme. Do not turn off the computer unless it appears to be active. Look for the disk activity light and listen for disk usage. If you must turn off the computer, pull the plug from the wall, rather than using the on/off switch. Look for notes, documentation, passwords, encryption codes, etc.

Investigator may wish to video-tape the entire evidence collection process. There are two schools of thought on this. The first is that if you video-tape the search and seizure, any mistakes can nullify the whole operation. The second school of thought is that if you video-tape the evidence collection process, many of the claims by the defence can be silenced. Sketch and photograph the crime scene before touching anything. Sketches should be drawn to scale. Take still photographs of critical pieces of evidence.

The state of California has equated hacker tools with burglary tools; the mere possession constitutes a crime.

Possession of a Red Box, or any other telecommunications instrument that has been modified with the intent to defraud, is also prohibited under USC Section 1029.

The hacker tools that you should be aware of include;

i) Password crackers
ii) Network sniffers
iii) Automated probing tools
iv) Anonymous remailers
v) War dealers
vi) Encryption and steganography tools.

Phones, answering machines, desk calendars, day-timers, fax machines, pocket organisers, electronic watches, etc., are all sources of potential evidence. If the case warrants, seize and analyse all sources of data, both electronic and manual.

Surveillance used in investigations

The two forms of surveillance used in computer crime investigations are physical surveillance and computer surveillance.

The physical surveillance can be generated at the time of the abuse, via CCTV security camera, or after the fact. When done after the fact, physical surveillance is usually performed undercover. It can be used in an investigation to determine a subject's personal habits, family life, spending habits, or associates.

The computer surveillance is done passively through audit logs or actively by way of electronic monitoring. Electronic monitoring can be accomplished via keyboard monitoring, network sniffing, or line monitoring. In any case, it generally requires a warning notice and/or explicit statement in the security policy, indicating that the company can and will electronically monitor any and all systems or network traffic.

One other method of computer surveillance that is used are 'sting operations.' These operations are established so as to continue to track the attacker, on-line.

To track and identify a hacker or remote intruder is very difficult. With caller ID, wiretap, etc., many hackers meander through communication networks, hopping from one site to the next, via a multitude of telecommunications gateways and hubs, such as the internet.

The investigative report should provide a detailed account of the incident, highlighting any discrepancies in witness statements. The report should be a well-organised document that contains a description of the incident, all witness statements, references to all evidentiary articles, pictures of the crime scene, drawings and schematics of the computer and the computer network, and finally, a written description of the forensic analysis. The report should state final conclusions, based solely on the facts, it should not include the investigator's opinions, unless he is an expert.

Industrialised nations restrict the export of specific technologies, including those with a direct military use and advanced technologies easily misused by other nations to suppress human rights, improve intelligence gathering, or counter security measures. Thus, an efficient relational database product might be restricted from export because oppressive third-world nations might use it to maintain data on their citizens. Restrictions on software export can sometimes be averted by finding a nation in which the desired product is sold legally without the export restriction.

New network technologies will make our networks increasingly intelligent, capable of enforcing complex compliance rules and allowing each enterprise to carefully craft the jurisdictions from which, through which, and into which its data will flow. Most jurisdictions will acquire the ability to detect cryptographic messages and to process cleartext messages even before they acquire the networking technologies that would honour an enterprise's routing requests. The result may be a long period of risk for those organisations determined to send and to receive whatever data they deem necessary through whatever jurisdictions happen to provide the most expeditious routing.

13

Police Records of Crime

Countries all over the world follow the same definitions of crime, the legal and administrative systems of each country often constrain the statistics that are available. Many countries have several police systems. Countries with a federal structure often have provincial police: others may have police whose jurisdiction only extends to particular areas of the country (e.g., the capital city, royal parks, safari parks) and other police may have jurisdiction over certain types of offences (e.g., fraud, illegal trafficking in antiques, environmental crimes).

The typical duties, even of regular police, may vary considerably from country to country. In fact, the day-to-day activities of the police officer may affect how and what is recorded as a crime, and even the level or rank of a police officer also contributes to what events are recorded as crimes. Examples of typical day-to-day activities of police in Thailand, where police have extensive crime and other recording responsibilities, demonstrate how crimes may or may not end up as recorded statistics.

There are many countries without national crime reporting systems that nevertheless utilise local police recording of crime as their source of crime statistics. Modern methods of countering crime require public confidence in all crime prevention agencies and government departments responsible for eliminating long term causes of crime—and not just the police. The amount of crime the public reports to the police is directly proportional to the confidence the public has in the police, especially in whether the police are likely to be able to solve the crime experienced.

The private security industry is very important, and very large numbers of such people are employed, often by the government. In many cases those in authority will choose not to take the case further, but rather will deal with it themselves without calling in the police. In such cases the authority will deal directly with the offender or by employing informal criminal justice proceedings. Such crimes are unlikely to be recorded by the official police, who would likely not regard them as part of their work load even if they knew about them.

As a country's development progresses, its ability to cope with more sophisticated crime recording systems will grow also. Better systems come with growth in the availability of telephones to the general population, and progress in education, both among those collecting the data and those analysing it.

Nations which have undergone many recent changes in their form of government and administration are unlikely to have stabilised their crime data collections. Developments in police technology are important: the easier it is to record crime, the more likely it is for crime to be recorded accurately and completely. This technology factor may contribute considerably to the body of data that is finally reported as a country's national statistics.

Definitions of recorded crime used in the fifth *UN Survey of Crime Trends and Operation of Criminal Justice Systems* are given below.

— *Intentional homicide*: Refers to death deliberately inflicted on a person by another person, including infanticide. Countries were asked to indicate whether certain categories were charged or prosecuted as "aggravated assault".

— *Non-intentional homicide*: Refers to death not deliberately inflicted on a person by another person. This includes the crime of manslaughter, but excludes traffic accidents that result in the death of persons.

— *Assault*: Refers to physical attack against the body of another person, including battery but excluding indecent assault. Some criminal or penal codes distinguish between aggravated and simple assault depending on the degree of resulting injury. Countries were asked to provide the major criterion for this distinction of it applied in their country.

— *Rape*: Refers to sexual intercourse without valid consent. Countries were asked to indicate whether statutory rape was included in the figures provided.

— *Theft:* Refers to the removal of property without the property owner's consent. Theft excludes burglary or housebreaking. It includes the theft of a motor vehicle. Shoplifting and other minor offences may or may not be included as thefts. Countries were asked to provide details.

— *Robbery*: Refers to the theft of property from a person, overcoming resistance by force or threat of force.

— *Burglary*: Refers to unlawful entry into someone else's property with an intention to commit a crime.

— *Fraud:* Refers to the acquisition of the property of another by deception. Countries were asked to give details of whether the fraudulent obtaining of financial property was included.

— *Embezzlement*: Refers to the wrongful appropriation of property of another which is already in one's possession.

— *Drug-related crimes:* Refers to intentional acts that may involve cultivation, production, manufacture, extraction, preparation, offering for sale, distribution, purchase, sale, delivery on any terms whatsoever, brokerage, dispatch in transit, transport, importation and exportation of drugs and isotropic substances. Separate statistics on possession and traffic were requested.

— *Bribery and corruption*: Refers to requesting and/or accepting material or personal benefit, or promise thereof, in connection with the performance of a public function or an action that may or may not be a violation of law and/or promising as well as giving material or personal benefit to a public officer in exchange for a requested favour.

— *Other:* Refers to serious types of crime completely different from those listed above and regarded as serious and frequent enough to require a separate category in the criminal statistics of a particular country. Countries were asked to provide details.

— *Crimes recorded by the police*: Refers to the number of penal code offences or their equivalent but excluding minor road traffic and other petty offences, brought to the attention of the police or other law enforcement agencies and recorded by one of those agencies.

GLOBAL VIEW OF CRIME

Reports of crime are dominated by property crime, mainly theft and burglary. Theft comprises around half of all reported crime and burglary a further 20 per cent. Personal crime constitutes a much smaller proportion, with assaults forming about seven per cent and robberies a further six per cent. Drug-related crime made up about six per cent. This general pattern varies greatly throughout the world, however. As a proportion of total reported crime, theft comprises as little as 20 per cent in some countries but over 60 per cent in others. Robbery comprises under one per cent in most Western European countries but over ten per cent in several Latin American countries.

Crime rates change at different rates for different offences and for different countries. Some of these changes, especially those between two different UN surveys, are almost certainly partly due to changes in the definition of what is reported to the UN, or to boundary or legislative changes in the reporting country. Changes for the period 1990-1994 are more stable because the figures all come from the Fifth UNCJS (UN Crime Trends and Operation of Criminal Justice Systems) More countries reported all increase in crime over the period 1990 to 1994 than reported a stable situation or a decrease. A large number of countries, however, showed a fall in crime over the period, with 17 out of 69 countries showing a fall in total crime and as many as 26 out of 60 countries showing a fall in robbery figures.

In contrast, only seven countries reported that drug offences had fallen and only 12 countries reported that assaults had fallen. Few countries showed stable crime rates over the period 1990-1994. The most stable offence type was rape, but even for rape only eight countries showed stability compared with 42 which showed a rise and 17 which showed a fall. Changes between the mid-1980s and the mid-1990s are more difficult to interpret.

A third set of countries reported more than twice as many homicides during the period. Few countries showed a stable situation and there was very little pattern in the level of change shown. There was more pattern in the reporting of rape offences, with about 40 per cent of countries reporting arise of between 10 and 50 per cent. Thirteen more countries reported rises of more than 50 per cent, and many of these will have done so because of police actions which show more sympathy to rape victims which has encouraged the reporting and recording of rape incidents to a greater extent than in the past.

Forty per cent of countries either reported a stable situation or a fall in the number of reported thefts. A further quarter of countries reported a rise of between 10 and 50 per cent, which is comparable with the five per cent year-on-year increase which some European countries such as England and Wales have reported for the whole of the twentieth century. Eight countries reported a more than doubling of the number of thefts, but some of these may have been due to changes in definitions.

CRIME RATES

Typically, about 50 to 60 countries reported a figure for the above mentioned crimes in 1994. These figures were converted to crime rates and then arranged according to the UN region in which the country was situated. The year 1994 was chosen as it is the latest date for which data are available. There was considerable variation for every offence, both between regions and even within regions. However, not too much should be read into the differences shown, because the number of countries reporting from each region, for each offence, was very different.

A region with fewer than three countries reporting for a particular offence was excluded for that offence. The extent of reporting from other regions was varied. Moreover the variation reported is not necessarily an indication that the actual occurrence of crime in those regions varies in the same way: we may simply be measuring a different propensity to report a particular crime in those regions or a regional variation in the way a crime is defined.

Rates of rape offences ranged from under ten to over 750 per million population, with well over half the countries reporting rates under 100 per million. The median reporting rate was 65 and three quarters of all countries reported a rate between 15 and 300 per million. The UN region with the highest median reporting rate was North America and the lowest was the Arab states. Although the median reported rates in all other regions were much more moderate, there was considerable variation within all these regions.

Assaults rates for individual nations ranged from under 100 to over 10,000 per million population, with well over half of the countries reporting a rate of under 1,000. The median reporting rate was 780 per million, and three quarters of countries reported a rate between 140 and 4,200. Different countries record an assault in different ways, with some holding to a medical definition (e.g., days off work) and others holding to a legal definition. Moreover, it is likely that in countries where there is a good deal of experienced violence and homicide, less serious assaults will be less likely to be reported.

Rates of homicide offences ranges between 18 and 230 per million population. There was quite a spread of rates reported in most regions. However, the lowest median reported rates were in Arab states and Western Europe, with the highest rates reported in Latin America and sub-Saharan Africa. Rates in Eastern Europe and in North America were about the same. Moreover, as a result of political change over recent times, the availability of illegal firearms is very high.

The region with the highest reported median rate for robbery was Latin America, closely followed by North America. East Asia and the African (sub-Saharan) regions reported rates around a half of American rates. Western and Eastern Europe reported much lower robbery rates, typically a quarter of those in America, and reported rates in the Arab states were extremely low.

The median reporting rate of theft offences was 59, and 90 per cent of countries reported a rate between three and 560 per 10,000. There were considerable variations in the median rates reported in the various UN regions. Theft rates were very much the lowest in the Arab states while moderate rates were reported in Sub-Saharan Africa, Eastern Europe and Latin America, and high rates were reported in Western Europe and North America.

Only 53 countries reported burglary rates, with the median reported rate just under 2,000 per million population. However, the variation was very great, with Western Europe and North America reporting rates of over 10,000, and with some Western European countries reporting rates twice as high as this.

In the case of fraud offences, the variation was less than most other offences, with Arab states reporting the lowest rate at 105 and sub-Saharan African states reporting a rate of 1,049. Fraud in Western Europe was higher than the median, with reported fraud in East Asia and Latin America being around the median.

The median reporting rate for drug-related crime was 531 per million population, with Eastern Europe and Asia reporting a median rate of under 200 and African (sub-Saharan) states reporting a rate of over 1,100. Arab states reported a rate of 376, and Western Europe reported a high rate of 934 per million.

The median rate reported for embezzlement was 122 per million population, with Western and Eastern Europe and Latin America reporting only a little more than this. The rates reported in sub-Saharan Africa were very much higher. Arab states reported very low rates.

CRIME AND URBAN LIFE

Measurement of urban and rural differences across countries presents special methodological problems.

First, the designation of areas as urban and rural varies from country to country and thus the international comparability of urban-rural is seriously impaired.

A second problem in the comparisons of urban and rural areas is the diversity of rural areas across countries, and very often even within one country. While urban areas tend to have common characteristics, such as urban centres, apartment buildings and main traffic arteries, rural areas cover everything from remote mountain villages and seaside resorts to high density settlements in relatively close proximity to urban agglomerations.

Another methodological issue concerns methods of recording crime. In most cases, crimes reported to the police are recorded on the basis of their place of occurrence. But police districts do not necessarily conform to the urban/rural subdivisions of the country. Jurisdiction of one police district may spread to both urban and rural communities and it would be very difficult, if not impossible, to properly distinguish an urban/rural breakdown for statistics provided by such a district.

In countries with more developed criminal justice statistics systems, though, these issues have been successfully resolved by introducing more complex coding procedures.

Illustrative statistics on urban/rural differences in the level and structure of crime are presented in the *Compendium of Human Settlements Statistics 1995* (United Nations, 1995). These statistics were collected from national statistical offices and compiled by the United Nations Statistics Division. Due to the methodological complexities of providing data on crimes reported to the police by urban/rural breakdown, not many national statistical offices were able to comply with the request for data.

These illustrative data indicate that crimes are reported more frequently in urban than rural areas. For example, in the Netherlands one crime is reported in urban areas every 37 seconds, whereas in rural areas the corresponding period is 117 seconds (almost two minutes). In urban areas of Cyprus, one crime is reported every three hours, compared to over 11 hours in rural areas. In some countries this difference is even more significant: in Poland, in a four- minute period there are over five reported crimes in urban areas and only one in rural areas.

The share of population living in urban and rural areas is not equal, so that it is necessary to provide crime rates in order to provide a balanced overview of the occurrence of crime. The crime rate reported here is a derived indicator showing the number of recorded crimes per 1,000 population in urban and rural areas, respectively. The crime rates vary significantly from country to country. Taking into account all the limitations of the data, statistics for these countries indicate that in both absolute (the total number of crimes) and relative terms (crime rates), crimes were much more frequent in urban than rural environments. These illustrative data from the few countries supplying urban and rural data suggest the importance of urban/rural location in explaining the levels of crime.

High homicide rates were reported for several Latin American cities, New York and Northern European cities, with lower rates for other European cities, and very low rates for Hong Kong, Tokyo, Nicosia and Cairo. More cities reported rates for robbery and although the pattern is less clear, there is much more variation than for homicide. It is not necessarily the same cities which are highest for both robbery and homicide.

A separate source of data also supports the notion that crime occurs at a much higher level in cities than in rural areas. These data were collected using a similar method to that of the UNCJS, requesting national correspondents of member countries to provide statistics (crimes recorded by the police) for a standard set of crimes from their official records. There are also many additional difficulties in comparing urban/rural crime rates.

Police districts often do not coincide with urban/rural distinctions and what may be defined as rural in one country may not be so considered in another. Those in close-knit rural communities may be less inclined to report crimes to the police, or in the "anonymous city" bystanders may ignore crime around them. However, even taking into account all these difficulties, there seems to be a preponderance of evidence to support the claim that crime is, generally speaking, distributed more heavily into urban areas in most countries for which there are data.

When countries were arranged by their level of income, theft rates were seen to rise sharply as income rose, with high income countries having a median theft rate of over 200 per 10,000 population, medium income countries having a rate of around 50 and low income countries having a rate of around two per 10,000. This mainly reflects the fact that there is a good deal more opportunity to steal in richer countries: however, it also reflects the likelihood that in countries with little wealth more possessions are held in common. Homicide rates show a very different pattern, with higher rates in medium and low income countries compared to high income countries.

The reasons for this are less easy to interpret; opportunities are the same in all countries, but better medical facilities and communications may save more lives in rich countries than in poor countries. The pattern of crime when compared with the economic development status of countries is difficult to assess. This is because there were very few countries reporting crime which were classified as being least developed. Median theft rates for industrial countries were over 100 per 10,000 population compared with under 20 for developing countries, and this finding holds even when development is measured either by income or the United Nationals Development Programmes (UNDP) development classification.

The median homicide rates for industrial countries and for developing countries were about the same in 1994 when measured by the UNDP development classification. However, when measured by income level, the medium income countries showed a rate of homicide much higher than the high income countries. It will also be noted that this finding does not conform with the Global Snapshot, where the homicide level is considerably higher for developed countries. Although there are several explanations for this difference, the main one is probably that the Global Snapshot included least developed countries within the developing country group.

Unrecorded Crimes

We have focused mainly on those familiar crimes of homicide, assault, rape, robbery, theft and burglary, with a brief mention of fraud and embezzlement. These traditional, official categories of crime have become over the years of the UNCJS reasonably widely accepted international categories. However, there has been much recent concern about types of crime that, because of their nature and mode of committal, are unrepresented in the official police records of crime. However, police recorded crime figures and household victim surveys have increasingly become regarded in recent years as insufficient to give a full picture of the varied amount of crime, of different sorts, that occurs.

There has been a need to produce measures of crime against sectors of the economy other than households and to took for methodologies that attempt to gather some figures for the whole area of organised, transnational and environmental crime. Three important methods of data collection are given below:

— There is the need to consider commercial victims, and this is covered by surveys of different types of commercial establishments.

— There has been considerable investment in surveys which ask offenders about their experience of offending.

— The final area of methodological development is the attempt to measure complex crime such as organised crime, transnational crime and terrorism.

Complex Crimes

The UNCJS has confined its data collection to statistics on traditional crimes. There is good reason for this: these crimes, mostly, are relatively simple discreet events. A homicide is a homicide; a burglary is a burglary. Even though there has been much discussion over the years concerning the definitions of these crimes internationally, it has generally proved possible for most participating countries to adjust their official records of crime to fit these definitions.

However, one can readily see that the definition of fraud, for example, is very broad and makes for much difficulty for national correspondents to provide statistics. This is because frauds of various kinds are not discreet events: rather, they may involve a long series of events all of which may be separate crimes in themselves the organised crime and transnational crime fit squarely into this category as well.

Organised Crime

Different authors have used slightly different definitions for organised crime, and this problem of definition has gotten in the way of attempts to collect information on this type of crime. The same problems also apply to transnational crime, which is in many ways related to organised crime, and to environmental crime. The UN has sponsored a whole series of activities, conferences and resolutions in the area of organised crime.

Documentation on this was most recently collated for the Ninth UN Congress in Egypt in 1995. In particular the papers for the world ministerial conference on organised transnational crime in November 1994 (included in the Congress papers) are an excellent summary of the position. Various attempts have been made by the UN to collect statistics on organised crime, but the most successful body for collecting data so far has been the European Union, which has been able to concentrate on a smaller geographical area.

The typology used in recent years by the European Union, and which seems likely to be copied by other groups. This typology defined 11 characteristics which typify organised crime, of which six must be present for an incident or series of incidents to be defined as organised. The latest published report of the European Union on organised crime concludes that present evidence clearly demonstrates the international dimension of organised crime.

The foreign origin of suspects and criminal groups is the predominant characteristic of organised crime. Member states identify organised criminal activity as a worldwide phenomenon operating across national boundaries which pose no significant obstacle to those involved. Historical, cultural and geographic factors, influence the distribution of organised criminal groups of foreign origin. Other features of organised crime covered in the European report include the following:

- — In some countries commercial business type structures were used in three quarters of the cases;
- — Violence is often used both between and within groups and on victims;
- — Influence is used in only a minority of cases, typically 10 to 20 per cent; and
- — Well over half of the organised groups were involved in money laundering.

An important general feature of organised crime is that the offences committed under this heading are typically prosecuted under the normal criminal code, in the same way as for other offences such as homicide, robbery or assault, etc., which are not "organised".

In most statistical data collections such crimes are not identified separately. However, there are many examples where different countries have attempted to analyse crimes which can be attributed to a particular phenomenon, whether organised crime or political violence.

Organised Crime in Europe

The European Union (EU) produces a situation report on organised crime every year. This is based on data sent in by member states and by the EUROPOL Drugs Unit. The availability of data and the usefulness of the annual situation report have improved greatly over the 1990s, but a good deal still needs to be done in developing a work able methodology for measuring and describing the amount of organised crime which exists, either in one country or a region such as Western Europe. The present methodology of the EU consists of the following definitions. At least six of the following characteristics must be present, three of which must be those numbered 1, 5 and 11, for any crime or criminal group to be classified as organised crime.

i) Collaboration of more than two people;
ii) Each with appointed tasks;
iii) For a prolonged or indefinite period of time;
iv) Using some form of discipline or control;
v) Suspected of the commission of serious criminal offences;
vi) Operating on all international level;
vii) Using violence or other means suitable for intimidation;
viii) Using commercial or businesslike structure;
ix) Engaged in money laundering;
x) Exerting influence on politics, the media, public administration, judicial authorities or economy; and
xii) Determined by the pursuit of profit and/or power.

Information on the following topics is required in country reports:

i) Characteristics of the suspects involved;
ii) Criminal activities:
iii) Places and regions of activity;
iv) Resources involved;
v) Use of violence;
vi) Use of "influence"; and
vii) Money laundering.

SELF-REPORT SURVEYS OF OFFENDING

Self-report surveys of offending have become more popular in recent years and despite a natural concern about whether people will admit, conceal or exaggerate offending, the results from such surveys have proved to be quite robust when compared with other estimates of crime.

A particular series of surveys on the self-reported offending of young people was conducted in various European countries during the early 1990s. At that time little was known about how many young people started offending; why some young people who committed offences stopped whilst others continued to commit crime as adults; what types of offences young people claimed to commit; and differences by age, sex, socioeconomic and psychological background. Differences in the way the data were collected in different countries have made the analysis of international comparisons from these surveys awkward and such results are not expected for some time.

The key points which came out of the survey in England and Wales in 1993 were as follows:

— Involvement in offending and drug use amongst young people is widespread.

— Every other male and every third female admitted to committing offences and the same numbers admitted using drugs at some time.

— The most offending is minor and is most drug use the confined to cannabis.

— Females aged 14 to 17 are nearly as likely as males to be involved in offending but as they get older, this offending drops off sharply in comparison with males.

— The rate of participation in property crime by males increases with age, whereas for females it declines.

— The seriousness and frequency of all offending by males and females declines with age.

The main influences on starting to offend are low parental supervision, persistent truancy and associating with others involved in offending.

14

Victim Empowerment

Victimisation surveys are direct sources of statistics concerning the operations of criminal justice systems. The surveys offer a clear picture of how the public views the criminal justice system as well as a number of other perceptions in regard to crime. There are a number of methodological problems relating to the measurement of crime using official records, just as there are also difficulties in using victimisation reports as a measure of crime. A special problem with victimisation surveys is that while they seem to overcome the thorny problem of the different legal definitions of crimes in different legal systems, they depend nevertheless on the cultural perception of crime that may affect the respondents.

Each measure of crime, whether victim survey or official record, is useful in its own right. The International Crime Victim Survey (ICVS), which was initiated in 1987, has been implemented so far in 55 different countries under the supervision of an international working group. In total more than 133,821 citizens have been interviewed within the framework of the ICVS.

In some countries attempts are now being made to survey commercial victimisation. These surveys ask both retail and manufacturing premises directly about the crimes they have experienced in a particular period of time. Major advantages of this approach include:

i) not all crimes are reported to the police by victims,

ii) police statistics do not separately identify the type of victim or gather much detail about the nature of the crime against commercial premises,

iii) although surveys of head offices are useful for gathering information kept centrally, individual premises may not report all crimes to head office, and

iv) surveys can measure the extent of repeat victimisation of the same premises and identify the factors that put some premises at greater risk than others.

Major disadvantages of the approach are:

i) the survey is relatively costly,
ii) only crimes of which the victim was aware can be covered by such a survey, and
iii) some types of theft and all types of fraud, are more difficult to detect and are therefore likely to be under-counted.

There are difficulties in using statistics of crimes recorded by the police for comparative purposes because of differences in legal definitions and recording practices. By bypassing the state agencies and interviewing individuals directly, survey researchers can overcome some of these obstacles. The credibility of the ICVS, however, hinges on whether citizens in different corners of the world share a set of basic norms defining criminal acts such as violence and theft.

In the current philosophical climate of post-modernism, the assumption of shared norms cannot be taken for granted. It is most questionable concerning forms of domestic violence against women since the definitions of such offences may be even more culture-bound than definitions of other crimes. Since the ICVS project originates from Western countries, cultural biases might have been introduced into its questionnaire and other instruments. To minimise such bias, researchers from various regions took part in evaluation sessions of the instruments used.

Although some questions were less relevant in some national settings than others, for example, questions concerning either cars or bicycles, respondents nowhere had serious difficulty in understanding the core questions on victimisations by crime. This result by itself lends some support to the assumption that certain basic concepts concerning conventional crimes are common, at least among the inhabitants of urban areas. In the last two sweeps of the survey, victims were asked to assess the seriousness of the incidents they reported to the interviewer. The assessments were made on a simple three point scale, indicating very serious, somewhat serious and not very serious.

Table 14. 1.

Ranking of crimes in terms of seriousness by victims.

Cases	*Africa*	*Asia*	*Eastern and Central Europe*	*Latin America*	*New World*	*Western Europe*
Car crimes	1	1	1	1	4	2
Joy-riding	2	2	2	3	5	4
Robbery	4	5	5	6	2	1
Violence against women	5	6	3	4	3	3
Sexual harassment	3	7	4	5	1	6
Motorcycle thefts	8	3	6	2	8	8
Burglary	7	9	7	7	7	5
Assault	9	4	8	8	6	7
Threats	17	12	12	9	11	11
Pick-pocketing	10	13	11	13	10	10
Bicycle theft	11	17	10	12	13	15
Theft from car	6	11	15	16	16	16
Car vandalism	14	15	17	17	17	17

Table 14. 1 presents the rank order of the different types of crime of the six global regions. On the basis of the mean scores, the crime types were subsequently rank ordered for all countries together and per region and country. Crime types which were rated as the most serious were given the highest rank. The results show how victims in various regions and countries rank different types of crime in terms of seriousness. The ranking of offences in seriousness terms shows a striking similarity across the regions.

Victims consistently hold violence against women, robbery with a weapon, motorcycle theft and sexual harassment as the most serious types of crime. Moderately serious were considered burglary, theft from car, pick-pocketing, car vandalism and threats. The least serious are considered car theft, joy-riding, robbery without a weapon and other personal theft. There are very few deviations from this overall pattern. The consensus on the seriousness of various types of conventional crimes must be based on a common understanding of the behavioural elements which make up these crimes and of their impact upon victims. It also implies that victims across the world apply similar standards for judging the seriousness of these incidents.

The results lend support to the underlying assumption of the ICVS that definitions, perceptions and normative judgements about conventional crimes are fairly universal. Although the legal definitions of conventional crimes differ, the meaning of basic concepts like street robbery, burglary or rape seem to be understood by the public in roughly the same way everywhere. There seems to be no *a priori* reason to refrain from comparative studies in this field.

DETERMINANTS OF CRIME

A major theoretical perspective currently used to understand levels of crime, explains the extent of offending, as broadly determined by factors, which increase the motivation to offend, or present criminal opportunities. Motivational pressures have been interpreted as emanating from socioeconomic strain. Indicators of such strain are unemployment, income inequality or dissatisfaction with income. Motivations to offend have also been linked to the process of modernisation, which is seen to weaken informal community control and impose modern norms of individualism and consumerism. The importance of criminal opportunities sterns from the notion that more people will be tempted to commit crimes if suitable opportunities for illegal profits abound.

This analysis is focused on three broad measures of the most serious forms of crime.

The first draws together the crimes which are rated as the most serious by victims (e.g., burglary, thefts of and from cars), and the three most serious categories of contact crimes (robbery with weapon, violence against women and sexual harassment). This combined measure we call from hereon more serious crime.

The second measure is the subset of contact crimes itself (robbery, sexual assault and assault).

Thirdly we will look at the correlates of violence against women in particular. In this analysis the data were used from all national and city surveys carried out between 1989 and 1996.

Urbanisation was the strongest factor explaining risks across different countries for more serious crimes. Victimisation by more serious crime is strongly correlated with increases in the proportion of the population living in larger cities. Lower affluence was significantly associated with higher risk of victimisation by more serious crime. This result provides a challenge to modernisation theory, which holds that less developed countries are characterised by lower levels of property crimes. The relationship between affluence and serious crime is mediated by the measure of socioeconomic strain: the proportion of young males who were dissatisfied with their household income.

In developing countries and the countries in transition there are more young males who feel economically deprived. This factor is strongly related to a high level of serious crime. The inverse relationship between affluence and serious crime is weakened, however, by an intervening factor. In more affluent countries people go out more often in the evening for recreational purposes. In a multivariate analysis this factor is positively related to high crime risks.

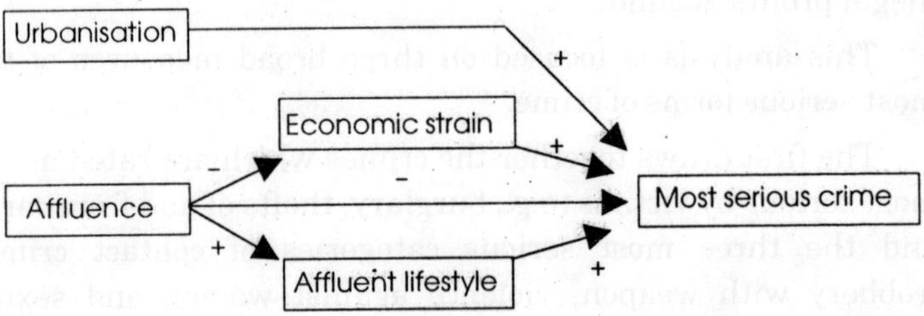

Figure 14. 1. Causes of serious crime according to ICVS 1989-1996 surveys

Factors urbanisation, economic strain and lifestyle accounted for 57 per cent of the variance in victimisation rates of 49 countries. With regard to contact crimes, economic strain was the strongest factor explaining risks. A second factor of importance explaining the level of contact crime per country was the rate of handgun ownership.

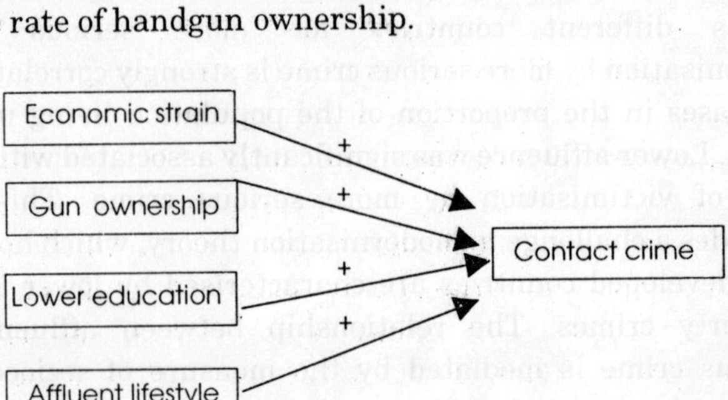

Figure 14. 2. Correlations of contact according to ICVS 1989-1996 surveys

In countries where more households possess one or more handguns the risk of contact crime is higher. Gun ownership is significantly related to both the level of robberies and the level of sexual incidents. It is not statistically significantly related to non-sexual threats/assaults. However, the relationship between gun ownership and threats/assaults with a gun is very strong. Statistically significant relationships were also found with lifestyle and level of education: risk of contact crimes are higher in countries where more people go out in the evening for recreational purposes and in countries where the average level of education is lower. The national homicide rates are clearly related to the level of gun ownership. The results of the ICVS analyses show that high levels of gun ownership such as in the USA, the former Yugoslavia, South Africa and several Latin American countries are strongly related to higher levels of violence in general.

Certain groups in society are more victimised than others for a variety of reasons. One of these groups is women, so that we looked at the correlates at macro level of violence against women. With regard to these risks economic strain was again the strongest predictor. In countries where more young males and others suffer from resource deprivation, more violence against women is committed.

The problems of economic strain or resource deprivation is related to violenced against women. Some economically deprived males seem to ventilate their stress and frustrations by assaulting women in their social environment. In the developing world, less sexual violence was measured in countries, where women are better educated, marry at a higher age and take contraception measures more often. In accordance with feminist perspectives, violence against women is more prevalent in countries where women possess low status.

Another factor which was found to be independently related to high risks of violence against women was the proportion of divorced women. This relationship is only found among the developed countries. Countries with the highest rates of violence against women in the Western world are the USA, New Zealand, Finland, England and Wales, and Sweden. In these countries the divorce rate is fairly high. There is no obvious causal interpretation of the statistical relationship between high divorce rates and violence against women in the more affluent countries.

Though at the micro level serious violence against women is strongly related to separation and divorce in the sense that women attempting to leave men are frequent homicide victims, the hypothesis that at the macro level a causal relationship exists between high rates of separation and divorce and serious violence seems to merit further scrutiny.

Affluence is positively related to most serious crimes only through the measure of lifestyle. The level of crime is determined by opportunity structures, such as an outgoing lifestyle and the ownership of cars or guns. Some of those opportunity structures are more common in more affluent countries. Others, like gun ownership, are unrelated to levels of affluence. The level of gun ownership is determined by cultural and legal traditions. In more affluent nations there is less economic strain, which reduces the propensity to seek profit by committing serious crime and/or violent crime. At the same time, though, a more outgoing lifestyle related to affluence may increase the supply of opportunities for certain forms of crime.

Thus affluence acts both as a brake on crime and a catalyst of it. The dual impact of affluence on serious crime explains why risks of crime are high in almost all urban areas of the world, regardless of the level of affluence. These results challenge the conventional notion that the problems of crime are automatically solved by economic growth. To increase urban safety, special policies and measures such as more stringent control of gun ownership are called for.

Some of the moderately affluent countries like South Africa, Argentina and Brazil seem to be in double jeopardy. In their main cities fairly large groups of economically deprived adolescents converge with well-to-do members of middle classes, providing ample opportunities for crime. In addition, the level of gun ownership is high. Similar animinogenic situations arise in Western countries and countries in transition where income disparities are growing under the influence of global market forces and guns are becoming more widely available.

VICTIMISATION RATES IN URBAN AREAS

More than half of urban respondents report being victimised by crime, no matter what part of the world. The key findings of the ICVS survey are the percentages of the public victimised by crime over the past five years from the day respondents are interviewed. To ensure comparability of the rates from national surveys and city surveys, five year rates per country were calculated for respondents living in cities with more than 100,000 inhabitants. Data from countries where the survey was carried out twice or more were averaged. The victimisation rates presented here give comparable information on the experiences of the public with crime over the course of five years in the period 1989-1996.

Half of urban respondents report being victimised by crime, no matter what part of the world they inhabit. The overall five-year victimisation rates are highest in Latin America and Africa, where three of every four citizens living in urban areas were victimised at least once. The overall victimisation rates are the lowest in Asian cities. Table 2 presents the urban five-year victimisation rates for four different types of crime for the six global regions.

Distribution of car-related crimes stands out from other crimes. The level of the latter crimes is determined by the availability of suitable targets. It is of interest that property crimes are higher in Africa, which runs against the popular assumption that where there is more property there is more to steal. Rather, the relatively high rates in Africa may reflect lack of security in dwellings and other aspects of social life.

Table 14. 2.

Percentage of public victimised by selected crimes: results of international crime surveys 1989-1996.

Cases	*Africa*	*Asia*	*Eastern and Central Europe*	*Latin America*	*New World*	*Western Europe*
Car crimes	22	8	28	30	45	37
Burglary	35	11	18	32	23	14
Other thefts	42	30	32	42	27	27
Contact crimes	32	13	17	36	20	16

Contact crimes are highest in Latin America and Africa. The level of contact crimes here is about twice as high as elsewhere. The level of contact crimes is fairly high in the New World countries (Canada, USA, Australia and New Zealand). It is the lowest in Asia and Western Europe.

For violence against men and women special rates were calculate. The first rate includes assaults where force was actually used. The second rate, for violence against women, includes both non-sexual assaults and sexual assaults, excluding less serious sexual incidents. Violence against women shows a different pattern than violence against men.

In the Western countries (Europe and the New World) men are as often assaulted as women. The level of violence is fairly high in the New World countries for both men and women. In the rest of the world there is a considerable gender difference: the risk of being assaulted is much higher for women than for men.

The risk of being assaulted for men in Latin America or Africa is roughly equal to that in the New World countries. But the risk for women is 50 per cent higher.

In Asian cities women are also more at risk than men. The violence problems of many developing countries specifically take the form of violence against women.

Assaults on women are more likely to be domestic in nature than assaults on men. In more than a quarter of these cases, the offender was known by name to the victim. In almost half the cases, the crime was committed in or near the victim's own home.

Domestic violence is a major social problem in Latin America, Africa and the New World countries in particular. The notion of high crime rates as unique features of some unfortunate nations is not supported. The experience of being criminally victimised has become a statistically normal feature of urban life all over the world, though the type of victimisation varies.

The rates of property crimes have gone down in many of the most industrialised countries. One possible explanation is that improved security has reduced the opportunities for crimes like burglary and car theft. In the rest of the world, the level of protection against crime is considerably lower. In these countries no decline in crime trends is yet in evidence. If present trends in protection against crime continue, the gap in levels of safety between developed countries and developing countries will become even wider.

Other sources of data also indicate that certain groups in particular countries may be more victimised than others, particularly in regard to minority groups and the young and commercial establishments, whose losses may be especially high.

The 1996 sweep of the ICVS included a question on the solicitation of bribes by government officials during the last year. The results show that this type of corruption is most diffused in Latin America (21.3 per cent), Africa (18.8 per cent) and Asia (14.6 per cent). The rate was moderately high in Central and Eastern Europe (10.7 per cent) and lowest in

Western Europe (0.7 per cent) and the New World countries (1 per cent). The high prevalence of street level corruption in developing countries and countries in transition adds to the burden of conventional crime in these parts of the world.

VICTIMS ROLE IN CRIMINAL JUSTICE

In recent times, criminal justice agencies in more and more countries have set themselves the task of rendering direct services to crime victims as an independent goal. Many other governmental and voluntary organisations have also improved their provision of services to crime victims. International standards for this were formulated in the UN *Declaration on the Basic Principles of Justice for Victims of Crime and Abuse of Power of 1985.*

By satisfactorily addressing the needs of victims that arise from their victimisation, state agencies can help to empower them. Such victim empowerment has been shown to be of great psychological and practical importance for victims. The acknowledgment and practical and emotional support given by criminal justice personnel helps them to cope better with the consequences of their victimisation and to regain their confidence in the state and the community at large.

Victims have a role beyond serving as a witnesses or providing evidence. The role is often of the nature of assisting at the trial, or formally appealing the prosecutor's decision not to prosecute or to dismiss the case. For example, in Hungary the victim can initiate the asking of questions at trial.

In several countries, however, the prosecutor will not carry through with proceedings unless the victim initiates action. Also, in nations such as China and Hungary, there are certain circumstances where a case may be prosecuted privately, and in Venezuela, there are certain situations when a case must be prosecuted in this manner. This is not the same as a civil trial, and still involves criminal charges.

In countries where the victim has a role in some part of the criminal justice system, it is usually in the preparatory proceedings or during the trial itself. The victim usually has no part in the sentencing phase of the process, where such a separate stage exists in the legal system in question. There are some exceptions, however. For example, in the Republic of Ireland the victim is allowed to make a victim impact statement, and in Republic of Korea it is constitutionally prescribed that a victim may present his or her opinion during the sentencing phase.

There does not seem to be a trend in terms of the type of nation which gives the victim a role in the criminal justice process. For example, there are both developed and developing countries that allow such a role, and there are also examples of both types of nations which do not allow the victim to play a part. Also, nations with political systems ranging from communist to democratic can be found among those in which the victim does have a role. Conversely, there are a wide range of governing styles represented among nations which do not allow victim participation in the process.

In England, there are specific helping agencies, such as Rape Crisis Centres, as well as a national umbrella organisation known as the National Association of Victim Support Schemes. It provides a national voice to the victim movement, and also gives help on a case-by-case basis to victims referred by the police. Also, there is a Criminal Injuries Compensation Board which oversees a programme for compensating victims of violent crime. This compensation occurs regardless of whether or not the offender is identified.

In US, although the victim has no direct role in criminal prosecution, has published a Victim's Charter which sets standards in order to guide criminal justice agencies in their interaction with victims.

In Cuba, there are organisations called Committees for the Defence of the Revolution (CDRs). These are neighbourhood associations organised at the block level, and offer services such as medical care, social welfare assistance and counselling services to crime victims. These polyclinics are organised into a nationwide system. Even though it is evident that there is concern for giving assistance to victims, Cuba has no specific victims' rights legislation.

UN Declaration on the Basic Principles of Justice for Victims of Crime and Abuse of Power of 1985

Access to justice and fair treatment

4) Victims are entitled to access to the mechanisms of justice and to prompt redress, as provided for by national legislation, for the harm that they have suffered.
5) Judicial and administrative mechanisms should be established and strengthened where necessary to enable victims to obtain redress through formal or informal procedures that are expeditious, fair, inexpensive and accessible.
6) The responsiveness of judicial and administrative processes to the needs of victims should be facilitated by:
    a) Informing victims of their role and the scope, timing and progress of the proceedings and of the disposition of their cases, especially where serious crimes are involved and where they have requested such information,
    b) Allowing the views and concerns of victims to be presented and considered at appropriate stages of the proceedings where their personal interests are affected, without prejudice to the accused and consistent with the relevant national criminal justice system,
    c) Providing proper assistance to victims throughout the legal process,

d) Taking measures to minimise inconvenience to victims, protect their privacy, when necessary, and ensure their safety, as well as that of their families and witnesses on their behalf, from intimidation and retaliation, and

e) Avoiding unnecessary delay in the disposition of cases and the execution of orders or decrees granting awards to victims.

7) Informal mechanisms for the resolution of disputes, including mediation, arbitration and customary justice or indigenous practices, should be utilised where appropriate to facilitate conciliation and redress for victims.

Restitution

8) Offenders or third parties responsible for their behaviour should, where appropriate, make fair restitution to victims, their families or dependents. Such restitution should include the return of property or payment for the harm or loss suffered, reimbursement of expenses incurred as a result of the victimisation, the provision of services and the restoration of rights.

9) Governments should review their practices, regulations and laws to consider resolution as an available sentencing option in criminal cases, in addition to other criminal sanctions.

10) In cases of substantial harm to the environment, restitution, if ordered, should include, as far as possible, restoration of environment, reconstruction of the infrastructure, replacement of community facilities and reimbursement of the expenses of relocation, whenever, such harm results in the dislocation of a community.

11) Where public officials or other agents acting in an official or quasi-official capacity have violated national criminal laws, the victims should receive restitution from the state

whose officials or agents were responsible for the harm inflicted.

Compensation

12) When compensation is not fully available from the offender or other sources, states should endeavour to provide financial compensation to:

a) Victims who have sustained significant bodily injury or impairment of physical or mental health as a result of serious crimes,

b) The family, in particular dependents of persons who have died or become physically or mentally incapacitated as a result of such victimisation.

13) The establishment, strengthening and expansion of national funds for compensation to victims should be encouraged.

Assistance

14) Victims should receive the necessary material, medical, psychological and social assistance through governmental, voluntary, community-based and indigenous means.

15) Victims should be informed of the availability of health and social services and other relevant assistance and be readily afforded access to them.

16) Police, justice, health, social service and other personnel concerned should receive training to sensitise them to the needs of victims, and guidelines to ensure proper and prompt aid.

17) In providing services and assistance to victims, attention should be given to those who have special needs because of the nature of the harm inflicted or because of factors such as those mentioned in paragraph 3 above.

RIGHTS OF VICTIMS IN CHINA

In Chinese criminal procedure law, crimes are categorised as publicly prosecuted cases and privately prosecuted cases.

Privately prosecuted cases are for some minor offences such as insult, defamation, abuse of family members, interference with force with the freedom of marriage and other minor offences against which the victim has conclusive evidence. Victims have different rights in these two categories of cases.

In the privately prosecuted cases, no public prosecutor finds an indictment before the court. The victim of crime brings a prosecution directly to court against his or her victimizer. The judge hears the case much as is done in civil procedure.

As one of the contesting parties, the victim has the following rights:

i) to withdraw prosecution from court against the victimiser,

ii) to bring a civil suit in the court on the damages for compensation by the victimiser,

iii) to authorize somebody to represent him or her in the court,

iv) to require the judge to call new witnesses,

v) to ask withdrawal of a judge or identifier,

vi) to question the defendant, witness and identifier, and

vii) to lodge an appeal against a sentence or decision.

Majority of crimes are prosecuted by public prosecutors. Before 1996, the publicly prosecuted cases were seen as the state's cases against the accused. In these cases, the victim was not one of the parties of the ongoing criminal lawsuit between the state and the accused, but seen as one of the participants in the proceedings and had fewer rights than he or she did in the cases prosecuted by the victim.

In April 1996, China revised its criminal procedure law. In the revised law, the victim in the cases prosecuted by public prosecutors is taken as one of the parties except that the public prosecutor and his or her rights have increased.

Rights to be accused: Traditionally, the state monopolises the right to accuse an individual who commits a crime, especially a felony, since crimes are considered as threats to the social order and hostile attacks to the state which represents all the people. The revised criminal procedure law, however, breaches this tradition. It provides that the victim of crime may prosecute directly in court his or her victimiser "if he or she has enough evidence to prove the defendant should bear criminal responsibility for his/her act that violates the victim's rights of person or property and that the police or the prosecutor's office has decided not to investigate the defendant's responsibility". (Article 170).

Right to ask withdrawal of judge, prosecutor or identifier: If the responsible judge, prosecutor, police officer, court clerk, court translator or identifier has any relationship which may impose negative impact on fair judgment, the victim may ask any of them to withdraw from the positions they are holding in the court (Articles 28-29).

Right to make statement on the facts of crime and question defendant, witnesses and identifier in the court: As the revised criminal procedure law provides, the victim may make a statement on the facts of the crime, the impact the crime has imposed on him or her and the punishment he or she hopes to be applied to the defendant. The victim may question the defendant, witnesses and identifier before the court if he or she wishes to do so during the court investigation of the facts of crime.

Right to ask prosecutor to contest a judgment: If the victim disagrees with the sentence or decision made by the court, he or she may ask the prosecutor to contest it, although the victim cannot appeal to a higher court. The prosecutor's office must make a decision on whether it will contest the judgment or decision within five days after it receives the request of the victim. A higher court will try the case as a case of second instance and make a new judgment or decision which may overturn the judgment or decision made by a lower court.

Restitution over fine: In March, 1997, China revised its criminal law one year after its criminal procedure law was amended. The revised criminal law provides that, if a defendant is ordered to make restitution to the victim and a fine has been imposed, and his or her property is not enough to pay both, he or she should pay restitution to the victim first (Article 36).

Limitation of prosecution not working after reporting to criminal justice systems by victim: The revised criminal law provides that the offender will not be prosecuted beyond the prescribed limitation of prosecution. However, if the victim reports the crime to the police, but the prosecutor's office or court does not put it on record for investigation, the limitation of prosecution does not apply.

REPORTING OF CRIME

According to the ICVS survey 1989-1996, for all crimes together, the reporting rates are the highest in the New World countries (54 per cent) and Western Europe (52 per cent). Reporting rates are moderately high in Africa (40 per cent) and in Central and Eastern Europe (35 per cent). Reporting of crimes to the police is less common in Asia (31 per cent) and Latin America (27 per cent). In the latter region the reporting rates vary a lot across countries. It is low in Bolivia and Brazil but moderately high in Argentina (42 per cent). In general reporting percentages are higher for serious property offences such as car or motorcycle theft and burglary than for other types of crime.

Reporting of burglaries and violence against women is highest in New World nations and Western Europe. The reporting rates are much lower in Asia, Central and Eastern Europe, Africa and Latin America. The difference is greatest for property crimes. The differences in reporting confirm the hypothesis that police figures in developing countries and countries in transition seriously underestimate the real level of crime. The numbers of property crimes are especially large in these countries.

The reporting rates for contact crimes are much lower than those for property crimes. Globally, 39 per cent of assaults on men are reported. The reporting rate of violence against women is even lower. Less than one in three instances of violence against women (non-sexual assaults and sexual assaults combined) are brought to the attention of the police (30 per cent). Police figures of various types of serious contact crimes reflect the small number of actual crimes ever reported to the police. Globally, the prevalence rate of serious violence against women, for example, is at least three times higher than indicated by police figures.

Analysis at individual levels shown that income level is the most important factor related to reporting of crimes. The second most important factor is the perceived seriousness of the offence. Other relevant factors are age, level of education and gender. Older, better educated and male victims are some what more likely to report crimes to the police.

Victimisations which are more serious and concern socially established victims are most likely to be reported. Cases of assault are more likely to be reported if they are more serious in terms of injury and/or perceived seriousness and if the crime was committed by a known person. Statistically significant but less important factors are age, affluence and gender. Victims whose victimisations were not reported to the police were asked about their reasons for non-reporting to the police. The main reasons for non-reporting were that the incident was not serious enough or that the police could do nothing.

Victims in developing countries and countries in transition are less likely to say that their victimisation was not serious enough for reporting to the police. This result is consistent with the higher seriousness scores given by crime victims in these countries. They more often say that the police could do nothing. Victims of burglary quite often seek assistance of the police in recovering property. This is most notably the case in developing countries and countries in transition. Many victims wanted the offender to be caught and punished. Many victims also referred to the moral obligation to report, especially in the western countries and Asia.

Insurance is a another reason for reporting in the more affluent countries. In the countries in transition this reason is often given by victims in Hungary (39 per cent) and the Czech Republic (50 per cent) where insurance is relatively common.

In most African and many Asian and Latin American countries only between 10 and 20 per cent of the respondents are insured against household burglary. In most industrialised countries the insurance rate is at least 70 per cent. These differences go some way in explaining the lower reporting rate in the developing countries and countries in transition. In the latter countries victims report not to back up insurance claims but in the hope that their property skill be reclaimed from the offender by the police. Financial considerations seem to play an important role in the expectations by victims of property crimes *vis-a-vis* the police.

Victims of contact crimes report to the police for different reasons. Victims of such crimes were especially concerned with stopping what happened. The moral obligation is again more in evidence in Asia than in Latin America. The results concerning, female victims of violence are similar. Globally, 50 per cent want to stop what happened and 28 per cent want to get help. There is little variation in this across regions.

Victims of violence often seek help from the police in a crisis situation. The lower levels of reporting of property crimes in Asia and Latin America and also in Africa and Central and Eastern Europe are related to a lower extent of insurance cover. Lack of confidence in the police seems another determining factor behind non-reporting of crimes. The latter seems of significance for victims of violent crimes in particular.

Satisfaction with Police Action

Police forces around the world clearly have a long way to go to adequately empower crime victims. Satisfaction with the police was markedly higher in the Western countries. Since victims of property crimes report for different reasons than victims of violence, the levels of satisfaction may be different as well. In the Western countries victims of contact crimes are less satisfied with the police response than victims of burglaries.

As a consequence the levels of satisfaction are less dissimilar across regions in the case of violent crimes than of property crimes. The opinions of victims of assaults/threats and violence against women show a similar pattern. The relatively high level of satisfaction, however, must be seen against the background of relatively low reporting of such crimes.

The most common reason for dissatisfaction with the police response was that the police did not do enough or did not recover the goods. Roughly one in five victims were unhappy that the police did not keep them sufficiently informed. Some other main reasons given for dissatisfaction show interesting differences.

In Asia, Latin America, Central and Eastern Europe and Africa, where satisfaction was relatively low, victims were more likely to be unhappy that the police did not recover their property or apprehend the offender. The reasons for dissatisfaction of Asian, African. Latin American and East European victims confirm that for them reporting is often motivated by the wish to reclaim stolen property in more affluent nations. This financial consideration seems less pertinent because more victims are covered by insurance. This factor might well be one reason for the higher level of satisfaction with the police in Western countries. Victims whose losses are covered by insurance are less concerned about the outcome of the investigation. Such victims primarily want to be treated efficiently and with respect. Against this background the relatively high levels of satisfaction of burglary victims in the West are somewhat less impressive.

The dissatisfied victims in Asia were most likely to be dissatisfied because of the impolite or incorrect nature of police. In many Asian countries relationships between the victims and the police are particularly strained. The reasons given for dissatisfaction by victims of contact crimes are fairly similar. The percentage of victims who felt the police did not do enough is high in all regions. The complaint that the police had been impolite was also mentioned by about 15 per cent of the victims, although this reason was given less often in Europe and the New World. Interestingly, this reason was most often mentioned by women who were victims of violence. Globally, one in five women who were dissatisfied mentioned this reason.

The police in most countries fail to satisfy the demands of a large part of reporting victims. Dissatisfaction is the highest among victims of burglaries and other property crimes in less affluent countries where victims are dependent on the police for recovering their property or claiming compensation. In all regions, dissatisfaction is also high among victims of contact crimes. Victims of violence report crimes to stop what was happening and/or to get help.

In the 1996 survey of ICVS, victims of more serious crimes who had reported to the police were specifically asked whether they had received support from a specialised agency. In most countries few victims had received such help. Of those who reported burglaries to the police four per cent had received help. The level of support was the highest in the Western European countries. The level of support in these countries is generally a good deal higher than previous sweeps of the ICVS.

Victims who had not received help from a specialised agency were asked whether they would have appreciated help in getting information, and practical or emotional support. Most victims of burglary and contact crimes reported that they would have welcomed specialised help. Two-thirds of victims of serious crimes who had reported to the police indicated an unmet need for help. Levels of demand were highest in Central and Eastern Europe, Asia, Africa and Latin America. There is obviously a huge gap between the need for such help and its actual provision.

The standards for victim empowerment of the UN Declaration of Basic Principles of Justice for Victims of Crime and Abuse of Power are not sufficiently implemented. In relation to this, many victims are reluctant to report crimes to the police. This lack of confidence in the police implies that crime victims have often no authority to turn to and feel alienated. Low reporting rates are also an impediment for effective crime prevention and control.

The chances of arresting the offender and getting a conviction are largely dependent on the information supplied by the victim. If many victims are doubtful whether reporting to the police will do them any good, as is clearly the case in most developing nations, the effectiveness of the police is severely undermined. For more effective criminal investigations the cooperation of the victims is essential.

Victims feel alienated with no authority to turn for help. Two-third of victims of serious crimes who had reported to the police indicated an unmet need of help. From the above discussions it can be find that risk of begin victimised is highest in third world countries. Less than half of the victims who reported their cases to the police were satisfied with the response.

Bibliography

Adelson, Lester, *The Pathology of Homicide*, Springfield, IL: Charles C. Thomas, 1974.

Alexander, Yonah, (ed.), *Middle East Terrorism: Current Threats and Future Prospects*, Aldershot, England: Dartmouth, 1994.

Alvazzi del Frate A., *Manual International Crime (Victim) Survey*, Rome: UNICRI, 1996.

_______________., "Preventing Crime: Citizens' Experience Across the World", *Issues and Reports* no. 9. Rome: UNICRI, 1996.

_______________ and Angela Patrignani, *Women's Vicitimisation in Developing Countries*, Rome: UNICRI, 1995.

American Law Institute a Model Penal Code, As adopted at the 1952 Annual Meeting of the American Law Institute at Washington, DC, 24 May 1962, 142.

Amnesty International, *The Death Penalty: List of Abolitionist and Retentionist Countries, July* 1997, London, UK.

Amnesty International, *The Death Penalty World Wide: Developments in 1996,* London, UK, 1997.

Andre, Bossard, *Transnational Crime and Criminal Law,* Chicago: Office of International Criminal Justice, University of Illinois at Chicago, 1990.

Anyebe, A.P., *Customary Law: The War Without Arms*, Enugu, Nigeria: Fourth Dimension Publishing Co. Ltd., 1985.

Applied Criminology Group, "Evaluation Report of the Boggart Hill Anti-burglary Initiative", *Report to the Multi-Agency Panel,* University of Huddersfield, UK, 1997.

Arlacchi, P., 1995, *Political Corruption and Organised Crime in Contemporary Italy*, Collected Works of the Seventh International Anti-Corruption Conference, Beijing, 1997.

Aromaa, K and Lehti, M., *Foreign Companies and Crime in Eastern Europe*, Helsinki, 1996.

Australian Bureau of Statistics, *Crime and Safety Australia*, ABS Cat. no. 4509.0, Canberra, 1994.

Baden, Michael M., *Unnatural Death: Confessions of a Medical Examiner*, New York: Random House, 1989.

Bennett, Richard R., Development and Crime: A Cross-national Time Series Analysis of Competing Models, *The Sociological Quarterly*, 32, 1991.

Bolz, Frank Jr., Kenneth J. Dudonis and David P Schutz, *The Counter-Terrorism Handbook: Tactics, Procedures and Techniques.* New York: Elsevier, 1990.

Brownmiller, Susan, *Against Our Will: Men, Women and Rape*, New York: Simon & Schuster, 1975.

Builta, Jeff and Richard Ward, *Violent and Terrorist Groups*, Office of International Criminal Justice (OICJ) at the University of Illinois at Chicago (UIC), 1996.

Canfield D.V., "Causes of Spalling of Concrete at Elevated Temperatures", *Fire and Arson Investigator* 34, June 1984.

Carey, Arthur, *Memoirs of a Murder Man,* New York: Doubleday, Doran, 1930.

Carlson, Ronald L., *Criminal Justice Procedure*, 5th ed. Cincinnati: Anderson, 1995.

Carroll, John R., *Physical and Technical Aspects of Fire and Arson investigation,* Springfield, IL: Charles C. Thomas, 1983.

Carter, Robert E., and A.J. McKechnie, *Arson Investigation,* Beverly Hills, CA: Glencoe, 1978.

Chalidze, Valery, *Criminal Russia: Essays on Crime in the Soviet Union*, Translated from the Russian by P.S. Falla. New York: Random House, 1977.

Clarke, R.V., (ed.), *Situational Crime Prevention: Successful Case Studies*, 2nd ed., Albany, New York: Harrow and Heston, Publishers, 1977.

______________ ,"Situational Crime Prevention", *In* M. Tonry and D.P. Farrington (eds.), *Building a Safer Society: Strategic Approaches to Crime Prevention*, Chicago: University of Chicago Press, 1995.

______________ , and G. McGrath, "Cash Reduction and Robbery Prevention in Australian Betting Shops", *Security Journal*, 1, 3, 1990.

______________ , *Situational Crime Prevention: Successful Case Studies*, Albany, New York: Harrow and Heston, Publishers, 1992.

Cole, George, *The American System or Criminal Justice*, 5th ed., Pacific Grove, CA: Brooks/Cole, 1989.

Cook, R., and R. Ide, *Principles of Fire Investigation,* Leicester, England: Institute of Fire Engineers, 1985.

Corkery, *The Theft of Firearms,* Home Office Research and Planning Unit Paper 84, 1989.

Cottone, James A. and S., Miles Standish, (eds.) *Outline of Forensic Dentistry,* Chicago: Year Book Med., 1982.

Cromwell, Paul E., James N. Olson and D. Aunn Wester Avary, *Breaking and Entering: An Ethnographic Analysis of Burglary,* Newbury Park: Sage Publications, 1991.

Curran, William J. and Donald Shapiro E., *Law, Medicine, and Forensic Science,* 3rd ed., Boston, MA: Little, Brown, 1982.

De, Haan D., "Determining the Point of Origin-Diagnostic Signs and Laboratory Analysis," *Fire and Arson Investigator* 36, June 1986.

De Forest Peter, R. E., Gaensslen and Henry S. Lee, *Forensic-Science: An Introduction to Criminalistics.* 2nd ed. New York: McGraw-Hill, 1995.

della Porta, D. and Y. Meny (eds.). *Democratic et Corruption en Europe*, Paris: La Dicouverte, 1995.

Devlin, Patrick, *The Criminal Prosecution in England*, London: Oxford University Press, 1960.

Dhokalia, R. P. and K. Narayana Rao (eds.), *Terrorism and International Law*, New Delhi: Indian Society of International Law, 1988.

Dictionary of Criminal Justice Data Terminology, 2nd ed., Washington, DC: Bureau of Justice Statistics, US Department of Justice.

DiMaio, Vincent J.M., *Gunshot Wounds: Practical Aspects of Firearms, Ballistics, and Forensic Techniques,* New York: Elsevier, 1985.

Ebbe, Obi N. I., "Criminal Procedure in Nigeria", *In Comparative and International Criminal Justice Systems: Policing, Judiciary, and Corrections*, Boston: Butterworth/Heinemann, 1996.

Ebbe, Obi N.I., "Power and Criminal Law: Criminalizing Conduct Norms in a Colonial Regime", *International Journal of Comparative and Applied Criminal Justice*, Winter, 9, 2, 1995.

Ebbe, Obi N.I., "Crime and Delinquency in Metropolitan Lagos: A Study of Crime and Delinquency Area Theory", *Social Forces*, 1989.

Eck, John, *Managing Case Assignments: Burglary Investigation Decision Model Replication,* Washington, DC: Police Executive Research Forum, 1979.

Egger, Steven, A., *Serial Murder: An Elusive Phenomenon,* Westport, CT: Praeger, 1990.

Ekblom, P. H., Law and M. Sutton, *Safer Cities and Domestic Burglary Schemes,* London: Home Office, 1996.

Environics, "Focus on Crime and Justice", *Focus Canada*, March, Ottawa, 1996.

Estrich, S., *Real Rape,* Cambridge, MA: Harvard University Press, 1987.

Fairchild, Erika S., *Comparative Criminal Justice Systems*, Belmont, CA: Wadsworth, 1993.

Farrington, D. P., *Understanding and Preventing Youth Crime,* York: Joseph Rowntree Foundation, 1996.

Fijnaut, et al. (eds.), *Changes in Society, Crime and Criminal Justice in Europe II: International, Organised and Corporate Crime*, The Hague, 1995.

Fischer, Barry A.J., *Techniques of Crime Scene Investigation,* 5th ed., Boca Raton, FL: CRC Press, Inc., 1992.

Flood, Susan, (ed.), *International Terrorism: Policy Implications,* Chicago: Office of International Criminal Justice, 1990.

Gabor, T., Welsh B. C., and Antonowicz D. H., "The Role of the Health Community in the Prevention of Criminal Violence, *Canadian Journal of Criminology,* 38, 1996.

Garland, David, *Punishment and Modern Society*, London: Oxford University Press, 1996.

Geason, S. and P. Wilson, *Preventing Retail Crime,* Canberra: Australian Institute of Criminology, 1996.

Geberth, Vernon J., *Practical Homicide Investigation: Tactics, Procedures, and Forensic Techniques,* 2nd ed. New York: Elsevier, 1990.

Gilmer, Welsey, Jr., The Law Dictionary, 6th ed. Cincinnati: Anderson, 1986.

Goldstein, Jeffrey H., *Aggression and Crimes of Violence,* New York: Oxford University Press, 1995.

Gottfredson, M.R. and Hirschi, T., *A General Theory of Crime,* Stanford: Stanford University Press, 1990.

Harry, O'Reilly, *Practical Burglary Investigation,* Chicago: Office of Security Programs, University of Illinois at Chicago, 1991.

Hazelwood, R., and Ann Wolkert Burgess, (eds.), *Practical Aspects of Rape Investigation: A Multidisciplinary, Approach*, 2nd ed. Boca Raton, FL: CRC Press, Inc., 1995.

______________, and Ann W. Burgess, *Practical Aspects of Rape Investigation—A Multidisciplinary Approach*, 2nd ed., Boca Raton, FL: CRC Press, Inc., 1995.

______________, Park Elliot Dietz and Ann W Burgess, *Autoerotic Fatalities,* Lexington, MA: Lexington Books, 1983.

Hickey, Eric, W., *Serial Murderers and Their Victims.* Florence, KY: Brooks-Cole Publishing Co., 1991.

Holmes, Ronald M., "Stalking in America: Types and Methods of Criminal Stalkers", *Journal of Contemporary Criminal Justice,* December, 1993.

Hughes, Daniel J., *Homicide Investigative Techniques,* Springfield, IL: Charles C. Thomas, 1974.

John, Eck, *Managing Case Assignments: Burglary Investigation Decision Model Replication,* Washington, DC: Police Executive Research Forum, 1979.

Johnson, Herbert A. and Nancy Travis Wolfe, *History of Criminal Justice*, 2nd ed. Cincinnati; Anderson, 1996.

Kalish, Carol B., *International Crime Rates*, Washington, DC: Bureau of Justice Statistics, 1990.

Karchmer, Clifford L., James Greenfield, and Marilyn Walsh E., *Enforcement Manual: Approaches for Combating Arson-for-Profit Schemes*, Washington, DC:US Department of Justice, Law Enforcement Administration, 1980.

Keppel, Robert D., *Serial Murder: Future Implications for Police Investigations,* Cincinnati: Anderson, 1988.

Kerbo, H. R. and M. Inoue, Japanese Social Structure and White Collar Crime: Recruit Cosmos and Beyond, *Deviant Behaviour,* 11, 1990

Kerry, J., (ed.), *Calling for Change: International Strategies to End Violence Against Women,* Publication no. 8., The Hague, Development Cooperation Information Department, Ministry of Foreign Affairs, 1994.

____________, "The BCCI Affair", Report to the Senate Foreign Relations Committee. Subcommittee on Terrorism, Narcotics and International Operations, Washington, DC: GPO, 1992.

Killias, M., Gun Ownership, Suicide and Homicide: An International Perspective, In Alvazzi del Frate *et al., Understanding Crime*, Rome: UNICRI, 1993.

Kleiman, Mark A.R., "Organized Crime and Drug Abuse Control", *In* Robert J. Kelly, Ko-Lin Chin and Rufus Schatzberg (eds.), *Handbook Organized Crime in the United States,* Connecticut: Greenwood Press, 1994.

Klotter, John C., Criminal Law, 4th ed. Cincinnati: Anderson, 1996.

Koss, P., "The Measurement of Rape Victimisation in Crime Surveys", *Criminal Justice and Behaviour,* 23, 1994.

Kress, Jack M., "Progress and Prosecution", *Annals of the American Academy of Political and Social Science,* 1994.

Kuhn, Andre, "Attitude Toward Punishment", In A. Alvazzi del Frate et al. (eds.), *Understanding Crime: Experiences of Crime and Crime Control,* Rome: UNICRI, 1992.

Lee, Goff M., "Comparison of Insect Species Associated with Decomposing Remains Recovered Inside Dwellings and Outdoors on the Island of Oahu, Hawaii," *Journal of Forensic Sciences*; 36:3 (1991), 748-753.

Leppard, David, *On the Trail of Tenor; The Inside Story of the Lockerbie Investigation,* London: Jonathan Cape, 1991.

Levin, J. and Fox J. A., *Mass Murder: America's Growing Menace,* New York: Plenum, 1985.

Long, David E., *The Anatomy of Terrorism,* New York: The Free Press, 1990.

Lunden, W.A., "Homicides in Canada:" *Police Journal* 60:2, April-June,1987.

Mac, Hovec, F.J., *Cults and Personality,* Springfield, IL: Charles C. Thomas, 1989.

Magee, Doug, *What Murder Leaves Behind: The Victim's Family*, New York: Dodd, Mead & Co., 1983.

McCarney, William P. and Robert James Fischer, "Arson Investigation: One Means of Preventing Future Fires," in *Critical Issues in Criminal lnvestigation,* edited by Michael J. Palmiotto, Cincinnati: Anderson, 1988.

Medea, Andra and Kathleen Thompson, *Against Rape,* New York: Farrar, Straus & Giroux, 1974.

Mirrlees-Black, C. and Ross A., "Crime against Retail Premises in 1993", *Research Findings* 26 Home Office, London, 1995.

_______________ , and Ross A., Crime against Manufacturing Premises in 1993", *Research Findings* 27, Home Office, London, 1995.

Moley, Raymond, *Politics and Criminal Prosecution*, New York: Minton, Balch and Co., 1995.

Mones, Paul, *The Dramatic True Story of the Detective Who First Used DNA Testing to Catch a Serial Killer* New York: Pocket Books, 1995.

Morse, Dan, Jack Duncan and James Stoutmire, (eds.), *Handbook of Forensic Archeology and Anthropology,* Pub. by editors, 1983.

Nalla, Mahesh K., "Criminal Justice System in Singapore", *In* Graeme Newman, Debra Cohen and Adam C. Bouloukos (eds.), *International Factbook of Criminal Justice System,* Bureau of Justice Statistics, 1996.

Newman, Graeme, *Just and Painful: A Case for the Corporal Punishment of Criminals,* NY: Harrow and Heston Publishers, 1994.

Newton, N. Minow, "Notable and Quotable," *The Wall Street Journal,* 4 February 1985, 22.

Nicholas, Groth, A., Jean Birnbaum, *Men Who Rape: The Psychology of the Offender* New York: Plenum Press, 1979.

Noon, Randall, *Engineering Analysis of Fires and Explosions,* Boca Raton, FL:CRC Press, Inc., 1995.

Norris, Joel. *Serial Killers,* New York: Doubleday & Co., Inc., 1988.

O'Connor, John J., *Practical Fire and Arson Investigation,* New York: Elsevier, 1986.

O'Neill, John P. "Terrorism." Speech Presented at the Office of International Criminal Justice (OICJ), University of Illinois at Chicago, 1996

O'Reilly, Harry, *Practical Burglary Investigation,* Chicago: Office of Security Programs, University of Illinois at Chicago, 1991.

Parikh, C.K., *Parikh's Textbook of Medical Jurisprudence and Toxicology: For Classrooms and Courtrooms,* Elmsford, NY Pergamon, 1980.

Parrot, Andrea and Laurie Bechhoffer, *Acquaintance Rape: The Hidden Crime,* New York: John Wiley & Sons, 1991.

Pope, Victoria, Trafficking in Women, *US News and World Report,* April 7, 1997.

Potas, I. et al., *Young People and Crime Cost and Prevention*, Canberra: Australian Institute of Criminology, 1990.

Reichel, Philip L., *Comparative Criminal Justice Systems: A Topical Approach,* Englewood Cliffs, NJ: Prentice Hall, 1994.

Ressler Robert K., Ann W Burgess and John Douglas E., *Sexual Homicide: Patterns and Motives*, Lexington, MA: Lexington Books, 1988.

Reuter Peter, *Disorganized Crime: The Economics of the Visible Hand,* Cambridge, MA: MIT Press, 1983.

Robert, K. Ressler, Ann W. Burgess and John E. Douglas, *Sexual Homicide: Patterns and Motives,* Lexington, MA: Lexington Books, 1988, 137.

Robert, R., Hazelwood and Janet Warren, "The Serial Rapist: His Characteristics and *Victims, FBI Law Enforcement Bulletin* 58:1, January, 1989, 10-17.

Roblee, Charles L. and Allen J. McKechnie, *The Investigation of Fires*, 2nd ed. Englewood Cliffs, NJ: Prentice-Hall, 1988.

Rogers, Spencer, L., *The Testimony of Teeth: Forensic Aspects of Human Dentition,* Springfield, IL: Charles C. Thomas, 1988.

Russell, Diana, (ed.), *The Politics of Rape: The Victim Perspective,* New York: Stein & Day, 1975

Rynearson, Joseph M. and Chisum, W. J., *Evidence and Crime Scene Reconstruction.* 3rd ed. Redding, CA: National Crime Investigation and Training, 1993.

Smith, Brent, *Terrorism in America: Pipe Bombs and Pipe Dreams*, New York: State University of New York Press, 1994.

Sparks, R.F., Germ H.G. and Dodd D.J., *Surveying Victims: A Study of the Measurement of Criminal Victimization*, Chicester, New York: Wiley and Sons, 1977.

Spitz, Werner U., *Spitz and Fischer's Medicolegal Investigation of Death: Guidelines for the Application of Pathology to Criminal Investigation*, 3rd ed. Springfield, IL: Charles C. Thomas, 1993.

Standing Committee on Justice and Legal Affairs, *Renewing Youth Justice*, House of Commons, Canada, 1997.

Stensrud, John R., "Interpretive Procedures in Police Investigations of Sexual Assaults:' in *Critical Issues in Criminal Investigation,* 2nd ed., edited by Michael J. Palmiotto, Cincinnati: Anderson, 1988.

Ted, R. Gurr, *Violence in America,* Vol. I, Newbury Park, CA: Sage, 1989.

The Govt. of India, 'Crime in India' New Delhi, *National Crime Records Bureau,* 1999.

Tritt, Howard, "Missing Children: What the Investigator Needs to Know." In *Critical Issues in Criminal Investigation,* 2nd ed., edited by Michael J. Palmiotto. Cincinnati: Anderson, 1988.

UNDCP,1996 "Illicit Drug Trafficking", Report of the Secretariat to the Commission on Narcotic Drugs. Document E/ CN.7/1996.

UNDCP, 1997, "Illicit Drug Trafficking", Report of the Secretariat to the Commission on Narcotic Drugs. Document E/CN.7/1997/4.

UNDCP, 1997, World Drug Report, UK: Oxford University Press.

Uniform Crime Reports, Washington, DC: Federal Bureau of Investigation, 1975-1990.

Uniform Crime Reports, Washington, DC: US, Department of Justice, Federal Bureau of Investigation, 1994.

United Nations, 1986, "Safeguards Guaranteeing Protection of the Rights of Those Facing the Death Penalty", *Economic and Social Council Resolution* 1984/50, 25 May.

United Nations, "The Standard Minimum Rules for the Treatment of Prisoners", *Resolution of First United Nations Congress on the Prevention of Crime and the Treatment of Offenders,* 1995.

United Nations, "Guidelines for the Prevention of Urban Crime", ECOSOC 1995/9, 1995.

United Nations, 1996, *The United Nations and Crime Prevention: Seeking Security and Justice for All,* New York: Department of Public Information, United Nations.

van Dijk Jan J.M., Opportunities of Crime: *A Test of the Rational interactionist Model. Report* for the Symposium on Economics and Crime of the Permanent Committee on Crime Problems of the Council of Europe, Strasbourg, November 28-31, 1995.

Vernon J. Geberth, "Final Exit Suicide Investigations," *Low and Order* 41(12), 67-70, Dec. 1993.

Waller, I., *Current Trends in European Crime Prevention: Implications for Canada,* Ottawa: Department of Justice, Canada, 1993.

Waller, I., Welsh and Sansfacon D., *Crime Prevention Digest: Trends and Payoffs for Selected Countries.* International Centre for the Prevention of Crime, 1997.

Waller, I., "What Reduces Residential Burglary: Action and Research in Seattle and Toronto", In H.J. Schneider (ed.), *Victim in International Perspective,* New York: de Gruyter, 1982.

Ward, Richard H. and Harold E. Smith, eds. *International Terrorism: Operational Issues.* Chicago: Office of International Criminal Justice, 1988.

Wardlaw, Grant, *Political Terrorism: Theory, Tactics and Countermeasures.* 2nd ed. Cambridge, England: Cambridge University Press, 1989.

Weisheit, Ralph and Sue Mahan, *Women, Crime, and Criminal Justice,* Cincinnati: Anderson, 1988.

Weiss, Michael, *Police Technology in Different Countries*, School of Criminal Justice, University at Albany, 1997.

Welsh, B. C. and Waller I., *Crime and Its Prevention: Costs and Benefits.* Ottawa: Department of Criminology, University of Ottawa, 1995.

Wemmers, Jo-Anne, *Victims and its Effects on their Attitudes and Behaviour*, Amsterdam: Kugler Publications, 1995.

White, G., "Corruption and the Transition from Socialism in China", *Journal of Law and Society*, 1996.

Willemse, Hans M. and Jaap de Waard, "An Evolutionary Psychological Perspective from Experience in the Netherlands, *Security Journal*, 1993.

Wilson, Margo and Martin Daly, "An Evolutionary Psychological Perspective on Male Sexual proprietariness and Violence against Wives", *Violence and Victims*, 8, 3, 1993.

Winer, Jonathan, Alien Smuggling: Elements of the Problem and the US Response, *Transnational Organised Crime*, 3, 1, 1997.

Women's Aid Organisation, *Draft Report of the National Study on Domestic Violence*, Kuala Lumpur, Malaysia, 1992.

World Bank, *World Development Report* 1997, New York: Oxford University Press, 1997.

Yallop, H. S., *Explosion Investigastion,* Harrogate, North Yorkshire, UK: Forensic Science Society Press, 1980.

Yereance, Robert A., *Electrical Fire Analysis.* Springfield, IL: Charles C. Thomas, 1987.

Yoshikawa, H., "Prevention as Cumulative Protection: Effects of Early Family Support and Education on Chronic Delinquency and its Risks", *Psychological Bulletin*, 115, 1, 1990.

Index